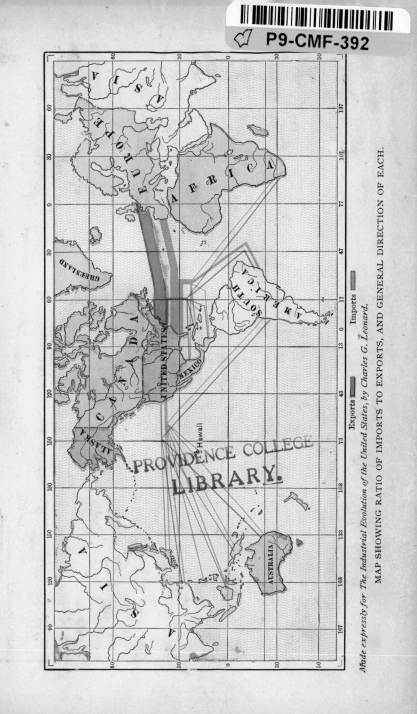

Made expressly for *The Industrial Evolution of the United States*, by *Charles G. Leonard.*

MAP SHOWING RATIO OF IMPORTS TO EXPORTS, AND GENERAL DIRECTION OF EACH.

Exports   Imports

SAMUEL SLATER.

"The Father of American Cotton Manufacture."

THE

INDUSTRIAL EVOLUTION

OF

THE UNITED STATES

BY

CARROLL D. WRIGHT, LL.D.

United States Commissioner of Labor

NEW YORK

CHARLES SCRIBNER'S SONS

1902

THE CAXTON PRESS
NEW YORK.

TO
PRESIDENT
FRANCIS A. WALKER.

PREFACE.

THE plan of this work comprehends a plain, simple statement of the leading facts attending the planting and development of the mechanical industries of our country. No attempt has been made to discuss some of the influences which have affected their development, such as the varied effects of tariff legislation, financial experiments, foreign policies, or economic conditions and principles. To have entered upon an ambitious field involving such important elements in the evolution of industry would have led to a work much more extensive than that contemplated. The results have been given, however, in such concise form as to present the general story of our industrial growth and the logical effects of such growth as shown in the various phases of the labor movement. Modern industry brought this movement as it is now understood into existence, and its influence upon future development will be important.

As invention has been the vitalizing principle of the factory system, it has been deemed wise to incorporate chapters on the influence of machinery. These chapters, the last three, are largely from addresses which I have made, and the line of thought followed in them is the result of extended observation and the wide study of facts, a study which has led me to change the conclusions reached by the earlier consideration of what I now see was a limited range of experiences.

The inception of great industries during the past quarter of a century and the building up of great manufacturing establishments are features which, however desirable in an exhaustive work, could not be treated in detail, but the figures showing the results of such undertakings have been freely used, and they tell the story of the general movement and of the distribution of industrial interests.

The details of the development of transportation are legitimate features of the evolution of industry, but they have been omitted, that a continuous general story might be told in such a way as to interest and instruct the class of readers for whom this work is intended ; but their great importance is recognized, as well as the importance of mining, agriculture, and other sources of our vast supply of raw materials.

In the preparation of this work I have had the skilful services of Messrs. Samuel C. Dunham and Charles W. Morris, Jr., in stenographic work, in proof-reading, and in the verification of names, dates, etc. I am also indebted to Mr. Wm. M. Steuart, late Chief of Division of Manufactures in the Eleventh Census, for the verification of figures taken from that and preceding censuses. All the maps and diagrams have been drawn by Mr. Charles G. Leonard especially for this volume, and many of the illustrations are from original sources.

C. D. W.

Washington, D. C., June 1, 1895.

CONTENTS.

ILLUSTRATIONS.

MAPS AND DIAGRAMS.

THE INDUSTRIAL EVOLUTION

OF THE

UNITED STATES.

INTRODUCTION.

LAND.—RESOURCES.—POPULATION.

BY THE definitive treaty of Paris, September 3, 1783, between the United States and England, the United States gained all the material objects of the Revolution and came into possession of an imperial estate of 827,844 square miles of territory.* This was the national domain March 4, 1789, when the new constitution went into effect and the federal government under it began its operations. It consisted of the thirteen original states and the territory claimed by some of them. The area of the United States since then has been greatly increased by purchase, by conquest, and by cession. The first great accessions were through the acquisition of the Louisiana and Oregon tracts in 1803-5, covering 1,171,931 square miles. The Florida purchase of 1819 added 59,268 square miles. From Texas in 1845 the United States gained 376,163 square miles, while the first Mexican cession added 545,-753 square miles, and the Gadsden purchase, in 1853, 44,064 square miles. In 1867 Russia, by purchase,

Land.

Accessions.

---

* I have used the areas of the original territory of the United States and all accessions thereto as given in the Federal Census Reports. They have been made with great care by Prof. Henry Gannett, of the Geological Survey and Geographer of the Census. The statements of no two authorities agree, the disagreement resulting from different estimates of boundary lines. The variation, however, is not very great. It seems wiser, therefore, to take the statements of the federal government.

National
domain.

ceded to the United States Alaska, with an estimated area of 532,409 square miles.* All these acquisitions, added to the original territory, make the total area of our national domain 3,558,009 square miles.†

Public domain.

The "public domain" of the United States, as distinguished from the "national domain," comprehends the lands within federal boundaries owned by the government and which were at its disposal for public purposes in various ways. The "public domain" is the name given by the General Land Office to these lands. Before any dispositions the public domain contained 2,889,179.91 square miles.‡ This vast quantity of land has been disposed of through sales to settlers, grants to states for educational and other purposes, and grants to railroads to aid them in building their lines, until there remains at the present time only 946,938 square miles subject to the disposition of the federal government.‖ Had the government retained all the public domain, it would now have at its disposal an area of lands somewhat less than that of the whole United States, excluding Alaska. It will be seen that the land element in the industrial development of the country has been amply sufficient to justify the prophecies of the statesmen who founded the government.

Resources.

The natural resources of the United States consist of almost every species of raw material produced by or from the earth essential to make a nation great in the three lines of development—agriculture, manufactures, commerce. The people in colonial days were quite content in the utilization of the natural resources of the soil and the forests. In the settlement of Virginia it was expected

---

* Estimate of Ivan Petroff, Special Agent of the Tenth Census.
† See map showing accessions.
‡ "The Public Domain," by Thomas Donaldson.
‖ Report of the Commissioner of the General Land Office, 1894.

that great gold mines would be discovered, and prospecting was at once begun. The results, however, were not satisfactory, and attention was turned to the exportation of timber, later on of tobacco, and afterward of cotton. The northern settlements exported manufactured timber in the shape of shingles, ship timber, and other products of the forest. The fisheries also added to the resources of the colonists, and as the settlements extended back from the coast, both north and south, various attempts were made, some successful and others unsuccessful, toward winning from nature what she had to give without going beneath the surface. The vast tracts of virgin forest supplied the material for building, as well as products for exportation. These simple natural products attracted settlers and gave them sufficient occupation, but as the country grew the discovery of iron and lead ores and of coal, and occasionally of gold and silver, increased the wealth of the country and aided in its wonderful development.* There are no estimates of the area of the iron, gold, and silver lands of the country that can be trusted, but the coal-fields east of the Rocky Mountain and Pacific tiers of states would cover an area of nearly one hundred thousand square miles, a territory a dozen times as large as the state of Massachusetts. The discovery of great quantities of gold in California in 1849 gave a new impetus to the development of our mineral resources, while the states of Nevada, Arizona, and Colorado have given of their wealth in great abundance.

The value of natural products can be stated in figures for the year 1889. In that year the farms gave $2,460,-107,454 worth of products for the support of our people and for foreign trade. The value of the products of all

Exportation of timber.

Gold, silver, and iron.

Wealth.

---

*For distribution of mineral products see map showing deposits of gold, silver, coal, and iron.

Total value of
natural
resources.

mining industries was $587,230,662 ; of the fisheries, $44,277,514; and of the forests, $446,034,761. This last value includes $8,077,379 worth of tar and turpentine, $403,667,575 worth of lumber and other mill products, and $34,289,807 worth of timber products not manufactured at mill. The total value of all these natural resources for the year 1889 was $3,537,650,391—certainly a vast product, representing labor, the profitable investment of capital, and the energy of the people. The wealth of the country, including all material evidences of wealth, like land, buildings, merchandise, and all forms of real and personal property, in 1890 amounted to $65,-037,091,197, of which amount $39,544,544,333 represents the value of real estate and the improvements thereon and $25,492,546,864 that of personal property, including railroads, mines, and quarries. Of course these great amounts are only approximately correct, there being many elements to preclude perfect accuracy, but they have been arrived at with great care and serve well their purpose to illustrate the development of the country as shown in property in existence. No comparative statements for any colonial period can be made. The per capita wealth at the present time is about one thousand dollars. It will be seen by these figures that the means for development are unlimited and indicate the activity of our people.

Population.

From the time of the first permanent settlement in Virginia in 1607 and in Massachusetts in 1620, the population of the colonies grew to be nearly four millions at the time of the adoption of the federal constitution, March 4, 1789. This constitution provided that a census of the people should be taken every tenth year, beginning with 1790. The first census showed a population of 3,929,-214. Mr. Bancroft, the historian, states that in 1775 the colonies were inhabited by persons "one fifth of whom had for their mother-tongue some other language than the English." The one fifth who could not claim the English mother-tongue came from France, Sweden, Holland, and Germany, the importance of the contributions being in the order named. Drawing the line at the date named, the beginning of our constitutional government, the descendants of the people then living now constitute what may be called popularly the true American stock. At the time of the first census (1790) about seven hundred and fifty thousand of the people of the United States were colored. The population for each decennial census was as follows :

American stock.

Census years.	Population.	Per cent of increase.
1790	3,929,214	. .
1800	5,308,483	35.10
1810	7,239,881	36.38
1820	9,633,822	33.07
1830	12,866,020	33.55
1840	17,069,453	32.67
1850	23,191,876	35.87
1860	31,443,321	35.58
1870	38,558,371	22.63
1880	50,155,783	30.08
1890	62,622,250	24.86

The population June 1, 1890, excluding Indians and other persons in Indian Territory, on Indian reservations, and in Alaska, was 62,622,250, as given in the foregoing table; but including these persons the aggregate population of the United States and its territories was 62,979,766.* It is probable that now, in the year 1895, the population is about sixty-eight millions. The average number of inhabitants to the square mile, taking the gross area, land and water surface, was in 1790, 4.75, while in 1890 it was 20.70. The increase of population

Present population.

---

* See map showing distribution of population at eleventh census (1890).

has come through natural increase and by immigration. Prior to 1819 no account was taken of the number of immigrants settling in the United States, but the accepted estimate gives the total number between the first census and the year 1819 as 250,000. Since that year the federal government has taken account of immigration; yet it has not been a correct one in all respects, on account

Immigration.

of the faults in the entries of total alien passengers, etc.; but since 1856 immigrants have been given separately, so that the movements in this direction for each year are now given with fair accuracy. Up to June 30, 1894, the total number of immigrants since 1790 was 17,363,977. Nearly one half of the number arriving since the year 1820 has come from Ireland and the German states, including Prussia, and of this half of the whole foreign immigration more than one half has come from the German states. The balance of the immigration has come from all parts of Europe and some parts of Asia, while the British possessions and South America have contributed a fair share. According to the census of 1890, the popu-

Native and foreign-born.

lation consisted of 53,372,703 native-born and 9,249,547 foreign-born, but the number of persons having one or both parents foreign-born was 20,676,046, or 33.02 per cent of the whole population. Taking this number and those whose grandparents were born abroad into consideration, it becomes quite evident that while in 1775 one fifth of the population of the colonies could not claim for their mother-tongue the English language, now one half cannot make such claim.

The strangers attracted to this country through the facilities for gaining land and through a desire largely to better conditions, have been assimilated with great facility, for the truth that strikes all observers who study to any extent the immigration to this country is that the descendants of recruits from all nationalities become in one or two generations thoroughly American. The exceptions are few and not sufficient to vitiate the general statement. This great population has spread itself over the whole country, it has multiplied the original thirteen states to forty-four, it has prospected every region, it knows where its richest deposits are to be found. Jefferson said it would be one thousand years before the Great Northwest would be settled, but he said this not foreseeing the great inventions which have made it possible for the people to settle in the remotest corners of the land. The pioneer element of the Anglo-Saxon race could not content itself until it had reached the utmost western boundary of its American inheritance. It has developed cities and founded states, like its Aryan

Distribution of population.

CENTERS OF POPULATION IN THE UNITED STATES AT EACH CENSUS FROM 1790 TO 1890.

ancestry in its march from the table-lands of Central Asia across and over the whole of Europe. In the forty-four states there are now 448 cities having a population of

Center of population.

more than eight thousand each, while in 1790, at the beginning of our federal existence, there were but six such cities. The urban population now constitutes 29.20 per cent of the total population, while in 1790 it constituted but 3.35 per cent of the total. The center of population has shifted westward. At the time of the first enumeration it was twenty-three miles east of Baltimore; to-day it is twenty miles east of Columbus, in the state of Indiana. It has moved westward 505 miles in one hundred years, and constantly along the 39th parallel of latitude, varying but a few minutes from that degree. The center of area, not taking Alaska into account, is in northern Kansas, approximately in latitude 39° 55'.

These elements—land, resources, and people—are the basic elements of our industrial evolution. With them alone, however, industrial development could not take

Urban population.

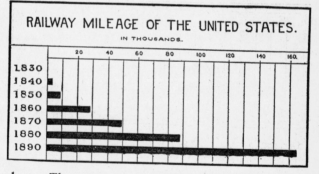

RAILWAY MILEAGE OF THE UNITED STATES.

IN THOUSANDS.

place. There must be added the vitalizing element of intelligence, inventive genius, and courage. The people of the United States have furnished these qualities; so the foundation for the story has been laid with abundant strength and proper proportions.

Railroad mileage.

The great influence of transportation is best illustrated by the mileage of railroads. In 1830 only twenty-three miles of railroads were operated in the United States, while in 1890 there were 163,597 miles, and in 1893 there were 173,433 miles.

This represents the means of carrying on internal commerce, but in addition to the railroads, water transportation adds largely to freight and passenger facilities. The navigable rivers and the Great Lakes all have their vast carrying trade ; but the development of the whole internal commerce is fully illustrated by the miles of railroad operated at different periods.

Means of transportation.

The resources of the country, resulting in the products that have been stated, have brought to the United States vast commercial relations. The exports for the year ending June 30, 1894, amounted to $892,142,572, while the imports, both free and dutiable, were valued at $654,-994,622. This great trade is represented on the accompanying map, and the countries of the world with which the United States has commercial relations are shown thereon.

Exports.

PART I.

THE EVOLUTION OF INDUSTRY:

THE COLONIAL PERIOD.

PART I.—THE EVOLUTION OF INDUSTRY:
THE COLONIAL PERIOD.

CHAPTER I.

THE INCEPTION OF INDUSTRIES.—SHIPBUILDING.

THE beginnings of great nations are usually shrouded in mystery and doubt. Tradition crystallizes into history or into what is accepted as such. The beginnings of industry are more in doubt than the beginnings of nations themselves. It is impossible to learn when the ordinary handicrafts which have been essential to the progress of man were developed to such an extent that they could be called handicrafts. Weaving, spinning, pottery, stone-working, even iron-working, and many other industries that to-day constitute the greatest and most important elements in our manufactures and commerce, cannot be traced to their starting-points.

The American nation has the advantage of most great nations, for its beginnings are clearly defined, its growth readily traceable, its expansion matters of record. Doubts may exist as to certain features of American history, but its great trend can be followed with clearness. Its industrial development forms part of its history, and constitutes one of its most interesting features. The study of the struggles of a people to establish themselves upon an independent industrial basis, the efforts of the infant state to free itself from the control of other states, fill the whole record with the greatest interest, and especially as all such efforts and struggles can be located and brought, as it were, to the family interest which surrounds the growth of our own people.

The American colonists were content to win from nature the things essential to a fairly comfortable existence. They came here that they might pursue their ways in accordance with their own likes. Whatever their motives in crossing the stormy western ocean, they knew well that they must win their way in all material things and must establish their own freedom in industrial matters. They were without capital and could pursue their simple industries only as individuals. The factory system had no place in the world then. They very naturally followed the conditions and circumstances of the home country, and their necessities resulted in the immediate introduction of industries which have flourished and made our country great. Their ambition at first was to be a prosperous agricultural people, as the old country intended them to be, yet they were obliged to carry along with agricultural pursuits mechanical work, that they might be housed and clothed.

Purposes of the American colonists.

The industries of the world were conducted under the domestic system of labor ; that is to say, the hand, supplemented with crude tools and machines, was used in the production of goods everywhere. They had at their command all the methods which the mother-country could command for producing goods ; at least, they brought with them the knowledge of handicrafts which enabled them to command the methods in existence. They found here the forests, which had no counterpart in the country from which they came, and they saw at once the opportunities for building their own little vessels and the prospect of shipping to the mother-country some of the products of the forests ; and

Early conditions.

while they had been led to believe that they would find on the American coast large deposits of mineral wealth which would reward their labors, they were soon obliged to turn their attention in other directions.   The London Company, which in 1607 planted the first colony at Jamestown, had stimulated the hopes of the discovery of gold.   They must have from the very first, however, had in mind the development, or the establishment at least, of manufactures.   From Stith's "History of Virginia"* it is learned that Captain Newport, in his second voyage, which took place late in 1608, brought with him work- men for the purpose of making pitch, glass, tar, soap- ashes, etc., which, the historian observes, had the country been peopled would have done well, but which proved only a burden and a hindrance to those not so engaged. He says that "no sooner were they landed, but the pres- ident dispersed as many as were able, some to make glass, and others for pitch, tar, and soap-ashes.   Leaving them at the fort under the council's care and oversight, he himself carried thirty about five miles down the river, to learn to cut down trees, make clapboards, and lie in the woods."   The council in London made serious complaint that gold and silver were not forthcoming, and made some threats of desertion if the expenses of the expedition were not defrayed by the ship's return.   Captain John Smith sent an answer by the ship, which was dispatched with the results of the pitch, glass, and soap-ash experiments and with what wainscot and clapboards could be pro- vided.   So this little cargo was, historically, the first ex- port which the colonies undertook, with the exception of a load of sassafras gathered near Cape Cod in 1608.   This cargo from Virginia was almost exclusively of manufac- tured articles.   Many of the experiments proved unsuc-

margin notes: 1608.

Skilled workmen.

First exports.

* London, 1753.

cessful, yet during their leisure time, as the historian states it, the Virginia colonists made clapboards and wainscot. Hemp, flax, and silk grass grew naturally, and some iron ore was sent to England and found to yield as good iron as any from other parts of the world.

By 1617 what works and buildings had been constructed at Jamestown had fallen to decay, the prospects of the country declining rapidly. The people had turned their attention from primitive manufacture to the cultivation of the tobacco plant. May 17, 1620, the company in London had a meeting, to which report was made of this attention of the colonists to tobacco-growing, and at which Sir Edwin Sandys, who had been treasurer of the company, made a statement that he had endeavored to turn the colonists from the cultivation of tobacco to the production of necessary commodities. He informed the company that for this purpose one hundred and fifty persons had been sent to set up three iron works; that directions had been given for making cordage, as hemp, flax, and more especially silk grass, grew in the colonies in great abundance, and were found upon experiment to make the best cordage and line that was manufactured. Each family was ordered to set one hundred plants of it, and the governor himself set five thousand. The colonists had also been advised to make pitch, tar, pot and soap-ashes, and timber for shipping, masts, planks, boards, etc., for which purpose men and materials had been sent over for erecting sawmills, although no sawmill was erected for many years. Salt works, which had originally been started, were restored, and the colony was generally imbued with new hopes of plenty, not only to serve the people with salt, but to supply the fisheries on the American coast.

It is evident that sufficient provision had been made

1617.
Decay of early
works.

Cultivation of
tobacco.

Cordage.

Salt works.

for the planting of the principal useful arts in Virginia, Useful arts in Virginia. for among the list of tradesmen who had settled there may be named husbandmen, gardeners, brewers, bakers, sawyers, carpenters, joiners, shipwrights, boatwrights, ploughwrights, millwrights, masons, turners, smiths of all sorts, coopers, weavers, tanners, potters, fowlers, fishhook-makers, net-makers, shoemakers, rope-makers, brickmakers, bricklayers, dressers of hemp and flax, tile-makers, edge-tool-makers, leather-dressers, men skilful in vines and in iron works and mining.   As stated in an old chronicle,* "the men sent have been, most of them, choice men, born and bred up to labor and industry ; out of Devonshire about one hundred men brought up to husbandry ; out of Warwickshire and Staffordshire above one hundred and ten ; and out of Sussex about forty, all framed to iron works, etc." This chronicle also says that "cotton-wooll and sugar canes, all of which may there also be had in abundance, with an infinity of other-more," were among the natural resources of the Virginia soil.

Many attempts were made to divert the colonists from Attempts to establish handicrafts. the production of tobacco and to establish in place of it the work of handicraftsmen.   These will be dealt with in a few illustrations.   Their history is full of romantic interest, illustrating the wants of the colonists and their heroic efforts to supply them.

The Virginia colonists were planters by nature and by training more than they were manufacturers, and they Planters in Virginia. started in the world with the idea that planting and agriculture generally were far more respectable than commercial and manufacturing pursuits.   As they grew they left their carrying trade to the seamen of the northern colonies, and while they had the raw material for many

* "A Declaration of the State of Virginia," 1620; Force's collection.

manufactures they were quite content to raise the material and let others work it into completed products. So the Virginia colonists rested dependent upon England for clothing, exchanging their increased staple, tobacco, for it and for such other necessaries as they found essential.

Settlement at Plymouth.
In December, 1620, another lot of colonists settled at Plymouth, where they found a sterile soil and very rugged climate, but from their way of living they early became interested in manufacturing and commercial enterprises. Like their neighbors in Virginia, they were obliged to turn their attention first to the cultivation of the soil for the supplying of the means of subsistence, but they, too, found timber in great abundance, and the converting it into marketable products offered resources for trade with the home country, especially as England's timber supply had been greatly wasted in the conduct of her iron works. This waste had been so wanton that means were taken as early as 1581 to restrain it. Thus the colonists at Plymouth and the others which settled in that vicinity became exporters of the products of forest industries.

Early exports from Plymouth.
The *Anne* was loaded at Plymouth on the tenth of September, 1623, with a cargo of clapboards and returned to England. The *Anne* was a small ship of one hundred and forty tons.* With her cargo there were beaver skins and other furs. So the two colonies immediately after their settlement were enabled to send the products of their own industry to England.

Shipbuilding.
The northern colony naturally took to shipbuilding ; first, because of the necessity of making small boats and vessels for their coasting, and, secondly, because they

---

* TONS BURDEN.—The tonnage or carrying capacity of a vessel; the quantity or number of tons of freight a vessel will carry: as, a vessel of three hundred tons burden. The internal cubic capacity of a vessel expressed in tons, now reckoned at one hundred cubic feet each.

found the means ready at hand from which vessels could
be constructed. The first vessel, barring some small
open boats built by De Soto's men, ever constructed in
this country by Europeans was a Dutch vessel named the
Onrest, a vessel of sixteen tons burden. This vessel was
built by Captain Adriaen Block, at Manhattan River, in
1614, and its building was necessitated by the destruction
by fire of one of four vessels which arrived in that year
from Amsterdam. It was in this little vessel, the *Onrest*,
or the *Restless*, that Captain Hendrickson discovered the
Schuylkill River in August, 1616. He also explored
nearly the whole coast from Nova Scotia to the capes of
Virginia. Mr. Bishop, in his excellent "History of
American Manufactures," relates that during the same
year (1614) in which the *Restless* was built, Captain John
Smith sailed for "North Virginia" with two ships and
forty-five men and boys, to make experiments upon a
gold and copper mine. Coasting along Maine in April,
they made some attempts at whaling, but failing in that,
they built seven boats, in which thirty-seven men made a
very successful fishing voyage. So the first attempt,
humble though it was, at the fishing business in this
country was made in American bottoms.

Within four years after the landing the Plymouth colony was joined by a carpenter and a salt-maker. These
men were sent out by the company in London. This
was in 1624. This carpenter built two shallops and a
lighter, and the salt-maker selected a site and erected
a building and made an attempt to manufacture salt
for the fishery, first at Cape Ann, and the next year
at Cape Cod, but his attempts were unsuccessful. In
1627 the Plymouth folks built a pinnace at Monamet,
now Sandwich, Mass. This was used for fishing, but
it was not till 1641 that the first vessel of any size

was constructed, which was a bark of fifty tons burden.

Shipbuilding by
Massachusetts
colony.
The first vessel built by the Massachusetts colony was *The Blessing of the Bay*, built at Mystic, now Medford, Mass., and launched on the 4th of July, 1631. · This vessel belonged to Governor Winthrop. It made several coasting trips, and it is related that upon one occasion, while passing Long Island, the sailors were greatly sur-

Indian canoes.
prised at seeing Indian canoes of considerable size, some of which were capable of carrying eighty persons. There was another vessel built at Medford in 1633, named the *Rebecca*, which was of sixty tons ; and another ship of

Shipbuilding at
Medford and
Marblehead.
one hundred and twenty tons was built at Marblehead by Salem people in 1636. At this time, on account of the peculiar state of affairs, the colonists were thrown upon their own efforts to secure a large proportion of the necessaries of life. The emigrant ships which had come from the home country, and which had constantly added to the numbers of the colonists, had supplied them with most of their provisions, other than corn and fish. The civil wars in England interrupted and practically suspended this supply ; so the colonists were obliged to resort to their own resources, as navigation had become precarious. As Governor Winthrop states in his journal, "the general fear of want of foreign commodities, now our money was gone, and that things were like to go well in England, set us on work to provide shipping of our own ; for which end Mr. Peter, being a man of very

At Salem.
public spirit and singular activity for all occasions, procured some to join for building a ship at Salem of three

At Boston.
hundred tons, and the inhabitants of Boston stirred up by his example, set upon the building another at Boston of one hundred and fifty tons. The work was hard to accomplish for want of money, etc. ; but our shipwrights were content to take such pay as the country could

make." Corn was made a legal tender for debt.

Vessels were built during the following years, notably in 1642, when five vessels of a considerable size were built at Boston, Plymouth, Dorchester, and Salem ; and in 1644, when some as large as two hundred and fifty tons were built at Cambridge. One of these took out a cargo of pipe-staves, fish, etc., to the Canary Islands. Quite a large vessel, three hundred tons burden, was built in 1646 at Boston.

By order of the court, on account of the rapid development of shipbuilding, which the court states was a

MARQUETTE DESCENDING THE MISSISSIPPI.

business of great importance for the common good, and following, as it asserts, the commendable course of England and other places, surveyors were ordered to be appointed to examine the ships to see if the work had been performed and carried on according to the rules of the art of shipbuilding. This was in October, 1641.

Shipbuilders were incorporated and the business flourished, for it appears that as early as 1665 Massachusetts

Incorporation
of shipbuilders.

had about 80 vessels of from 20 to 40 tons, about 40 from 40 to 100 tons, and about a dozen ships above 100 tons, making in all over 130 sail. The business was regulated by law and at the same time encouraged. The evidence of the prosecution of the shipbuilding business was all along the coast—at Salem, at Newburyport, New Bedford, Salisbury, everywhere where harbors, opportunity, and supplies were convenient. These statements are true of the district of Maine, which was then and for a long time a part of Massachusetts, whose coves, bays, and streams near the seaboard and whose great supply of timber made shipbuilding the attractive industry.

Ships built in
Massachusetts.

A century before the Declaration of Independence the number of ships which had been built along the Massachusetts coast and belonging to the people settled there numbered thirty vessels between 100 and 250 tons, 400 of from 30 to 100 tons, and 300 between 6 and 10 tons.

THE "HALF-MOON" ON THE HUDSON.

CHAPTER II.

SHIPBUILDING (*Concluded*).

CONNECTICUT started her shipbuilding interest as early as 1640, when the General Court of that colony declared that it was necessary for the comfortable support of the plantations that a trade in cotton-wool be set upon and attempted. The governor of the plantations, Edward Hopkins, undertook the finishing and setting forth of a vessel to those parts where cotton-wool was to be obtained. The first cruiser employed by American colonists was built in 1646, or a little after, by the New Haven and Hartford colonies, to cruise in Long Island Sound for the purpose of preventing encroachments by the Dutch. This vessel carried ten guns and forty men. Shipbuilding flourished in Connecticut, the leading place for such enterprise being at New London, on the Thames. The first actual merchant vessel was built there by merchants of New London and Newport, which cost, exclusive of iron work, etc., £200, and many vessels of various sizes, but all small, were built for voyages to the West Indies, to Newfoundland, and even to Europe. The barks of that day were small vessels, the name being applied to anything that was larger than an ordinary boat. The pinnaces and shallops were deck boats of perhaps twenty tons. The largest vessel built at New London was named *New London*. It was called a ship, was of seventy tons burden, and was the largest vessel that had been built up to that time, 1666. Whale-fishing

Shipbuilding in Connecticut.

Pinnaces and shallops.

in boats along the coast had been pursued by the colonists, and of course the boats for this industry were in demand. Besides New London, Essex, in Saybrook township, started the shipbuilding industry, and small vessels were also built at Sea-Brook, Killingsworth, and New Haven.

A very interesting story is told of an invention which was made in colonial days, and while it does not particularly belong to the development of industry in general, it nevertheless has a bearing on the early application of the inventive genius of this country. The story may be found in the "Transactions" of the American Philosophical Society, and in Silliman's
Early
submarine
vessel.
Journal for 1820. It relates to a submarine vessel contrived by David Bushnell, of Saybrook, for the purpose of blowing up the enemy's ships. Skilful mechanics had previously made inventions of submarine boats, but Bushnell's invention was different from any previous attempt. His design was perfected while he was a student of Yale College, and he carried out his plans in 1775, after his graduation. Silliman's Journal describes Bushnell's invention as "a machine for submarine navigation, altogether different from anything hitherto devised by the art of man. This machine was so constructed that it could be rowed horizontally at any given depth under water, and could be raised or depressed at pleasure. To this machine, called the
The *American*
Turtle.
American Turtle (from its resemblance to two upper tortoise shells placed in contact), was attached a magazine of powder, which was intended to be fastened under the bottom of a ship, with a driving screw, in such a way that the same stroke which disengaged it from the machine, should put the internal clock-work in motion. This being done, the ordinary operation of a gunlock at the

distance of half an hour, or any determinate time, would cause the powder to explode, and leave the effects to the common laws of nature.'' It was this same Bushnell who sent a fleet of kegs down the Delaware to destroy British ships, which incident furnished the origin of the humorous song well known as ''The Battle of the Kegs.''

The Connecticut shipbuilding industry was carried on with considerable energy until the War of the Revolution, when it declined, increasing up to that time, as it did in other states.

Rhode Island began the shipbuilding industry in 1646, Narragansett Bay furnishing convenient places for the construction of vessels, Newport, Bristol, Warren, Providence, and places on the Providence and Taunton Rivers flourishing in consequence. *Shipbuilding in Rhode Island.*

New Hampshire took part in the industry, the building of ships having been a prominent branch of business from the very first settlement of the province. *In New Hampshire.*

The *Restless*, built by Adriaen Block in 1614, has already been referred to, and was probably the first vessel built with a deck ever constructed in this country by Europeans. From this the student of the development of industry would naturally expect to find New York in later years the leading shipbuilding port, especially as the colony was settled under the auspices of Amsterdam, the mercantile metropolis of Europe ; that it was not so was probably owing to the administration of the home company, which stood in the way of taking advantage of the many facilities for shipbuilding. The Knickerbockers, who came after the Dutch adventurers, did build, however, many small vessels, sloops, etc., for the prosecution of the Indian trade. These vessels were used in the sounds and rivers of the colony and in the bays along the coast ; but the restrictions which existed *In New York.*

delayed the opening of the shipbuilding industry, and as late as 1652 New Netherlands had but one small wharf. The accounts of the early shipbuilding there are very meager, and while the shipping interest, after restrictions were removed or modified, grew to extensive proportions, just how much of it was the result of home industry cannot be clearly stated ; but in 1683 there were three barks, three brigantines, twenty-six sloops, and forty-six open boats enrolled by name, and in 1686, according to an official report of the governor, there were then belonging to the province nine or ten three-mast vessels of about eighty or one hundred tons burden, two or three ketches, a bark of about forty tons, and about twenty smaller vessels of twenty to twenty-five tons each. These, except the sloops, traded with England, Holland, and the West Indies, a large proportion of which trade was conducted in vessels built in the colony.

Number of vessels in 1683.

Near the end of the seventeenth century the shipping of New York had grown to considerable proportions, the colony possessing forty square-rigged vessels, sixty-two sloops, and sixty boats. These vessels, with a population not exceeding 6,000, show that the builders of New York were alive to their advantages, and at the time of the Revolution Poughkeepsie and Albany had become prominent in shipbuilding ; and when thirteen vessels of the frigate class were ordered by Congress in December, 1775, the *Congress*, of twenty-eight, and the *Montgomery*, of twenty-four guns, were ordered to be built at Poughkeepsie. Many of the vessels built at the port of New York were of large size.

Extension of shipbuilding in New York.

War vessels.

Space will not admit of mention of the shipbuilding industry on the western lakes, but the development of interests necessitated the construction of vessels of various size to navigate those waters. The first mention of any vessel built on interior waters, although there may have been some account prior to this, is that of a small vessel of sixty tons, whose keel was laid on the 26th of January, 1679, at the mouth of Cayuga Creek, on the American side of the Niagara, and six miles above Shipbuilding on the lakes.

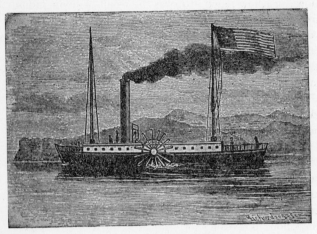

FULTON'S "CLERMONT," 1807.

the falls. It was at this place that the adventurers who accompanied Fathers Tonti and Hennepin, under Sieur de la Salle, finished and equipped with seven small cannon and the usual armament of a man-of-war the first vessel that ever set sail upon Lake Erie. The name given this vessel was the *Griffin.* A schooner of forty feet keel was launched June 28, 1755, on Lake Ontario, and was the first English vessel built on that lake, while the first American vessel built thereon was at Hanford's Landing, in 1798. The *Washington* was built at Four Mile Creek, near Erie, Pa., on Lake Erie, in 1797, and was the first national vessel ever built on that lake. During the Revolution many vessels of different sizes First English vessel on the Great Lakes.

were built on the lakes, and prior thereto, as different expeditions made it necessary, vessels had been constructed for the navigation of the lakes.

New Jersey began the building of ships as early as 1683, the industry being carried on at Salem and Burlington largely, although it is undoubtedly true that vessels had been built on the Delaware prior to that time. It was a principal occupation at Little Egg Harbor, in Burlington County. The *Governor Livingston*, a fine schooner, was fitted out as a letter of marque in 1779 and 1780.

Pennsylvania established the shipbuilding industry at a very early period, and some vessels were built at Philadelphia in 1683, the year after the arrival of William Penn. A shipyard was commenced at the foot of Vine Street soon after. Six years after the founding of Philadelphia she freighted ten vessels with provincial products for the West Indies; yet, as time went on, the industry did not flourish as it did in some of the more

northern parts, and during the year just prior to the Revolution but few vessels were built there. At the time of the Revolution Philadelphia had become the first in naval archi-

BELL'S STEAMBOAT, "COMET," 1812.

tecture, however, and the city originated huge raft-ships. They were immense structures, designed for carrying great quantities of timber, to be broken up at the close of the voyage. Of the thirteen frigates ordered by Congress in 1775, the *Washington* and *Randolph*, of thirty-two guns each, the *Effingham*, of twenty-eight, and the *Delaware*, of twenty-four guns, were built at Philadelphia. The keels of other war vessels were laid at Philadelphia, and many smaller vessels built and equipped. The development of shipbuilding through invention has rested very largely upon the inventive genius of residents of Philadelphia. These matters belong to a later date, however, than colonial days.

The state of Delaware early saw the establishment of shipbuilding. This occurred especially in the locality of the present city of Wilmington. Certain it is that as early as 1642 shipbuilding, boatbuilding, and cooper work were carried on upon Cooper's Island, but the first vessel for foreign trade, which was a brig named the *Wilmington*, was built in 1740. The industry was also carried on at New Castle as early as the time of the settlement by Penn. The *General Washington*, a fine ship of 250 tons, was launched from the shipyard of William Woodcock, in Wilmington, in 1790. Wilmington has acquired a wide reputation in shipbuilding, all classes of vessels being built there. *In Delaware.*

There are but few particulars of shipbuilding in the middle and southern colonies, the result, probably, of the tendency to agricultural pursuits rather than to commerce and manufactures ; but after the earlier years Maryland improved her facilities for shipbuilding. They were unsurpassed by those of any other province. The business progressed rapidly, and Maryland built as early as 1769 twenty vessels, with an aggregate of 1,344 tons. Only small craft had been built prior to this time. In 1772 eight vessels were built in Maryland, a number equal to that built in Pennsylvania at the same time. During the War of the Revolution, Maryland was exceedingly active in fitting out cruisers, and one of the *In Middle and Southern States.* *In Maryland.*

first frigates ordered by Congress, the *Virginia*, of twenty-eight tons, was built by the Maryland ship-builders. Others were ordered there in later years, while the old *Constellation* was built at Baltimore for the federal government.

In Virginia. The shipbuilding industry of Virginia has already been noticed in slight degree, a few barks, pinnaces, etc., having been built there prior to 1621. The business, however, did not make much progress, probably the ordinances in prohibition of commerce, under acts of

Parliament, having much to do with the slow progress made there. Nevertheless, the Virginians turned some of their attention from the soil to commerce, for it is recorded that in 1769 she produced twenty-seven sail of new vessels, while the Continental Congress

"Old Ironsides."

ordered two frigates, of thirty-six guns each, to be built in Virginia, and the old frigate *Chesapeake* was laid at Portsmouth.

Shipbuilding materials. About the close of the last century shipbuilding had increased considerably in the southern colonies, and so much so that Maryland, Virginia, and North Carolina each surpassed New Hampshire, while Virginia and Maryland had more manufactories of cordage and cables, used so largely in building ships, than any two of the states of

New York and New Hampshire, New Jersey and Connecticut.   Georgia and the Carolinas supplied most excellent material for ships, which material was used by
the shipbuilders of the Middle and Northern States.
The southern colonies had great advantages in these
directions.   Cedar, pine, live-oak grew in abundance
and gave the very best materials for serviceable ships,
and in 1740 the Carolinas began seriously to attend to
shipbuilding, five ships being built in that year, and
twenty-four square-rigged vessels, besides sloops and
schooners, were constructed between the years 1740 and
1779.   Some vessels had been built in Georgia as early
as 1741, and a new era in shipbuilding, resulting from
the discovery of extensive supplies of live-oak, began
in 1750.   When the Revolutionary War broke out
South Carolina availed herself of her facilities, as shown
in her activity in fitting out cruisers for the defense of
American coasts.   It is to be regretted that the data
of the shipbuilding interests in the southern colonies are
not as extensive as those for the northern colonies, but if
the southern colonies lacked in the building of ships, they
certainly made up in furnishing the very best material
for their building.

Shipbuilding
materials in
southern
colonies.

The industry in the whole country prior to the Revolution, when, of course, shipbuilding was suspended to a
large degree, except for war purposes, was satisfactory
and showed the enterprise of the colonists.   The record
is a flattering one and is a fitting statement with which
to close this brief account of the shipbuilding of the
colonies.   The account for all the colonies for the year
1769, the only year for which a summary is found, at
least just prior to the Revolution, shows that 389 vessels
had been built, having an aggregate of 20,000 tons
burden.   Of these New Hampshire built 45 ; Massa-

Shipbuilding
prior to the
Revolution.

chusetts, 137 ; Rhode Island, 39 ; Connecticut, 50 ;
New York, 19 ; the Jerseys, 4 ; Pennsylvania, 22 ;
Maryland, 20 ; Virginia, 27 ; North Carolina, 12 ; South

Ships built in
different
colonies.

Carolina, 12 ; Georgia, 2.   The whole number of vessels built in all the colonies in the year 1772 was 182.
These figures show the development when the Revolution opened.

While the history of shipbuilding during colonial
days would occupy chapters, this account, brief as it is,
has been given much more length than can be devoted
to general industries, because it was the first industry to
attract the colonists other than the planting of the soil.

Shipbuilding
the first
mechanical
industry.

It was the first of the mechanical industries to which
they paid their attention to any profitable degree.

A Modern Atlantic Liner.

CHAPTER III.

TEXTILE INDUSTRIES.*

IT IS impossible to determine when the manufacture of cloth was first undertaken by the colonists. The records of shipbuilding and other industries give positive dates in most instances ; but a careful search of documents and records fails to disclose the time of the earliest efforts to produce their own clothing. There is no doubt, however, that with the earliest ships that came to the southern and northern colonies there came the spinning-wheel and the hand-loom, although no mention is made of their advent. *Spinning-wheel and hand-loom.* It is true, too, that the colonists depended for some time upon the mother-country for textiles. They soon learned the way of the savages and their skill in utilizing the furs of animals, but they could not have entered to any great extent upon the spinning of yarn and the weaving of cloth.

The old home of the woolen industry was Holland, and England had received her best workers in wool from that country ; so the colonies had men entirely familiar with weaving. They brought men to Virginia *Sheep-raising in Virginia.* in 1607 who were accustomed to sheep-raising and who knew the intricacies of the manufacture of cloth from wool fibers. The Virginia colony was the first to introduce sheep, while the Dutch West India Company brought them to New Netherlands as early as 1625.

* For a detailed account of the woolen industry, see " Manufacture of Wool," by S. N. D. North, *The Popular Science Monthly*, June, 1891 ; for an account of cotton and woolen manufactures, see Bishop's " History of American Manufactures," Vol. I, and "A National History of American Manufactures."

None were brought to the Plymouth colony, so far as can be learned, at as early a date as that, but the Massachusetts colony imported them about 1633, and in order to protect them from wolves and Indians kept them on an island in Boston Harbor. Governor Winthrop stated that the Plymouth folks had about forty sheep brought to them from Boston in 1634. Strangely enough, the year before they felt obliged to forbid the exportation of sheep ; so they must have had a few at that time. The

Massachusetts colony had succeeded in acquiring about one thousand sheep by 1642. Dependence had before that been largely upon importations from Malaga. The

flocks of sheep increased everywhere, until, taking all the colonies together, the accounts show that in 1661 they had nearly one hundred thousand. It is evident, therefore, that at this time the colonists were in a position to make a very large proportion of their own clothing. The raising of wool increased, and with it, as a natural result, the manufacture of cloth.

THE SPINNING-WHEEL.

It is not known how many sheep there were in the

country at the time of the adoption of the constitution, but twenty years later there were ten million.

The first mention of the presence of the spinning-wheel and the loom occurs in the records of the Massa- chusetts colony, in an inventory in 1639, relating to four yards of home-made cloth, at six shillings per yard, and two spinning-wheels are mentioned in another inventory in 1638, the spinning-wheels being set down at three shillings. The colonists of New Netherlands could not make woolen, linen, or cotton cloth, or weave any other textiles, and this prohibition was under heavy penalty, any one making such goods being banished and arbi-

First mention of spinning-wheel and loom.

THE HAND-LOOM.

trarily punished as perjurers. This was the restriction of the home government.

Prohibition of cloth-making.

Governor Dudley, of Massachusetts, in writing home in 1631, stated that clothes and bedding must be brought to the colony until the development of industry enabled them to be produced there ; yet a year or two later the colonial people, from their small clippings, must have commenced the spinning and weaving of wool, and the

ten years following saw emphatic progress in the efforts
to supply clothing made in the houses of the colonists.
Hemp and flax were produced in sufficient quantities to
enable the people to make the clothing they absolutely
needed ; nevertheless, the farmers gave their preference
to foreign cloth, which they bought with their own wares.

Beginning of
the manu-
facture of
wool.

The domestic manufacture of cloth was not general, but
it is safe to say that the manufacture of wool in this
country was practically begun in the period from 1632 to
1642.

An event occurred in 1638 which gave the Massachusetts colony quite a start in the woolen industry. This
came through the expulsion from Yorkshire, England, of
Pastor Ezekiel Rogers and his flock. These people had
some capital, and on founding the town of Rowley they
set up a woolen and fulling-mill.* This little town was
incorporated in 1639, and in it the homespun industries
of America were commenced. Quite a number of the

First fulling-
mill.

Rogers people were familiar with the manufacture of
woolens, and the fulling-mill which they built was the
first one erected in the North American colonies. John
Pearson was the builder, and the year was 1643. This
little mill was in operation as late as 1809. Although
these people came from the woolen districts of England,
they used in their homes flax and cotton, as well as wool.
Governor Winthrop, in one of his letters, says that Rowley exceeded all other towns, although the manufacture
of wool was general. There is a tradition, amounting to
fact almost, of the erection of a fulling-mill in 1640 at
Salem. The presence of fulling-mills indicates that the

---

* FULLING-MILL.—A power machine for fulling and felting felts and woven
fabrics, to improve their texture by making them thicker, closer, and heavier.
Such mills operate by means of rollers, stampers, and beaters, of various
forms and usually of wood, which beat, roll, and press the fabric in hot suds
and fullers' earth, felting it together till the required texture is obtained. An
unavoidable result of the process is a reduction in length, in width, and, in the
case of hats, of size.

weaving of cloths was sufficient not only to clothe the people in the vicinity but to give a surplus for trade.

The Massachusetts colonists also profited by the troubles which existed in England at this period, on account of which there was a less supply of cloths than usual ; so the government of the colony made inquiry concerning the number of persons who would buy sheep and took means to encourage the raising of flocks. Some tide-mills* were erected, notably one at Guilford, Conn. Another stimulating incident was the fact that the English government put an export duty of three shillings four pence on every piece of woolen broadcloth and prohibited the exportation of sheep, wool, and woolen yarns from England. This stringent legislation led the Massachusetts General Court in 1656 to order the people of the towns to turn their attention to spinning and weaving. Home manufactures became an absolute necessity, and the other colonies followed the example of Massachusetts, fulling-mills being erected here and there. Every effort was made to stimulate the woolen industry, herdsmen being provided by law or under town orders and bounties given for the destruction of wolves. Later on woolen manufactories were set up in different places ; so that by the time of the adoption of the constitution the northern colonies were producing considerable quantities of woolen cloth, one establishment at Hartford, Conn., in the year ending September, 1789, having produced 5,000 yards of cloth, some of which was sold at five dollars per yard. General Washington visited this particular factory during his tour in the Eastern States in 1789, and he writes in his diary that the work seemed to be going on with spirit, and that while their broadcloths

Restrictions of English laws.

Necessity of home manufactures.

Washington's visit to Connecticut.

---

* TIDE-MILL.—A mill supplied with power by means of a water-wheel operated by the tide, either directly in flowing through a tideway, or indirectly in flowing out of a tidal basin.

were not of the first quality, yet they were good. He testi-fied also to the quality of coatings, cassimeres, serges, and everlastings, and ordered a suit of broadcloth to be sent to him at New York. Tradition gives it that in making his speech to Congress in January, 1790, he wore a full suit of broadcloth made at the Hartford fac-tory. Another cloth-dresser at Hartford, Robert Pier-pont, in 1789 finished on one press over 8,000 yards of cloth.

Woolen manu-facture in Virginia.

Virginia made early attempts to stimulate the manufac-ture of woolens, and as far back as 1662 passed laws for the encouragement of that industry. Her first fulling-mills, however, were not erected until about 1692. Gov-ernor Andros, during his administration, made great efforts to develop textile manufactures, but his successor, Governor Nicholson, was opposed to such efforts, and advised Parliament to pass orders prohibiting the making of cloth in the colonies. From this it is deducible that considerable quantities of domestic cloths were manufac-tured—enough, at least, to affect the importation of English goods. At this period (the close of the seven-teenth century) the imports and exports of Virginia and Maryland were greater than those of all the other colonies combined. Before the close of the colonial period Vir-ginia had fulling-mills in various localities.

In Penn-sylvania.

Pennsylvania took action similar to that of her sister colonies to encourage the production of woolen goods. That state certainly did its share in the early efforts of the colonies to produce what they might need for their own wear. There were many fulling-mills in the state by the middle of the eighteenth century, and broadcloths were produced in Philadelphia in the latter half of that century. Philadelphia introduced the manufacture of

Introduction of spinning-wheel irons.

spinning-wheel irons, the production of which at the

close of the colonial period amounted to 1,500 sets, most
of them being for use in families, and not in woolen
establishments. Lancaster, Pa., had erected fulling-mills
at a very early date, and was the largest inland town in
the country at the time of the adoption of the constitution. It then had 700 families, 234 of which were manufacturers, including many weavers of woolen, linen, and
cotton cloth.

New Jersey, too, came in for her share in the develop-
ment of textiles, but not at so early a date as some of the *In New Jersey.*
others, of course. The Quakers who came to Jersey
from Yorkshire and London, in England, and who settled
at Salem, Burlington, and other parts of West Jersey,
about the year 1677, lost no time in commencing the
manufacture of cloth. A colony was established on the
Delaware, under a charter from the court of Sweden,
granted in 1640. By the terms of this charter the
people were permitted to engage in all manufactures and
in all commerce, domestic and foreign, and Governor
Printz, who soon afterward came to the colony, was instructed by his government to do all in his power to promote the propagation of sheep, with the view of exporting wool to the home country. After this Swedish company came under the proprietary government of Pennsylvania, it is learned from a letter to a Swedish official,
written in 1693, that the wives and daughters of the colonists employed themselves in spinning wool and flax,
and many of them in weaving. They had a few sheep,
eighty in number, probably as early as 1663, and were
well supplied with wool at the time of the writing of the
letter just mentioned.

Rhode Island, the present home of the manufacture of
some of the best woolen cloths in the country, took *In Rhode Island.*
active part in developing the woolen trade, and South

In South Carolina. Carolina, by its first Provincial Congress, was urged to encourage manufactures. Premiums were offered for the making of wool-cards* and for woolen cloth. A fulling-mill was erected in that state before 1790 for dressing fine and coarse woolens. This was on Fishing Creek,

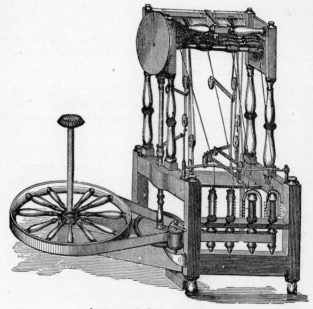

ARKWRIGHT'S SPINNING MACHINE.
From the original drawing.

Premiums offered. near the Catawba River, and the spinners and weavers of the colony in that vicinity kept the fulling-mill busy in dyeing, fulling, and pressing, all these processes being

---

*WOOL-CARD.—A brush with wire teeth, used in disentangling fibers of wool and laying them parallel to one another preparatory to spinning. In hand-cards the wires are short and are passed slantingly through leather, which is then nailed upon a board. Two of these brushes are used, one in each hand, and in use are drawn past each other, the fibers being between them. In the carding machine, which has superseded hand-carding, the cards are formed by hard-drawn wire staples, each furnishing two teeth, drawn through leather and bent at a certain angle.

performed in excellent manner by the settlers from Great Britain, who were fully conversant therewith.

What has been said relates almost entirely to the starting of the woolen industries. Cotton-spinning and weaving very naturally kept pace with the manufacture of woolen cloths. Cotton was an indigenous plant in the southern portion of the colonies, and so nature offered the opportunity for the utilization of a fiber which constitutes the basis of the great civilizing cotton industry. It is probably true that in the older country the use of the cotton fiber antedates that of the animal fibers, and especially is this true of flax and some of the vegetable fibers which require treatment involving more intricate processes than cotton before the finished cloth can be produced; but its use was recognized at a very early date by the colonists, for when the Pilgrims were earnestly trying to produce their first crops of Indian corn cotton was being raised by the colonists in Virginia. Purchas, the historian, relates that in the year 1621 cotton was planted in this country.

The Massachusetts colonists received their first supply from Barbadoes, in 1633, and some cotton goods were made up for home wear in the New England colonies as early as 1643. South Carolina had cotton under cultivation as early as 1664, or it may be two years later. If one refers to a work entitled "Cotton in the Middle States," published in 1862 by Dr. G. Emerson, of Philadelphia, he will find that long before the Southern States took up the culture of cotton the plant was raised on the eastern shore of Maryland, in the southern counties of Delaware, and at various points in the middle colonies; yet it was regarded as an ornamental plant as late as 1736 and many years after, and its cultivation was confined to gardens. According

Cotton-spinning and weaving.

Cotton-raising.

First supplies of cotton.

Cultivation of cotton in Maryland and Delaware.

to the work just cited, many families in Maryland who came from Sussex County, Delaware, wore clothing made of cotton of their own raising, spinning, and weaving. But the culture of cotton in this particular section of the colonies gradually diminished. The Middle States could not compete with the more Southern States in raising this staple. Mr. Madison, representing Virginia in the convention which was held in Annapolis in 1786 for the purpose of taking under consideration the means which could be adopted for recuperating the finances of the country, stated it as his opinion that "from the results of cotton-raising in Talbot County, Maryland, and numerous other proofs furnished in Virginia, there is no reason to doubt that the United States will one day become a great cotton-producing country."

Decrease of cotton culture in Maryland and Delaware.

From these and other facts which are ascertainable, it is clearly seen that the cultivation of cotton which first drew the attention of the colonists took place on the peninsula between the Delaware and Chesapeake Bays, then crossed to western Maryland, thence to Virginia, and finally found its home in the far South. No exportations of this great staple of any consequence were made until the year of the Constitutional Convention—1787— when Charleston, S. C., sent three hundred pounds to England. There was no reason why the cotton industry should not have been established in the colonies on a larger scale than it was and at an earlier date, unless it be, perhaps, the difficulty which existed of separating the cotton from the seed. This process was carried on both by hand and by rude machinery—a difficulty which was overcome in the opening years of the constitutional period by the invention of the saw-gin by Whitney.

Cotton cultivation transferred farther south.

Whitney's saw-gin.

CHAPTER IV.

TEXTILE INDUSTRIES (*Concluded*).

In 1774–75 Alexander Hamilton published some pamphlets, in one of which he used the following language:

With respect to cotton, you do not pretend to deny that a *Hamilton's views of cotton manufacture.* sufficient quantity may be produced. Several of the southern colonies are so favorable to it that, with due cultivation, in a couple of years they would afford enough to clothe the whole continent. As to the expense of bringing it by land, the best way will be to manufacture it where it grows, and afterwards transport it to the other colonies. Upon this plan I apprehend the expense would not be greater than to build and equip large ships to import the manufactures of Great Britain from thence. If we were to turn our attention from external to internal commerce, we would give greater facility and more lasting prosperity to our country than she can possibly have otherwise. . . . . If by the necessity of the thing manufactures should once be established and take root among us, they will pave the way still more to the future grandeur and glory of America.

Another difficulty which prevented the growth of the cotton industry along lines equal to the growth of the wool manufacture resulted from the peculiar attitude of the home country. Prior to the decade of years beginning with 1760 the cotton cloths of England were made in the same way that the woolen cloths were made—that *Methods in use by colonists.* is, by hand machinery. The colonists used the same methods, and thus produced coarse grades of cotton cloths.

During the decade of years from 1760 to 1770 the inventive genius of England brought out the wonderful series of spinning and weaving machines which revolutionized the textile industries, but England took great pains that none of these machines should reach her colonists; so, although waking up to the importance of the cotton industry at a late period in their history, the colonists made no headway in establishing it in their midst, and the colonial period closed with no particular advance having been made, and it was only during the earlier

Invention of cotton machinery in England.

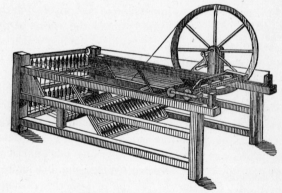

HARGREAVES' SPINNING-JENNY.

years of the succeeding period, beginning with the adoption of the constitution, that the American people overcame the existing obstacles.   They made great efforts to secure English machines, but the legislation of England prohibiting the exportation of machines, tools, or plans, and even the immigration of men who knew how to build machines, presented difficulties which they could not overcome.   Some of these difficulties aided in bringing about a frame of mind which led to a conclusion that great efforts must be made to secure industrial independ-

Efforts to secure cotton machinery in America.

ence, and the colonists actually attempted to introduce
spinning machines as early as 1775. Mr. Aitkin, who
published the *Pennsylvania Magazine*, brought out in the
year just named a cut of what he called "a new invented machine for spinning of wool or cotton," and he
said in a note accompanying the cut that he had seen
the machine perform and was convinced of its usefulness.
Mr. Christopher Tully was the maker of the Philadelphia
machine, but whether it had anything to do with the
setting up of a manufactory in that city for the production of woolen, cotton, and linen goods, in which the
machine was used, it is impossible to determine ; but the
factory was commenced in 1775, and the efforts of the
association which erected it constitute the first actual attempt to manufacture cotton goods by new methods in
the United States.

Spinning machinery.

The provinces urged the manufacture of textile machinery, cotton-cards, etc., and in 1775 there was undertaken at Norwich, Conn., the manufacture of iron wire
for the making of cotton and wool-cards. Card teeth
were made by hand in 1777 by one Oliver Evans,
of Philadelphia, and Jeremiah Wilkinson, of Cumberland, R. I., was engaged in the manufacture of hand-
cards. Evans invented a machine by which he could
turn them out at the rate of 1,500 per minute. So before the Revolution the cotton industry was fairly well
under way. The war brought many appeals from Congress to increase the supply of wool and other materials
and for the expansion of the manufacture of cloth. The
armies needed clothing, and Congress had to rely upon
the people of the colonies to supply it.

Card teeth.

Effect of war on cloth manu- facture.

While the first attempt to manufacture cotton goods
on any scale occurred in Philadelphia, the second
attempt was made in Worcester, Mass., in 1780, and a

Early attempts at cotton manu- facture.

spinning-jenny* on the English pattern was procured. This machine and that in use at Philadelphia were in all probability brought over prior to the legislation of Great Britain which prohibited their exportation from that country, for the accounts of manufactures nowhere

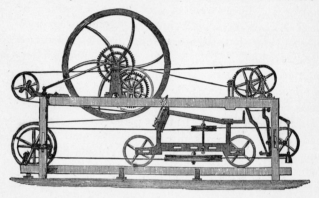

CROMPTON'S MULE-JENNY (specification drawing).

give any evidence of any other English-made machines having been used in the United States at any time prior to those just mentioned. The use of textile machinery belongs to the period following the Revolution.

The use of flax and hemp by the colonists was very

---

* SPINNING-JENNY.—A machine for spinning wool or cotton. It has a series of vertical spindles, each of which is supplied with roving from a separate spool, and has a clasping and traversing mechanism by means of which the operator is enabled to clasp and draw out all the roving or roll simultaneously during the operation of twisting, and to feed the twisted threads to the spindles when winding on—the whole operation being almost exactly like hand-spinning, except that a large number of rovings are operated upon instead of a single one.

SPINNING-MULE.—A machine invented by Samuel Crompton, in which the rovings are delivered from a series of sets of drawing-rollers to spindles placed on a carriage which travels away from the rollers while the thread is being twisted, and returns toward the rollers while the thread is being wound. It draws, stretches, and twists at one operation. So named because it was a combination of the drawing-rollers of Arkwright and the jenny of Hargreaves.

SPINNING-JACK.—A device for twisting and winding a sliver as it comes from the drawing-rollers. It is placed in the can, in which it rotates, the sliver being wound on a bobbin.

general. They produced a coarse kind of mixed fabrics in which linen or hemp thread largely entered as material. Linen subserved nearly all the purposes for which cotton is now employed, and for this reason the cultivation of flax and hemp plants received great attention.* The linens were of very coarse texture. The kerseys, linsey-woolseys, serges, and druggets consisted of wool variously combined with flax or tow, and formed the outer clothing of a large part of the population during the colder season. Hempen cloth and linen of different degrees of fineness, from the coarsest tow-cloth to the finest holland, constituted the principal wearing apparel, outward and inward. The inner garments and the table and bed linen of nearly all classes were almost entirely supplied from the serviceable products of the household industry. The materials were mostly grown upon the farms of the planters, and the breaking and heckling of the flax were done by the men, while the carding, spinning, weaving, bleaching, and dyeing were performed by the wives and daughters of the planters, the women taking great pride in the products of their industry. The laborers dressed in home-made goods of hemp or flax, and coats, or doublets, and breeches of leather or buckskin were also worn. Felt hats, coarse leather shoes, with brass buckles, and sometimes with wooden heels, were part of the equipment of the workingmen.

General use of linen.

Methods of spinning flax

Laborer's dress.

The Scotch-Irish of New Hampshire undertook to manufacture linen goods, for they were familiar with this industry. The foot-wheel was used by them for spinning the flax, and these men, wherever they were, undertook to improve the linen manufacture. They introduced a better knowledge of the cultivation and manufacture of flax and linen and of spinning flax. Most of the proc-

* See Bishop's "History of American Manufactures."

esses of manufacture were manual operations, only crude and imperfect implements being used, and much of the woolen cloth was worn without shearing, pressing, or any other finish. As a result of the efforts of the Scotch-Irish, a public meeting was called in Boston, when a committee was appointed to consider the pro-

Spinning school in Boston.

priety of establishing "a spinning school or schools for the instruction of the children of the town."* A large, handsome brick building was erected on the east side of what was Long Acre, now known as Tremont Street, near Hamilton Place. At the opening an immense concourse assembled, and the women of Boston, rich and poor, appeared on the Common with their spinning-wheels, vying with each other in the use of the instrument. Subscriptions were raised for the support of the project, and the Assembly, in 1737, laid a tax on carriages and other luxuries for the maintenance of the institution. After a few years of active work the building was abandoned, and it was afterward used as a manufactory for worsted hose, metal buttons, etc.

Hon. Daniel Oliver started a spinning school at Boston about the same time, for the employment of the poor.

Public spinning in New York.

The city of New York in 1734 passed an ordinance for the erection of a poorhouse, which was furnished with spinning-wheels, leather and tools for shoemakers, knitting-needles, flax, etc., for the employment of the inmates.

Linen manufactures.

Linen manufacture prospered fairly well in the other colonies, the cultivation of flax and hemp being much attended to in Pennsylvania, where the German and Irish people had settled in large numbers. These manufac-

---

* For an account of this experiment recourse has been had to Bishop's excellent " History of American Manufactures."

tures did not flourish so well in the South, because, while the soil was well adapted for hemp and flax, the profits of tobacco culture discouraged other industries ; so the clothing of the southern colonies, as linen, woolen, silk, hats, and even leather, came from the old country. The expense of labor probably had something to do with these matters, because the raising, dressing, and manufacture of flax and hemp involved a large amount of labor simply to bring the material into such shape that thread could be made of it. The scarcity of labor hindered manufactures in all the colonies. Some forms of industry, of course, afforded the means of purchasing foreign merchandise on fairly easy terms, thus reducing the inducement to undertake the manufacture of goods. This operated to retard the development of the textile industries, as well as others. The efforts to cultivate silk and to make silk goods met with but little success. Some of the colonists brought with them a knowledge of silk-raising and silk manufacture, but the accounts of this industry are so meager that one cannot state positively the extent to which it was developed.

Effects of expensive labor.

Silk.

Indigo was introduced and helped to make the textile industries more profitable and easy, but they could not compete with agriculture, commerce, and the fisheries, which were the great strong arms of the colonies.

Indigo.

The close of the first century of the colonies found them hampered by the laws of the mother-country. While the first attempts to make a portion of their own clothing had not drawn much attention to the colonists from English merchants and manufacturers, their subsequent efforts did draw such attention, and on account of complaints that were made to the Board of Trade, that wool and woolen manufactures of Ireland and the North American plantations were being exported to foreign

Manufacturers hampered by laws.

markets formerly supplied by England, the British Parliament passed a law in 1699 which for the first time
recognized such manufactures in the colonies.   This act,
known as 10 and 11 Wm. III., c. 10, provided that
"after the first day of December, 1699, no wool, wool-
fels, yarn, cloth, or woolen manufactures of the English
plantations in America shall be shipped in any of the
said English plantations, or otherwise loaden, in order
to be transported thence to any place whatsoever, under
the penalty of forfeiting ship and cargo, and £500 fine
for each offense ; and the Governors of the Plantations
and Officers of Customs and Revenue there are to see
this Act, as it relates to the plantations, duly executed."
The total population of the American colonies when this
prohibition was placed upon them was probably about
260,000.   Under such prohibitions the struggle was a
hard one, and with courage, persistence, and ingenuity
the colonists went on in their way ; yet when the eighteenth century drew to a close and their political independence of Great Britain had been won and a new constitution adopted, the country found itself still subject to
Great Britain in most industrial matters.

CHAPTER V.

PRINTING AND PUBLISHING.

INDUSTRY is always allied to the diffusion of knowledge; so its development must necessarily require the printing press. Primitive wants are supplied that com-

Alliance of industry and knowledge.

BENJAMIN FRANKLIN.

fort may be secured, but general knowledge and the evolution of industry must go hand in hand ; so the first colonists, while working diligently to demonstrate their

Provision for education.

capacity, not only to provide their wants, but to export their products, had regard for posterity, and provided at an early day for the best interests of education and the diffusion of knowledge.

First press.

The first printing press in the country was established at Cambridge, Mass., in 1639, provision having been made for a college at that place the year before. The Virginia colonists had made provision for a college at an earlier date, 1619, but the plans of the Virginians were not allowed to be carried out. The first issue of any printed matter was from the Cambridge press, in January,

First printed matter.

1639, when a small pamphlet, "The Freeman's Oath," was printed.* There was brought out an almanac for the year 1639 from the same press, while in 1640 the first book appeared. It was called "The Bay Psalm

First book.

Book." It went through many editions, being a popular work, both in America and England, and in the latter country an edition was published soon after its appearance in the colonies, the latest edition being printed in 1754.

First original composition.

In 1640 Mrs. Anne Bradstreet, the wife of Simon Bradstreet, who afterward became governor of Massachusetts, and who was a daughter of the celebrated Thomas Dudley, brought out a volume of poems, which was the first original composition printed in America.

Second press.

The second press which was brought into use in the colonies was sent over in 1655, accompanied with all the necessary materials for printing. This press was designed particularly for printing the Bible and other books in aboriginal tongues and for the purpose of aiding Rev. John Eliot in his missionary work with the Indians.

That great aid to the spread of printed information, the

---

* Isaiah Thomas, " The History of Printing in America," Worcester, Mass., 1810.

copyright, was first applied in 1672, under the General Court of Massachusetts, when John Usher, a bookseller, was given the privilege of publishing a revised edition of the laws of the colony.

A second press was set up at Boston by one John Foster, in 1674, and he had the honor of printing the first book, so far as known, ever printed in that town.

The third printing press which the colonies could boast, and the very first that was erected outside of the Massachusetts colony, was set up in Philadelphia, in the year 1686, by William Bradford. This was at a place now known as Kensington. Some of the authorities give it that his earliest publication was an almanac for the year 1687.

Third press.

New York's first press was established in 1693, and this was by the same Bradford who had set up the press in Philadelphia in 1686. Bradford, after his removal to New York, was appointed printer to the government, being allowed £50 from the public treasury. He held this situation for nearly thirty years, and was also during the same period public printer for the province of New York.

New York's first press.

The first attempt to publish a newspaper in the colonies occurred at Boston on September 25, 1690, when a sheet entitled *Publick Occurrences, both Foreign and Domestick*, appeared. This publication, which was printed by Richard Pierce and published by Benjamin Harris, and which was to have been issued monthly, never went beyond the first number, being suppressed by the government.

First newspaper.

The first paper of which there is any record of its having gone beyond the first number was the *News-Letter*, published on April 24, 1704, by one Green, in Boston, for John Campbell, postmaster of that town.

Printing in Maryland.

Second news-
paper in the
colonies.
The second newspaper was the *Boston Gazette*, issued in
Boston.   This was printed by James Franklin, a brother
of Benjamin Franklin, and was published December 21,
1719.

The *New York Gazette* was published October 16,
1725, by the Bradford already referred to.

The first regular printing done in Maryland was by
William Parks, in 1727 or 1728.   A press had been set
up at Annapolis in 1726, and on this Parks printed a
complete collection of the laws of Maryland.   The next
year he began the publication of the *Maryland Gazette*.
Parks also established a press at Williamsburg, Va., in
1729, and did the first printing in that colony.

South Carolina.
South Carolina's first press was set up at Charleston,
by Eleazer Phillips, of Boston, in 1730.

Rhode Island.
Rhode Island's first press was at Newport, and was
established by Benjamin Franklin's brother James, in
1732.

New
Hampshire.
North Carolina.
Other colonies had presses at later dates—New Hamp-
shire in 1756 ; and North Carolina in 1754-55, through
the establishment of a press at Newbern, by James Davis.

Delaware.
Delaware's first press was established at Wilmington
in 1761, by James Adams.

Georgia.
Georgia came into the printing business the last of the
old states, a press being set up at Savannah in 1762, by
James Johnson.

The great rival towns for printing were Philadelphia
and Boston, the publishing business of the two cities
being nearly equal prior to the Revolution.   Benjamin
Franklin, America's greatest typographer, shared the successes of the two cities.   Born in Boston, and receiving
his first instructions in the art of printing in the establishment of his brother James, he carried his knowledge
to Philadelphia and gave that city his illustrious services,

his industry, wisdom, and talent making his skill and reputation known throughout all the colonies and the home country.

An enterprising undertaking for the primitive colonial press was the bringing out of the first German Bible. This was printed at Germantown, Pa., in 1743, by Christopher Saur, and was the first Bible printed for the European population in the American colonies. Three years' labor had been spent upon the work, which was of quarto form, containing 1,272 pages. It was the heaviest publication which had been issued from the press in Pennsylvania.

First Bible printed in America.

The first American Bible in the English language was carried through the press at Boston in a private way by Kneeland and Green, about the year 1752. It was chiefly made by Daniel Henchman, probably

THE FRANKLIN PRESS.

First Bible in English.

the most flourishing bookseller of the American colonies prior to the Revolution. He it was who built the first paper-mill in New England, although the first paper-mill erected in the American colonies was built in Pennsylvania, the date of its erection not being clearly ascertainable.

First paper-mill in the American colonies.

The General Magazine and Historical Chronicle for

all the British Plantations in America was the first journal having a literary character published in this country. This was in 1741, the publication being a duo-decimo monthly, at twelve shillings a year. Benjamin Franklin was the printer and editor. It had but a short life, being published only six months. After Franklin brought out his magazine John Welbe published *The American Magazine* in opposition to Franklin, but Welbe's enterprise did not continue long.

First daily newspaper in America.

The *Pennsylvania Packet*, or *General Advertiser*, was the first daily newspaper published in America. This was published in Philadelphia, and first appeared as a weekly in November, 1771, being printed by John Dunlap.

The *Philadelphia Gazette*, established in Philadelphia in 1788 by Samuel Relf, was the first daily evening paper.

Newspapers in Pennsylvania at time of Revolution.

At the breaking out of the Revolution there were nine newspapers in Pennsylvania, of which six in English and one in German were published in Philadelphia, one in German at Germantown, and one in English and German at Lancaster.

In Massachusetts.

At this period there were seven newspapers published in Massachusetts, of which five were at Boston, one at Salem, and one at Newburyport. Connecticut had four and Rhode Island one, while New Hampshire could claim but one, which was published at Portsmouth. There were, therefore, thirteen newspapers in New England at that time.

In New York.

There were four newspapers published in the province of New York at the date named, three in the city of New York and one at Albany. Maryland had two, one at Annapolis and one at Baltimore. There were two in the colony of Virginia, two in North Carolina, three in South Carolina, and one in Georgia.

The colonists could therefore boast, at the time of their movement against the mother-country, of thirty-seven newspapers. Many of the efforts to establish periodicals in the colonies were failures, the entire number between 1704 and 1775 being less than one hundred, of which three fourths were newspaper sheets and the balance magazines of some kind or form. Twenty-two of the whole number were begun in Massachusetts and fourteen in other New England states. Pennsylvania had twenty-two, New York sixteen, and the other colonies or provinces twenty-two. Many of them, however, had but a brief existence, while some continued for a respectable period, exerting a varied influence on the public mind. Materials were costly and were mostly imported ; the price of labor was high and the country sparsely settled, so that but small circulations could be secured, and a general taste and leisure for reading had not been fully cultivated. Another obstacle which the printers and publishers were obliged to meet during the latter part of the colonial period was the legislation of the mother-country.

Number of newspapers in the colonies.

High price of labor. Small circulations.

Under the Stamp Act of March, 1765, all pamphlets and newspapers were subject to a duty of one half-penny, and all such, after November 1st of that year, were required to be printed on stamped paper. A publication not exceeding six sheets was subjected to a tax of two shillings, and the same tax was imposed upon all advertisements. Two pence a year was fixed for almanacs, if printed on one side of a sheet, and four pence on all others. Dr. Franklin was in London at the time of the passage of the act, having been sent there as colonial agent. In a well-known letter referring to this act, Franklin says : "The sun of liberty is set ; you must light up the lamps of industry and economy." The party to whom he wrote responded : "Be assured we

Tax on publications.

Obstacles in
the way of
printing.
shall light torches of quite another sort.'' The act of
March, 1765, was repealed in 1766, but in 1767 Parliament made another law imposing a duty on paper as well
as some other articles. Much embarrassment was experienced under the workings of this last act. On the
other hand, later on the Continental Congress, which
met in September, 1774, at Philadelphia, forbade printers
to execute any printing for the adherents of the British
administration. So the printing business of the colonies
was hedged in, like most other industries, and printers
had to overcome not only great natural but artificial and
political barriers.

All these causes made literary enterprises somewhat
dubious. The science and skill displayed in advertising
in modern times were not thought of in colonial days.
The whole number of printing presses in the country
prior to the Revolution could not have been much above
Printing and
bookselling
combined.
forty. The printers mostly combined bookselling with
their business, while not a few engaged in the selling
of groceries, fancy articles, and a general assortment
of goods. Some, indeed, were large dealers in general
merchandise, keeping for sale not only domestic but
imported books. The staple supply of the colonial
bookstores consisted of works on law, medicine, history,
and some of the minor departments of science and
general knowledge. Ninety-two booksellers had carried on business in Boston prior to 1775, while eighteen
Booksellers in
New England,
New York, etc.
houses were engaged in like business in other parts of
New England. The names of a dozen concerns appear
for New York, and thirty-eight for Philadelphia, while
Maryland, South Carolina, and Georgia added six to the
list. This list, however, is far from complete, but it indicates the development of a business which has become
in our day one of enormous proportions.

Some of the early colonial printers undertook the business of bookbinding in connection with their other work, the first attempts in this direction being upon Eliot's Indian Bible, as early as 1663. The edition of the Psalms, which has been mentioned, was bound in parchment. More than a third of all the booksellers who carried on business in Boston had binderies of their own. This feature of the business was not so general in the other colonies, for in New York there were but few who did binding in connection with their business as booksellers or printers. In Philadelphia there were several who carried on this feature of the book business, and in Charleston, of the three booksellers there at the close of the colonial period, two executed their own binding.

Bookbinding.

In connection with these brief historical facts a question might arise as to the literary character of the colonists. There were many persons of good repute for their learning and ability who sustained this character. Many of them had been educated in European universities. Some of these names are found in the "Transactions" of the Royal Society of London and those of the American Philosophical Society. The *Bibliotheca Americana*, in 1789, gives us a pretty clear insight as to the character of some of these men, and from their names and their calling the progress made in literature and in various departments of knowledge and art is learned. The following quotation is taken from the *Bibliotheca Americana :*

Literary character of the colonists.

The people of North America have now professors in every art and science, with adequate salaries ; and, whatever they may want to import, men of eminence in literature are not of the number. At the head of their philosophers and politicians, stands the venerable Franklin. In the first class, the ingenious Lorimer must not be forgotten. In mathematics, the self-taught Rittenhouse. In divinity, Weatherspoon. In history, criticism, and policy, the modern Tacitus (Payne). In poetry, Barlow, Smith, and Ray. In painting, West. In law and oratory—how shall I enumerate them? Take the first class. In Georgia, George Walton; German Baker, in Virginia; Jennings, in Maryland; Lewis, Bradford, and Chambers, in Pennsylvania; Boudinot, in Jersey; Hamilton and Bird, in New York; Johnson, in Connecticut; and Parsons, in Massachusetts.

CHAPTER VI.

SAWMILLS.—BUILDINGS AND BUILDING MATERIALS.

MANY industries other than those already referred to were planted by the colonists. Sawmills and the manufacture of lumber gave opportunity for the employment of labor and the exportation of the products of the forest. As seen in a former chapter, the first efforts of the colonists outside of raising food were expended in the manufacture of clapboards for exportation, and both the Virginia and the Plymouth settlements sent home cargoes of these articles. They were made by hand, for in those early days there were no other means of manufacturing. Naturally, the abundance of timber led to the erection of crude sawmills. Artisans were sent as early as 1620 to Virginia to set up sawmills, so that the making of boards and clapboards, which had been accomplished by hand-labor as early as 1609, might be expanded and the exports increased. When it is known that a man could easily make by hand 15,000 clapboards or pipe-staves in a year, which were worth in the colonies £4 per thousand and in the Canaries £20, it will be understood how desirable it was to have sawmills, and yet as late as 1650, when the value of clapboards was that just stated, there was no sawmill in Virginia, nor does the record show the erection of any permanent mills for some years after that date. For the Carolinas and Georgia, however, the accounts are clearer, although the dates of the erection of the first mills are not ascer-

Sawmills stimulate exportation.

Crude sawmills.

tainable.   Acts were passed in South Carolina as early as 1691 for the encouragement of the erection of engines for propagating the staples of that province, and a few years later (in 1712) for encouraging the building of sawmills and other mechanic engines ; yet the sawmill does not appear to have come into extensive requisition in Carolina during colonial times.

Turning to the northern colonies, we find that the first sawmill erected in New England was in New Hampshire, near what is now known as Portsmouth, where a sawmill was built prior to the year 1635 ; at least this is the first distinct account found of a sawmill in New England. Among the skilful mechanics sent to the colonies in 1628–29 were those who knew how to erect and operate sawmills.   Some accounts give it that one was built in 1633, and mention is made of mills generally at even earlier dates, but they have not been described.   But well-authenticated accounts indicate that just prior to 1635 a sawmill was erected, as stated.   During the first fifty years after the settlement at Plymouth sawmills were erected in different parts of New England, the many streams offering facilities for running them, and before the century expired saw and grist-mills were found at convenient points in most of the northern colonies, and

in fair proportion in the others.   Rhode Island, Connecticut, and New York engaged in this work, and in some places wind sawmills were erected, an account of the latter colony, published in 1708, relating that a Dutch-built mill to saw timber would do more work in an hour than fifty men in two days.   Sawmills were also

erected in Delaware, while New Jersey found it essential to have mills of her own.   There seems to be no information, however, concerning the introduction of sawmills in Maryland ; but water-mills, for grinding corn,

were erected in that colony by public subscription in
1639. In many places grist-mills were built alongside of
sawmills in order that the same power which moved the
one might be utilized in moving the other.

The product of the sawmill was considerable, the
official value of different kinds of lumber exported from
all the colonies in 1770 being $686,588. These exports

PLYMOUTH, 1621.

consisted of boards, plank, scantling, timber for masts,
spars, staves, headings, hoops, and poles. After the close
of the colonial period (in 1792) there were exported
65,846,024 feet of lumber, 80,813,357 shingles, 32,039,-
707 hoops, staves, and headings, while of timber, consisting of ship and other timbers, frames of houses, etc.,
large quantities were sent out.

The primitive development of the lumber industry
naturally closes with the colonial period, for when the
next period opened a new power had arisen and a new
element grown into the development of industry—

steam; but the account of the grist and flour-mills, necessities to the existence of the people, can only be told in detail.   In general it may be said that nearly all of the colonies erected windmills for the grinding of grain—all of the colonies, or nearly all of them, encouraging the industry—and while the colonists were exporting very considerable quantities of lumber, as just stated, which, of course, were over and above their own wants, they had succeeded, at the close of that particular period in our history, in sending abroad large quantities of flour and other bread-stuffs, the exports from Philadelphia alone amounting in 1789 to 369,668 barrels of flour.   Some of the mills, especially those in operation near Philadelphia, made not only bolted flour, but ground chocolate, snuff, hair-powder, and mustard, and pressed and cut tobacco, by water-power.   The total exports of bread-stuffs from all of the colonies cannot be stated for the year closing the colonial period, but the total export of flour in 1791 was 619,681 barrels, besides which there were sent abroad over 1,000,000 bushels of wheat.

Use of wind-
mills.

Exports of
cereals.

The first habitations of the colonists were naturally crude affairs.   They had plenty of timber with which to build their houses, but they had to wait for other building materials before any ornamental buildings or those having anything that might be called artificial finish could be erected.   Log houses and stockades—buildings erected of crude hewn timber—were all that could be obtained.   The progress of social life is marked as much, if not more, by domestic architecture as by almost any other line, except, it may be, the textile industry.   So the first dwellings of the colonists could claim but little advance over the primitive wigwams of the savages, and, in fact, in many cases were simply temporary huts, like

Early
dwellings.

Domestic
architecture.

the huts of the savages. The Indian huts had thatched roofs and walls, with warm mats hanging about, and were, perhaps, in the inclement northern climate, more comfortable than the dwellings of the white people.

The transition marks one of the clearly-defined features of industrial development, and this takes the dwellings from the rude habitation to the capacious frame house and to the mansion of stone or brick—accomplishments secured only by much toil and patience and years of waiting. When a people pass beyond the rude hut the development of many features of industry begins, and the manufacture of building materials and of everything that can be used in adorning dwellings becomes a necessity. Our forefathers were not of a class who were willing to dwell always in log cabins. The log cabin is a temporary habitation, and has no relation to future development, except as a temporary convenience. When

Development of dwellings.

the erection of dwellings which shall last for years begins, architecture, however primitive, must be cultivated, that the dwellings may represent the taste and the intelligent progress of the people building them. So the manufacture of boards, brick, lime, and everything entering into the building trades

THE FIRST CHURCH ERECTED IN CONNECTICUT. HARTFORD, 1638.

Dwellings represent intelligent progress.

must be provided. It has been seen how the sawmill grew and developed in the colonial days, furnishing one of the profitable branches of business, both through the supply of the colonists and the manufacture of lumber for exportation.

Stone and bricks.

The first stone and bricks which were used in the colonies were brought from England, and were chiefly used in the building of fireplaces. Ten thousand bricks were imported by Massachusetts in 1629. Imported bricks were also used in the erection of dwellings, and there are houses in different parts of the original territory whose owners now boast of the fact that the bricks used in their construction were brought from England.

Virginia first to make bricks.

Virginia was the first colony to make bricks. This occurred as early as 1612. The first brick-kiln in New England was set up at Salem, Mass., in the year 1629, the same year in which a sawmill was started.

Limestone and marble.

The discovery of limestone and marble was made at an early time, for in the year just named (1629) limestone, freestone, and marble were found to exist in the eastern part of the Massachusetts colony. The

First brick house in Massachusetts.

first brick house in Massachusetts, probably, was built in Boston in 1638, as near as the records allow the mention of a particular date. A brick watch-house

In Plymouth.

was built on Fort Hill, in Plymouth, in 1643. The bricks for this were furnished at eleven shillings per thousand. Some writers refer to the fact that as early as 1647 lime, brick, and tile-making were among the independent trades that were pursued in New England. The town of Medford, on the Mystic River, the town being called Mystic at that time, had some brickyards and sent the product to Boston. Mention is found of spacious houses, having brick, tile, slate, and stone settings, existing in colonial towns in the fifties of the seventeenth century, and as early as 1667 the Massachusetts General Court undertook the regulation of the size and manufacture of bricks. Ten years later a brick college building was erected at Cambridge, while the first brick meeting-house was erected in 1694, to take the place of a wooden one in Brattle Street in Boston. Brick-kilns were started in the Maine district previous to 1675, but most of the towns were supplied with wooden dwellings and buildings.

Under the Dutch, many of the buildings in New York were made of bricks, but the material was imported from Holland. A church edifice was erected in 1642, of stone. *Brick buildings in New York.*

Some of the early buildings in New Jersey were constructed partly of bricks, but mostly of split trees, the buildings having the appearance of stockades, although they were covered with shingles and plastered inside. Barns built in this way cost about $25 each. Farmhouses were built in a very cheap manner, stone being used for the chimneys. In 1721 freestone was quarried at Newark—probably the first in the country. Its value was recognized, and it was sent to neighboring colonies. William Penn's manor-house, which was situated a few miles above Bristol, in Bucks County, Pennsylvania, was built of bricks, and according to his own statement cost over £5,000. The materials, however, were largely brought from England. *In New Jersey.*

The southern colonies do not seem to have developed much in the way of brickmaking or stone-cutting ; yet, while wooden buildings were largely used in the Carolinas and other southern colonies, there were near the close of the colonial period some spacious brick houses in southern towns. They had a very superior quality of clay, and the manufacture of potters' ware was commenced about the middle of the eighteenth century. So, as the ambition of the colonists grew relative to their habitations, the industries necessary to meet the ambition developed accordingly, and not only was the production *In southern towns.*

Exportation of bricks.

of bricks at the close of the colonial period equal to the demand for home consumption, but small exportations were made. These exportations were chiefly to the West Indies.

Glassmaking.

While bricks, stone, and lime were produced, the necessity for having glass made at home was felt. Some of the artisans sent to Virginia made an attempt to produce glass as early as 1609. It was an expensive article to import, on account of the breakage which was likely to occur. This fact stimulated the colonists to efforts to produce their own glass, but another and a more curious cause was the facility with which glass trinkets, beads, etc., could be used with the Indians in trading for furs, skins, and lands; so glassmaking was one of the earliest industries established in this country, and the first of these, as stated, was in Virginia in 1609, when a glass furnace was erected about a mile from Jamestown. In

First in Virginia.

all probability this was the very first manufactory of any kind erected in this country. The business was prosecuted with some success, but the glass enterprise was conducted under difficulties. The fuel and the alkaline salts required, while cheap, necessitated the employment of labor, which was very scarce, and labor was the chief cost of glassmaking.

First in northern colonies.

The first glass that was made in the northern colonies was produced in Braintree, Mass., at a village called Germantown, but glass bottles were the only articles made. The first glass works in that colony were commenced in Salem, Mass., about 1639, and the persons interested in this undertaking were granted several acres of ground for the purpose of promoting the manufacture. It should be understood that window-glass and even mirrors and glassware were not common in England fifty years before the settlement of the colonies, for as late as

1661 country houses in some parts of Great Britain had no glass windows, and even ambitious palaces were but partly supplied with glazing. Few attempts were made to introduce the extensive manufacture of glass in colonies other than those named. On Manhattan Island there were some glassmakers among the early settlers, and one or two attempts were made in Pennsylvania prior to 1700, and between that time and the adoption of the constitution there were quite a number of works erected here and there ; but it cannot be said that there was very much progress made prior to the Revolution. Although the demand increased and the use of glass had become an almost universal necessity, it was a scarce article during the War of Independence, the most of that used prior thereto having been brought from the old country.

Glassmaking in New York and Pennsylvania.

Scarcity of glass during the Revolution.

CHAPTER VII.

THE IRON INDUSTRY.

METALS were essential in the building trades as well as for domestic purposes. The colonists, however, did not have much knowledge either of the working or of the uses of iron. They had expected to find great quantities of the precious metals. At the time America was colonized the use of iron was increasing greatly in the old country. Information was received by the council in London, in 1610, that iron ore existed in Virginia and that it had been found even upon the surface of the ground. This, it is stated, had been tested in England and found to be of excellent quality. In 1619 workmen familiar with the manufacture of iron, to the number of one hundred and fifty, were sent to Virginia for the avowed purpose of erecting iron works, and smelting furnaces were erected on Falling Creek, a branch of James River, in that year, but in May, 1622, the works were destroyed by the Indians, and a general massacre of the workmen and their families occurred. The Indians seemed to have a very jealous fear of works, whether for the manufacture of iron or for other purposes. The destruction of the Virginia works and the slaughter of the people connected therewith of course discouraged the colonists, and no other attempt at the production of iron was made for several years.

In the northern colonies the search for iron ore had been carried on, and it had been discovered in some

Iron ore in Virginia.

In northern colonies.

parts of the Massachusetts colony as early as 1630, but no attempt was made to produce iron until some fifteen years later. Bog-iron ore* was discovered in Lynn, where numerous peat-bogs were found, and this bog-iron ore supplied the first furnaces of the Massachusetts colony, whose first attempts to manufacture iron were made in Lynn or its vicinity. The colonists were suffering from a scarcity of iron both for use in the manufacture of wares and tools and for the erection of their buildings. To supply this demand furnaces were started, as stated. Later on attempts were made at Braintree, and a grant was secured for the encouragement of iron works to be set up there. This grant was not surveyed and laid out until January, 1648. There has been much discussion whether the first forge was set up at Lynn or at Braintree, but the Lynn historian, Mr. Lewis, insists that the first works were erected at that place, on the west bank of the Saugus River. This was probably in 1643 or 1644. According to Governor Winthrop, whose statements relative to these works were made in 1648, the production was fairly encouraging, the works yielding about seven tons per week. The works at Lynn involved much expense, and the members of the company did not live in the immediate vicinity ; so

Bog ore in Lynn.

First iron works in Massachusetts.

---

* BOG ORE.—A variety of iron ore which collects in low places, being washed down in a soluble form in the waters which flow over rocks or sands containing oxide of iron, and precipitated in a solid form as the waters evaporate. It is deposited in the bottoms of ponds as well as swamps, and is found in beds now dry, above the level at which it must originally have been collected, or else these are the product of springs which have now disappeared. Bog ore contains phosphorus, arsenic, and other impurities, which greatly impair its qualities for producing strong iron. The pig metal obtained from it, called cold short, is so brittle that it breaks to pieces by falling upon the hard ground; but the foreign matters which weaken it also give to the melted cast-iron great fluidity, which causes it to be in demand for the manufacture of fine castings, the metal flowing into the minutest cavities of the mold, and retaining the sharp outlines desired. Bog ores are very easily converted into iron, and when they can be procured to mix with other kinds of ore, they produce a very beneficial effect, both in the running of the furnace and in the quality of the iron. For these reasons, as also for the cheapness with which they are obtained, it is an object to have them at hand, though they seldom yield more than thirty to thirty-five per cent of cast-iron.

but little profit was realized.   The enterprise was prose-cuted at different times, however, and the works were not finally abandoned until after more than a century from their commencement had elapsed.   The works at Brain-tree continued in operation for a period equally as long.

According to Mr. Lewis, the author of an excellent his-tory of Lynn, Mass., one "Joseph Jenks deserves to be held in perpetual remembrance in American history as being the *first* founder who worked in brass and iron on the western continent.   By his hands the first models were made, and the first castings taken of many domes-tic implements and iron tools.   The first article said to have been cast was a small iron pot, capable of con-taining about a quart.   Thomas Hudson, of the same family with the celebrated Hendrick Hudson, was the first proprietor of the lands on the Saugus River, where the iron foundry stood.   When the forge was established he procured the first casting, which was the famous old iron pot, which he preserved as a curiosity and handed down in the family ever since."   The legislature of Massachusetts granted Mr. Jenks a patent, May 6, 1646, for the making of scythes and other edged tools, while in October, 1652, the same Mr. Jenks was employed by the government of Massachusetts to make dies from which to supply the deficiency of specie by a silver coinage.

Bog ores were found along the coast in the vicinity of the small ponds and the marshes ; so furnaces and forges for smelting and working up the metal which was obtained from the swamps and surrounding hills were quite com-mon in colonial days.   Some of the ponds, especially those in Middleboro, Attleboro, Carver, Scituate, Hali-fax, and neighboring towns, it is said, supplied from one hundred to six hundred tons of ore annually, the crude iron contained in the ore being about twenty-five per

Marginal notes:

Iron enterprise at Lynn, Mass.

At Braintree.

First iron article.

Massachusetts patents for edged tools.

cent. Many works sprung up wherever bog ore could be found, and its uses were applied in very many directions.

Copper ore was discovered near Salem by Governor Endicott in 1648, and some smelting* works were erected by him about 1651, but the discovery proved of little account.

The number of iron works in New England, according to the returns for 1731, was six works for hollow-ware and nineteen forges or bloomeries† for bar-iron. There were no pig-iron furnaces nor any refineries for pig metal, but refineries came into use during the next score of years. Rolling and slitting-mills‡ were in existence in Hanover, Milton, and Middleboro in 1750. The rolling-mills produced mostly nail-rods, from which spikes and large nails were made. But these mills suffered under the legislation of the mother-country, through the prohibition, by act of Parliament, of the erection of slitting or rolling-mills, plating forges, or steel furnaces.

A forge was erected in Rhode Island by Joseph Jenks, but this was destroyed in 1675, during the Wampanoag

Marginal notes:

Copper

Iron works in New England.

In Rhode Island.

---

* SMELTING.—The act of obtaining the metal from an ore by a process that includes fusion ; also, in a more limited sense, to reduce by fusion in a furnace.

† BLOOMERY.—An establishment in which wrought-iron is made by the direct process, that is, from the ore directly, or without having been first introduced in the form of cast-iron.

FURNACE.—A structure in which to make and maintain a fire the heat of which is to be used for some mechanical purpose, as the melting of ores or metals, etc.; specifically, a structure of considerable size built of stone or brick, used for some purpose connected with the operation of smelting metals. Furnaces are constructed in a great variety of ways, according to the different purposes to which they are to be applied.

FORGE.—An open fireplace or furnace, fitted with a bellows or some other appliance for obtaining a blast to urge the fire, and serving to heat metal in order that it may be hammered into form. Forges differ from foundries and blast furnaces in their products being articles of wrought-iron, while those of the latter are castings.

FOUNDRY.—A manufacturing establishment in which articles are cast from metal.

‡ SLITTING-MILL.—A mill in which iron bars or plates are slit into nail-rods, etc.

ROLLING-MILL.—A metal-working establishment using, in connection with heating-furnaces, systems of steel rollers for forming metal into sheets, bars, rods, or wires.

war. Several other iron works, as well as some other manufacturing enterprises, were destroyed during the course of this war, greatly reducing the resources of the colonists in Rhode Island.

The bog ore which supplied the furnaces was not of a quality sufficiently tough for the production of good nails, spikes, and tools.

The shipbuilding around Plymouth and Narragansett Bay increased the demand for all kinds of iron products ; so the colonists were stimulated in their efforts to discover ores in such abundance that this demand might be supplied.

Manufactures of iron in Rhode Island.

Rhode Island made considerable progress in this direction, for toward the close of the eighteenth century the manufactures of iron, which at that time included very many articles, such as bar* and sheet-iron steel, nail-rods, and nails, farming implements, stoves, pots, and other castings, and household utensils, iron-work for ships, anchors, and bells, were important products of industry. Slitting and rolling-mills, anchor forges, nail-cutting machines, and several mills were erected at Pawtucket Falls, some of which were carried on by water. There were in operation toward the close of the century screw-cutting machines and hollow-ware furnaces. The militia companies of the colony were supplied with muskets as early as 1775 by Stephen Jenks of North Providence.

Attempts to make cut nails.

One Jeremiah Wilkinson, at Cumberland, was the first to make the attempt to cut small nails from sheet-iron. In this Wilkinson used old Spanish hoops. Wilkinson

---

* PIG-IRON.—Iron in oblong masses, or pigs, as turned out by the smelting furnace ; so called because the molten metal is run into a long mass with shorter ones attached to it at right angles, the long one being called the sow, and the shorter ones the pigs.

BAR-IRON.—Wrought-iron rolled into the form of bars.

ROLLED-IRON.—Iron passed between steel rolls of different sizes, according to the shape desired to be imparted to the metal.

also made pins and needles from wire which he himself drew out. These articles were very scarce and expensive. If, therefore, they could be made by the colonists and sold without the intermediary expenses of transportation from the old country a good market could be secured.

The colony of Connecticut at a very early date (1651) encouraged the discovery of minerals within its territory, *Iron in Connecticut.* for it is recorded that on motion of Mr. Winthrop, who was the prime mover in the organization of the company which undertook the first iron works at Lynn and Braintree in 1643, or thereabouts, and who had received a grant for a settlement and iron works in Connecticut, the Assembly of Connecticut passed an encouraging *Encouragement offered by Connecticut.* act which declared that, "whereas, in this rocky country among these mountainous and rocky hills there are probabilities of mines of metal, the discovery of which may be of great advantages to the country in raising a staple commodity ; and whereas, John Winthrop, Esq., doth intend to be at charges and adventure for the search and discovery of such mines and minerals, for the encouragement thereof, and of any that shall adventure with the said John Winthrop, Esq., in the said business, it is therefore ordered," etc. It granted to him, his heirs, associates, partners, and assigns, forever, the lands, timber, and water within two or three miles of any mines of lead, copper, tin, antimony, vitriol, black lead, alum, stone, salt, or salt springs he might discover, if he should set up any works for digging, washing, melting, or other operations required for such metals or minerals, provided it was not in a place already occupied. The government of Connecticut again, in 1663, offered encouragement to any one who would undertake the discovery of mines and minerals, and the act of 1663 was renewed in 1672, but the records do not give any very definite information as to the success which rewarded either the research of Mr. Winthrop or that which resulted under the acts of 1663 and 1672. This encouragement was offered by the General Court.

Prior to this the Assembly of New Haven, seven years before the date of the charter of Mr. Winthrop, gave encouragement to the manufacture of iron in Connecticut, for on the 30th of May, 1655, it was ordered, "that if an iron worke goe on within any part of this jurisdiction, the persons and estates constantly and onely imployed in that worke shall be free from paying rates," and the same year an order was passed concerning the manufacture of steel. This is believed to have been the first attempt at the production of steel in the Connecticut colonies. The General Court acquiesced in these privileges, and in the following May exempted the persons from rates for ten years and ordered that the property invested in the manufacture of steel should not be attached for the individual debts of those involved in the undertaking, at least to such an extent as to hinder the work or damage the other proprietors. So iron works grew in the Connecticut colonies, the government thereof making provision for the encouragement, through exemptions and otherwise, of the development of the industry. Slitting-mills were erected at Stony Brook as early as 1716, and these were probably the first works erected subsequent to those just recorded.

First attempt at the production of steel in the Connecticut colonies.

The efforts to obtain ores led to the discovery in Connecticut of two deposits of copper, which it was confidently hoped would give a profitable yield. One of these copper mines was found at Simsbury, now the town of Granby, and after some struggle was successfully worked until 1773. This mine furnished the ore

Discovery of copper in Connecticut.

for some copper coins which were struck in 1737 and 1739, by Samuel Higley, a blacksmith of Granby. These coins were current for many years, and were known as the " Granby coppers."

Mr. Higley, in May, 1728, was granted a patent for ten years for making steel, the condition of the patent being that the petitioner should improve the art within two years after the date of the act of the legislature granting the patent.

Bells were cast in a foundry for that purpose, at New Haven, in 1736, by Abel Parmlee. **Bells.**

Connecticut's most valuable deposits of iron ore were found in the northwestern part of the state, bordering on New York and Massachusetts, Sharon, Salisbury, and Kent being the most favored townships.

As late as 1740 Mr. Philip Livingston of Albany, N. Y., who had received a grant of a large tract of one hundred acres, and who had set up a furnace or bloomery at Limerock, where pig-iron, common iron kettles, etc., were made as early as 1736, erected iron works at Ancram, in Columbia County, New York, some twelve miles northwest of the Connecticut mines, and in 1762 a blast furnace was built at the outlet of Wanscopommuc Lake, in Salisbury. **Iron in New York.**

With these beginnings the manufacture of iron in Connecticut progressed with good results, so that at the close of the colonial period Connecticut was doing fairly well in that industry, but in addition to iron and its manufactures steel is said to have been made by several parties. Many bloomeries and small works for a variety of manufactures in iron were established on the small streams traversing Connecticut, the forges in the southern part of the state being chiefly supplied with bog ore, while in the interior other kinds of ores, especially the **Progress of iron manufacture in Connecticut.**

hematitic ores found in the northeastern part of the state, gave an impulse to trade. To this day Connecticut is noted for the extent and variety of its manufactures of metal small wares.

Berlin, in Hartford County, Connecticut, is stated to be the first place in this country where tinware was manufactured. This was in 1770, by Edward Patterson. Many of the industries which make Connecticut what it is were started in a small way during the latter part of the eighteenth century, but, as already intimated, they related very largely to the manufacture of metal wares.

Place of the first manufacture of tinware.

The Dutch colonizers of New York made no successful attempts at the manufacture of iron, although they did stimulate prospecting for iron and other ores. The first iron works in New York were erected, as already stated, by Mr. Philip Livingston, at Ancram, who obtained his ore largely from Salisbury, Conn. A company of German miners, who came to this country between 1730 and 1750, were among the earliest explorers of the metalliferous regions of the highlands. They made many excavations and, it is said, set up some iron works in Orange County during the period named, for in 1750 Governor Clinton, in reporting to Parliament, stated that there was a plating-forge with a tilt-hammer at Wawaganda, in Orange County. It was the only mill of that kind in the province, and had been built four or five years before the year named. In the same year some works were built in the town of Monroe, for the manufacture of anchors. These anchors were made from the iron ore found at the south end of Sterling Mountain, and the mines there became very productive. The metal was strong, and was afterward largely used for the manufacture of cannon, bar-iron, steel, etc.

First iron works in New York.

Manufacture of anchors.

Cannon.
Bar-iron.
Steel.

Mr. Peter Townsend was the first man to produce steel in the province of New York. This he made first from pig and afterward from bar-iron, using the German method. He became the proprietor of the Sterling works before the Revolution. It was from the ore from the mines which supplied the Sterling works that the enormous iron chain which was used in 1778 as an obstruction across the Hudson at West Point was forged. This chain weighed 186 tons, and under the direction of Col. Timothy Pickering, one of Washington's staff, was produced and delivered in six weeks. According to all accounts this immense chain remained unbroken throughout the Revolution, and some of its links are preserved among the revolutionary relics at Newburgh. These works became historic in their influence upon the progress of the war. Other works were erected by Mr. Townsend and his associates in 1777. These men also owned other mines, especially the Long mine, which was discovered in 1761 by one David Jones.

First steel produced in New York.

Iron chain across the Hudson.

Governor De Lancey, in obedience to a royal proclamation, in 1757 sent to England an account of the iron works of the province of New York as they existed from 1749 to 1756. In this account is a statement furnished by Robert Livingston, Jr., son of the first proprietor of the Ancram iron works, which have been mentioned. This statement indicates that these works were the only ones in the province then carried on. According to this account the amount of iron made at Ancram for the years named was over 3,300 tons.

Besides the Livingston works iron manufactories sprung up at Copake, Hudson, and other places. William Hawkshurst advertised in 1765 that he had erected a refinery and great hammer for refining the Sterling pig-iron into bars, and he announced that flat, square,

Pig-iron refinery.

and bar-iron, cart, wagon, chair, and sleigh-tire, mill spindles, anvils, pots, kettles, forged plates, weights, and many other articles could be supplied to his customers in New York.

Encouragement of iron industry. Societies were formed at this time for the encouragement of the iron industry, premiums being offered for products of skill. Among these was the Society of Arts, which opened a fair for the sale of domestic products. Other portions of the province of New York, under the demands which were stimulated by the increasing population, the necessities of building both ships and houses, and other things, developed the iron industry to a considerable extent, not only supplying the home demand, but even exporting to some extent, the shipments of iron from the port of New York amounting to 2,400 tons of pig and 750 tons of bar-iron in 1775 ; but it was not until after the Revolution that the industry assumed great proportions. Then in the northern part of the state iron ore was discovered and utilized and the industry firmly established, although the general progress in the state, so far as the iron industry was concerned, did not equal in the last century that in New England and Pennsylvania.

Manufacture of guns. The manufacture of guns was carried on to some extent, muskets and rifles being made in considerable quantities for the Indian trade, while the armories at Albany were employed by the government at the commencement of the Revolution.

Iron in New Jersey. It is quite impossible to give any precise date for the erection of the first iron works in New Jersey, but the earliest in that province belonged to Col. Lewis Morris, whose brother Richard and himself were the ancestors of the Morris family so well known in the early history of this country ; but near 1655 one Henry Leonard, who had worked in the first iron works in the country, those at Lynn, Mass., which have already been described, came to Jersey, and is said to have been the first to set up a forge in that province. It was not until the next century, however, that much progress was made, during which, and prior to the close of the Revolution, many important works were established, some of which were erected at the very close of the seventeenth century. When the eighteenth century closed ten mines were being worked within the limits of Morris County alone, which contained two furnaces, three rolling and slitting-mills, and about forty forges with two to four fires each. Many of the counties during the last quarter of the eighteenth century found ore in fair abundance, and of course forges were erected for working it. The village of Troy, in Hanover County, had a bloomery forge, built in 1743, while the Beach Glen bloomery, three miles north of the village of Rockaway, was built in 1760. A little above Milton the Russia and Hopewell bloomeries were set up, the former in 1775 and the latter in 1780. Randolph, Mount Hope, Morristown, Boonton, Dover, and other towns, have for a very long time been busy in the manufacture of iron. Iron works were erected at an early date on the Ringwood and Pequannock Rivers, and a charcoal furnace was erected prior to 1770 on the Morris County side of the Pequannock. So at other places Jersey did her share in the early evolution of the iron industry, and to such an extent as to place her on a very firm basis when the new era after the adoption of the constitution was opened.

Iron works in Morris County, N. J.

Charcoal furnace.

CHAPTER VIII.

THE IRON INDUSTRY (*Concluded*).

Iron in Pennsylvania.

THE great iron-producing state of Pennsylvania did not develop her mineral resources at as early a period as her more northern neighbors, yet at an early time her anthracite and bituminous coal gave her great advantages in the production of iron ; in fact, while accounts appear of the knowledge of the existence of iron ores during the seventeenth century, there does not appear to be any distinct account of the erection of forges or furnaces during that century. Mr. Swank, in his work, "History of the Manufacture of Iron in All Ages" (and he is corroborated by Bishop and others), states that the settlers on the Delaware, under the successive administrations of the Swedes and Dutch and the Duke

No efforts prior to 1682.

of York, appear to have made no effort to manufacture iron in any form down to 1682. From Mr. Swank's work and others it is learned that in the "Journal of a Voyage to New York," in 1679 and 1680, by Jasper Dankers and Peter Sluyter, who then visited the Swedish and other settlements on the Delaware, it is expressly declared that iron ore had not been seen by them on Tinicum Island or elsewhere in the neighborhood. Dankers states : "As to there being a mine of iron ore upon it, I have not seen any upon that island, or elsewhere ; and if it were so it is of no great importance, for such mines are so common in this country that little account is made of them." But under William Penn the manufacture of iron in Pennsylvania had its beginning. In a letter written by him to Lord Keeper North, in July, 1683, he mentions the existence of "mineral, of copper, and iron in divers places" in Pennsylvania, and in 1685, speaking of the prospects of trade, he says : "I might add iron, because there is much of it." It is probably true that Penn had iron works at Hawkhurst and other places in Sussex, but it is in 1692 that the first mention of iron having been made in Pennsylvania is found, although this is only a mention.* The first authentic account, however, of the first attempt which was successfully carried out in the making of iron in Pennsylvania shows that it was in 1716. This was a bloomery forge, which was constructed by Thomas Rutter, on Manatawny Creek, in Berks County. The next iron enterprise in Pennsylvania was undertaken by Samuel Nutt, an English Quaker, who, in 1717, about the same time that Rutter built his forge on the Manatawny, erected one on French Creek, in the northern part of Chester County. Accounts state that as early as 1719 the iron at this point promised well.

First attempt to make iron in Pennsylvania.

Mr. Swank gives the third iron enterprise in Pennsylvania as the Colebrookdale furnace, erected about 1720 by a company of which Thomas Rutter, who has already been mentioned, was the principal member. This furnace was located on Ironstone Creek, in Colebrookdale township, Berks County, the site of which is marked at the present time by cinder. By 1728 the iron industry of Pennsylvania had developed to such an extent that it was really on a firm foundation, for the colony exported 274 tons of pig-iron to the old country in 1728–29. After this date forges and furnaces

Exports of iron from Pennsylvania.

---

* See "History of the Manufacture of Iron in All Ages," by James M. Swank.

were erected rapidly in the Schuylkill valley and other
eastern portions of Pennsylvania. The history of their
erection, the struggles of their progress, their periods of
success and adversity, are all connected with the development of the state.

The iron industry of Pennsylvania crossed the Susquehanna at a very early date, yet not early enough to bring

Iron west of the Susquehanna. the great development into the colonial period, only a
few forges and bloomeries having been erected in the
western part of the state prior to the Revolution. There
was a bloomery in York County in 1756 and a forge on
Codorus Creek in 1770. A furnace and forge were built
at Boiling Springs, in Cumberland County, a little after

Nucleus of the Carlisle iron works. 1762. This formed the nucleus of the Carlisle iron works.
A forge is supposed to have been built at Mount Holly
in 1756, and another in the same county in 1770. These
are the principal works that were erected west of the
Susquehanna during the colonial period.

The iron manufactures of the state took many forms.
Furnaces, foundries, rolling-mills, nail works, wire-mills,
and manufactories of metallic and other materials had a
rapid growth. The amount of iron exported from Philadelphia in the year ending April 5, 1766, was 882 tons
of bar, worth £26 per ton, and 813 tons of pig-iron,
worth £7 and 10 shillings per ton. In the three years
preceding the war, ending January 5, 1774, the exports
were respectively 2,358, 2,205, and 1,564 tons.

Manufacture of nails in Pennsylvania. The manufacture of nails was begun at an early date
in Pennsylvania, certainly as early as 1731, while anchors
were made as early as 1755. Works for drawing wire
were erected in 1779.

Manufacture of small arms in Pennsylvania. Small arms were manufactured in Philadelphia, Lancaster, and other places. The mechanics of Philadelphia
acquired a reputation for inventive skill, as evidenced in

the construction of machines and instruments. This inventive skill was undoubtedly stimulated largely by the ease with which ore could be secured for the manufacture of iron. One of the earliest evidences of this inventive development is found in the employment of a fire-engine, which was recommended by Samuel Preston, one of the early mayors of the city of Philadelphia. This was in December, 1719.

The first experimental steam-engine built in America was made in Philadelphia in 1773, by Christopher Colles.

Experimental steam-engine.

Carding machines, cotton-gins, spinning-jennies, and other textile machinery, were made in Philadelphia, while many other valuable inventions were developed and applied practically by the mechanics of that city.

Carding machines.

There do not appear to have been works of any extent erected in Delaware during the seventeenth century, but as early as 1726 mention is made in some accounts of Governor Keith, of Pennsylvania, being the proprietor of iron works in Newcastle County. Mr. Bishop thinks they were probably at Newcastle, the oldest town in the state, or on White Clay Creek or its branches. In the latter part of the eighteenth century a rolling and slitting-mill was erected at Wilmington, a place which had achieved a good deal of importance as one of the active centers of colonial industry, but its development in iron, whatever it has, took place after the colonial period closed.

Iron in Delaware.

Extensive deposits of bog-iron ore were found throughout the whole eastern shore of Maryland, and other kinds of ore were found in other parts of the state. These ores were described as early as 1648 and their uses and advantages understood by the English settlers of Maryland, but the mechanic arts did not find a home in that state at a very early date, notwithstanding the legis-

In Maryland.

lature in 1681 endeavored to turn the industry of the colony into that channel. The manufacture of iron probably commenced not many years after this legislative

encouragement, although the earliest forges of which any very positive mention is made were found at Principio, at the head of Chesapeake Bay. This was known to have been in operation prior to 1722. A rolling-mill, which was in operation at the time of the Revolution, was erected in the colony as early as 1742. This was on Big Elk River, five miles north of Elkton. Other works were built at various times, at somewhat long intervals, during the colonial period, a furnace being erected in 1734 at the head of Back River. A slitting-mill was also set up in the same vicinity in 1778. Cannon were

cast in Maryland as early as 1780, at a furnace called Northampton. This was situated about ten miles west of Baltimore. The Maryland records have it that this particular furnace ran seventy years upon a single deposit of brown ore. Other furnaces and some forges were erected in Anne Arundel County at as early a date as those just mentioned, and other counties had forges and slitting-mills built in the last century.

The preparations to provide for the war which were made in the colonies in the summer and autumn of 1776 stimulated the furnaces and gun-shops, wherever they

were, and the forges and the slitting and plating-mills and other iron works of the colonies which had survived the parliamentary restrictions of 1750 found plenty of work. Maryland had eight furnaces and nine forges at that time, that colony, with Virginia, exporting over 2,500 tons of pig-iron yearly to England ; so the iron industry of Maryland was quite an important one when the war broke out. On the 1st of July, 1776, the Maryland Convention authorized the Council of Safety to lend the proprietors of an air furnace in Frederick County the sum of £2,000 to encourage them to prosecute their cannon foundry, and it added in the authorization, "with spirit and diligence." Small cannon and swivels were ordered in the same year and month from the furnace and iron works in Baltimore County. The pig-iron of Ridgely's furnace had the reputation of being the best made in the state, and the gun-makers of Massachusetts purchased some of it at £10 per ton. At the close of the last century there were probably seventeen or eighteen forges for the manufacture of iron in Maryland, and these works existed in six counties of the state ; but the western part of the state did not develop the industry until after the close of the colonial period. Allegany County, which now has some of the richest mineral and iron-producing localities in the state, was not developed until later.

Reputation of pig-iron in Maryland.

Number of forges at close of the seventeenth century.

In all probability the very first attempt to manufacture iron on the American continent was made in Virginia, as early as 1619. Brief mention of this has been made and of the disastrous termination of the enterprise through the massacre of the operatives by the Indians. No other attempt was made during the seventeenth century, and it was not until 1715 that the iron industry was practically commenced on any permanent basis in that colony. Mr. Bishop and other writers give an account of a visit of Col. William Byrd to the iron mines and furnaces of Col. Alexander Spottswood, on the Rappahannock. Colonel Byrd stated that he was informed by Colonel Spottswood that he was not only the first in this country, but the first in North America, who had erected a regular furnace, and that they had run altogether upon bloomeries in New England and Pennsylvania till his example had made them attempt greater works. Other

First attempt at iron-making in Virginia.

accounts would lead to the supposition that these works were erected prior to 1724. At the time of Colonel Byrd's visit there were, according to his host's statement, four furnaces in Virginia, but there was no forge.

Iron ore west
of the Blue
Ridge.

Early in the last century deposits of brown hematite iron ore appear to have been opened in several places in the great limestone valley of Virginia, west of the Blue Ridge. Pine forge, three and a half miles north of Newmarket, in Shenandoah County, was built, according to a statement in Lesley's " Iron Manufacturer's Guide," in 1725, and there was also one erected in 1757, on Mossy Creek, fifteen miles north of Staunton, while a furnace was built not far from the forge in 1760. From a work entitled " Notes on Virginia," published in 1781, there is obtained a very good idea of the condition of the iron works of Virginia at that time :

The mines of iron worked at present are Callaway's, Ross's, and Ballandine's on the south side of James River, Old's on the north side in Albemarle, Miller's in Augusta, and Zane's in Frederick. These two last are in the valley between the Blue Ridge and North Mountain. Callaway's, Ross's, Miller's, and Zane's make about 150 tons of bar-iron each in the year ; Ross's makes also about 1,600 tons of pig-iron annually ; Ballandine's, 1,000 ; Callaway's, Miller's, and Zane's, about 600 each. Besides these, a forge of Mr. Hunter's at Fredericksburg makes about 300 tons a year of bar-iron from pigs imported from Maryland ; and Taylor's forge, on Neapsco of Potomac, works in the same way, but to what extent I am not informed. The undertakers of iron in other places are numerous, and dispersed through all the middle country. The toughness of the cast-iron of Ross's and Zane's furnaces is remarkable. Pots and other utensils cast thinner than usual of this iron may be safely thrown into or out of the wagons in which they are transported. Salt pans made of the same, and no longer wanted for that purpose, cannot be broken up in order to be melted again unless previously drilled in many parts.

The development in the colony brought many other

furnaces and forges into existence before the close of the
century, Virginia taking its place in the development,
and during the Revolution performing its part in the
manufacture of material necessary for the conduct of the
war. The Assembly of Virginia at different times encouraged the erection of mills and iron works ; so that
when the Revolution stimulated the southern colonies to
pay increased attention to manufactures Virginia was
ready to adopt new measures. Among other features a
resolution was passed in August, 1775, providing " that
in case the British Ministry attempts to enforce the Act
of Parliament preventing the erection of plating and
slitting-mills in America, the Convention will recompense
to the proprietors of the first two of such mills as shall
be finished and set to work in this Colony all losses they
may respectively sustain in consequence of such en-
deavours of Administration."

The Virginians were no whit behind the other colonists in their zeal to provide the troops which the Continental Congress was called upon to supply, although
Virginia depended more upon her own resources for the
cannon and small arms necessary to provide her troops
than did some of the others.

North Carolina has an abundance of good ore in some
parts, and it was first discovered by the colony sent out
by Sir Walter Raleigh, but no great progress was made
in the erection of furnaces or forges until late in the colonial period, although it is known that several iron
works were in operation before the Revolution. They
were on the belts of the middle and western districts,
but just where they were established is not quite clear ;
yet they must have existed some years prior to the war,
as there was exported to England as early as 1728–29 a
small quantity of pig-iron—about one ton—and in 1734

Development of
iron works in
Virginia.

Encouragement
in Virginia.

Iron in North
Carolina.

another small shipment was made. But no authentic accounts of the location or the dates of early iron enterprises in North Carolina are to be found. The colonial period, therefore, gives but little in the way of the development of this industry in that colony ; nor is there any accessible information relative to the manufacture of iron in South Carolina. The industry was commenced

Skilled labor dear.

at a late date in the latter state. Skilled labor was dear and met with little encouragement ; so the expense of iron works prevented their establishment. As the southern colonies were devoted to agriculture, the demand for iron was less than in the more northern colonies. There was not, therefore, the stimulation to the research for ore or to the establishment of iron works when it was discovered. The first iron works in South Carolina were erected in the year 1773, but they were

First iron works in South Carolina.

destroyed by the Tories during the Revolution. To encourage the manufacture of iron the colony offered a premium of £1,000 for the erection of a bloomery that should first produce one ton of good bar-iron. For the second and third forges of the same kind, the sums of £800 and £700, respectively, were promised; but it was not until some years after peace was declared that iron works on any large scale were erected. These consisted of the Æra furnace, built in 1787, and the Etna, erected the following year.

Iron in Georgia.

The resources of Georgia in iron, gold, and coal are ample enough, but the development of iron manufacture did not take place during the colonial period. Georgia was the youngest of the colonies, and it is very natural that she should have no iron history during the colonial period. The last of the thirteen colonies to be settled, it could not be expected that such an industry should receive much attention.

While great quantities of bar-iron, steel, and nails were used by the colonies before the war and imported from other countries, nevertheless they exported bar and pig-iron in very respectable quantities. For fifty years prior to the Declaration of Independence these exports had been going on, the quantities ever varying, sometimes from one cause and sometimes from another—often, however, owing to the restrictive legislation of the mother-country. The total amount of bar and pig-iron exported in 1728, and this was from Pennsylvania, Maryland, Virginia, and Carolina, was 1,127 tons and a few hundred weight, while in 1775 the exports of bar and pig-iron from all the colonies amounted to 3,912 tons, the highest exportations being in 1771, when they reached 7,525 tons and some hundred weight. With the Declaration of Independence, these exportations dropped at once, amounting in 1776 to a little over 316 tons. Nearly all of these exportations, it should be remembered, were to England. To Scotland and Ireland there were exportations of small quantities.

Exports of iron.

In this review of the development of the industries of the colonies the attempt has not been made to give in detail the facts for all trades and industries, but only to show the leading features connected with the establishment of those industries which in after years have constituted the bulk of the manufactures of the United States. The textiles, which now lead in magnitude, the lumber, saw, and planing business, iron and steel manufacture, the building trades, printing and publishing, flour and grist-mills, with boots and shoes added, employ 56 per cent of the total capital of the United States invested in manufactures at the present time, and their product is 64 per cent of the entire product ; yet all of these industries had their origin, to a certain extent, in

Review of industries during colonial period.

the colonial days. The manufacture of boots and shoes was begun at a very early date, even to the extent of exporting small quantities, shoes being exported as early as 1651 by some of the merchants of Boston, who had obtained a few, chiefly manufactured of calf-skin, from Lynn, where the business had already been undertaken. Of course the tanning of leather was a necessity. With the colonists were to be found handicraftsmen of all trades, and every hamlet had its own shoemaker, blacksmith, etc. These small trades flourished as the colonies developed and as the greater industries became important.

Shoe manufactures in Massachusetts.

The magnitude of the manufactures of the country at the time the constitution was adopted cannot be stated with exactness. The exports of all kinds amounted to nearly $20,000,000, but just how much of this was furnished by the mechanical industries cannot be stated, although the amount must have been in the vicinity of $1,000,000, because a few years later, when there were returns, it was found to be over $1,300,000. To state the amount of manufactures would be mere guesswork, and an estimate can be reached only by considering the amount of exports and the value of manufactures at later periods. Reasoning from such facts as are obtainable, it is probable that the manufactures of the United States at the close of the colonial period amounted to about $20,000,000.* The matter was well summed up by Alexander Hamilton, the first secretary of the treasury, who in January, 1791, submitted to the House of Representatives as comprehensive a report as was possible on the manufactures of the states. This well-known report gives much in detail the facts relative to the dif-

Exports, 1789.

Value of manufactures, 1790.

---

* Mr. Tench Coxe made an estimate in 1790 fixing the annual value of the manufactures of the United States for that year at more than $20,000,000.

ferent industries which then flourished. The report showed a most gratifying increase in the manufactures of the country, whether they were conducted for purely domestic purposes or for the supply of trade, and the advancement which each had made was clearly pointed out.

Before the Revolutionary War the injurious competition with foreign countries had been an almost insurmountable hindrance to the establishment of manufactures, and at its close, when the stimulus of the war was withdrawn, very many attempts undertaken during its progress were abandoned, the abandonment resulting not only from renewed competition with the mother-country but from the combined effects of low prices and the scarcity and the high price of skilled labor and machinery. As will be pointed out in a future chapter, in dealing with the establishment of the factory system, the American manufacturers were unable to contend with the new forces coming into existence in Europe, and especially in England, without legislative protection. How they overcame these obstacles will be shown after the treatment of the colonial period.

Conditions at close of the Revolution.

CHAPTER IX.

LABOR AND WAGES.

Early conditions.

THE colonists, both North and South, while preserving many of the customs and habits of their old home, undertook in some things to break entirely away from them. Among these attempts to surround themselves with new conditions, with a hope of avoiding some of the difficulties experienced in their past lives, they undertook to conduct their work on the community basis. Each colonist was to do his share toward the support of the whole, the result of the combined work being for the benefit of all. Pure and simple communism seemed to be the aim, so far as labor and its results were concerned; but Captain John Smith, after a very brief experience, found such a system would not succeed, and after some bitter complaints declared that "he that will not work shall not eat," while the Plymouth colony, after nearly three years of experimenting on the community basis, came to the same conclusion, finding that the drones among them benefited equally with the industrious. So labor was relegated to its old conditions, and wages were paid for services rendered. The slave system in Virginia, however, which early took root, prevented many complications which arose in the northern colonies, and few attempts were made to regulate wages by law, while the Pilgrims were imbued with the idea that nearly every condition—social, industrial, and political—could be fixed by statute and all the affairs of the

Experience in Virginia.

In Plymouth.

community regulated in exact ways. They were exclusives in every respect. They did not care to have with them people who were not considered as proper citizens, and the colonial records are full of examples of town and general legislation excluding from the benefits of citizenship certain persons thought to be undesirable. They proposed to build a state where human nature should be regulated into obedience to the opinions and wishes of the majority ; so they very naturally undertook to regulate wages by law, following in this practice the attempts of England at various times to prevent mechanics and laborers from charging too high a price for their services.

Attempts at regulation of wages.

The Massachusetts Bay colony, as early as 1633, adopted a statute, through the General Court, commanding that carpenters, sawyers, masons, bricklayers, tilers, joiners, wheelwrights, mowers, and other master workmen (as they were then called, but, as they would be designated to-day, journeymen) were not to receive more than two shillings per day, each paying his own board, or if furnished with living they might receive fourteen pence per day. The constable, with two others associated with him, was to fix the rates of pay of inferior workmen in the same occupations. The best laborers were allowed eighteen pence per day, while the poorer ones were rated by the constable, as in the case of inferior workmen in the trades. Skilled tailors were paid twelve pence per day, but the poorer ones were paid eight pence per day, with their living. The whole day was the time, but allowances were made for food and rest. Whenever an employer paid wages beyond the amounts established by law, or whenever a workman received such extra wages, he was subjected to penalties. The law undertook to say that there should be no idleness, and idleness was subjected to penalty.

In Massachusetts.

Wages of tailors.

Curiously enough, in the year 1634 the clause of the statute imposing a penalty of five shillings upon those who paid wages above the court rates was repealed, and towns were authorized to appoint a board of three men to adjust wages when the employers and employees could not agree as to the rates for work done under the law. In 1635, finding that the statute did not work exactly as it was expected, some men were fined for receiving two shillings and six pence per day, but this rule gave little satisfaction, and later in the year the law was repealed. There was plenty of work to do, while labor was in demand. Many workmen were brought over from England in the early days, under contract to work out their passage money after arriving. The practice of apprenticing boys, even at an early age, some of them not older than seven years being bound until twenty-one years of age, was common, and the service they had to render was severe, as was also the discipline they had to undergo for conduct that was not approved. These apprentices were entitled, under custom, to a suit of clothes on attaining their majority, and this practice was continued until very recent times.

Strange to say, the experience of the three years mentioned did not convince the Massachusetts Bay colonists of the futility of undertaking to fix economic conditions by statute, and so in 1636 towns were authorized to fix wages within their respective jurisdictions. It was impossible for the settlers to believe that legislation was not essential. Free trade in labor was not acceptable. But the collapse in prices which occurred in 1640 brought them to another position, and they were taught that local option in the fixing of wages was not sufficient to control prices of commodities ; so laborers were commanded by the

Towns authorized to fix wages.

Labor in demand.

Free trade in labor not acceptable.

General Court to reduce wages in accordance with the reduction of prices, and in Plymouth colony, as late as the year 1639, laborers were fined for taking wages beyond the limits. These attempts led them into all sorts of vague notions as to the power of law. No sooner did one statute fail than it was re-pealed and some other attempt made in like direc-tion, but generally reversing what had gone before. Mr. William B. Weeden, in his work, "The Economic and Social History of New England, 1620-1789," has brought together very many instances of attempts to regulate social and economic conditions, and the reader is referred to that work for more general details than can be recited in the present volume. Speaking of these attempts, he calls attention very forcibly to the fact that the administration of government in the colonial days consisted largely in meddlesome interfer-ence with daily affairs, and that the colonists were ever trying to so adjust the burdens of the state that their own backs and those of their poor dependents might be galled the least possible ; yet he states, with wisdom, that the intuitive sagacity of the men of those early days seldom failed in indicating the finally tenable grounds of legislation. In the light of these statements it will not appear strange that legislation was aimed at the regula-tion of dress and even to minuter affairs that concerned the household and not the public.

Notion that law could fix wages.

It is impossible to state definitely the average wages paid in any class of work, but for a long period two shillings per day may be considered as a fair average for mechanical labor. It was natural, under the primitive conditions surrounding the colonists, that labor should be performed in exchange for goods and produce, under a system of barter, and this system was superinduced, to

Average wages.

a certain extent, by legislative interference. The attempt to have each town regulate its own wages resulted in the working people seeking new abodes and attempting to live independent of legislative restriction. Speaking of the time of 1640 and later, and of Massachusetts, it is ascertained that the General Court found by experience that labor could not and would not be controlled. Winthrop says the legislation "held not long." But Massachusetts and Plymouth were not alone in these attempts, for the Connecticut court fixed detailed prices for artificers and workmen during the same period. Some of the regulations of the towns were to the effect of making one shilling and six pence per day the wage for common labor. Mowers received two shillings and carpenters one shilling and ten pence, while a man using two yoke of oxen received six shillings for eight hours of labor. Wheelwrights, under the regulations of Hingham, in the Massachusetts Bay colony, were brought to two shillings per day. But through it all and for many years there seemed to be great anxiety whenever labor undertook to fix its own price, and if a man by any means was enabled to secure wages out of the ordinary line he was looked upon with suspicion.

All through the seventeenth century skilled workmen and laborers were subjected to these annoying regulations, both in fixing wages and in imposing fines for excess. But the law did not stop here, for it prohibited excessive prices by dealers. It is learned from the records of the Massachusetts colony that an edict was issued in 1645 that workmen were not to be forced to take wine in part payment for their services, while in 1672 the General Court forbade laborers to demand liquors as a part of their wages. This latter movement was to offset the restriction on the laborers,

Effect of attempts to regulate wages.

Wages of mowers.

Skilled workmen subjected to annoying regulations.

but legislators found then that the toilers of the land grew more and more independent with the lapse of years and that it was futile to undertake to control them in what they should receive for their services. At this time (1672) common laborers were paid two shillings, as they were forty years before. Women were paid from four to five pounds per annum. Indians who worked in the fields were paid eighteen pence per day. These wages continued, for the records show that a common laborer in New England earned two shillings per day at the close of the century, and two shillings and three pence to three shillings in New York. Skilled labor in the mother-country received rather less compensation. With the opening of the new century labor received more in this country, one John Marshall, of Braintree, being paid about four shillings per day from 1697 to 1711. He was what would be called an "all-around man," doing some work on farms, making laths in the winter, and working as a painter and carpenter and a maker of bricks.

Wages of common laborers 1672.
Of women.
Of Indians.

Wages in the Virginia colony during the same period were computed at ten pounds sterling per annum. It is somewhat remarkable that wages remained so steady during all of the seventeenth century, and in fact there was no great change until far into the following century. The wages of farm laborers were very generally taken as the standard from which the wages paid to mechanics, tradesmen, and other laborers were to be computed. *
At the close of the colonial period agricultural laborers were paid only about forty cents per day, and this was very little in excess of their wages in the middle of the century, the average wages from 1752 to 1760 being thirty-one cents per day, while butchers in 1780 were paid but thirty-three and one third cents per day, and

In Virginia.

In 1752.
In 1760.

* See Felt's "History of Massachusetts Currency."

carpenters fifty-two cents. Ship and boatbuilders, when the colonial period closed, were paid about ninety cents per day, and shoemakers seventy-three cents. Blacksmiths were paid nearly seventy cents per day. These illustrations are sufficient to show the general conditions, so far as wages are concerned, of laborers during the colonial period. *

The value of a day's wages cannot be estimated by the amount represented in money. That is what political economists call the ''nominal'' wage. The real wage must be determined by considering the prices which the laborer is obliged to pay for the necessaries of life, and when these are considered it will be found that although work was plenty and laborers scarce, the workingman was obliged to pay comparatively high prices, thus reducing his real wage. The records give ample material for price quotations. In 1630, in the northern colonies, while a master mechanic was paid on the average, we will say, two shillings per day, he was obliged to pay from ten to eleven shillings per bushel for corn and fourteen shillings per bushel for wheat, while a good cow was worth twenty-five pounds. Many things, however, were low, a pound of butter costing but six pence and a pound of cheese five pence, and the price of corn and wheat varied greatly, for in 1633 corn could be bought for six shillings per bushel; yet in 1635 twelve shillings was the price.

The prices of commodities varied much more than the price of labor. Taking a few quotations from 1740 we find that carpenters and mowers, who received two shillings and six pence per day, paid about six shillings per bushel for corn. Summer wheat was

* See " History of Wages and Prices in Massachusetts," 1752–1883, by the author. Boston, 1885.

seven shillings per bushel and rye six shillings, while later in the year corn could be purchased for four shillings. This latter commodity fell two or three years later to two shillings and four pence per bushel, but meal was fourteen shillings per bushel. In 1640 a cow cost but five pounds, while sheep could be bought for ten shillings a head, and yearling swine for twenty shillings. These prices, however, are not very perfect indications of trade prices, as they are often taken from schedules of property which might have been sold under some stress ; yet they indicate something of what labor was called upon to expend for a living. In 1646, if a workingman wished to send his child to school, he had to pay four shillings per quarter. Indian corn is quoted at all sorts of prices, up to ten or twelve shillings and down to two shillings per bushel, at different periods ; but in the closing years of the seventeenth century it was quoted at three shillings per bushel, while wheat was selling at five shillings and rye at two shillings and six pence per bushel, pork at three pence per pound, and beef at two pence per pound. A hogshead of cider could be bought for one pound and seven shillings, selling for from six to seven shillings per gallon. There was less variation in prices from 1700 to the close of the colonial period, although during the Revolutionary War fluctuations were, of course, great ; but the year before the war began, that is, in 1774, corn was worth about three shillings per bushel and wheat about six shillings per bushel, and at the close of the war corn could be bought at from three shillings to three shillings and ten pence per bushel, and in 1789, while carpenters were receiving three shillings and four pence per day and common laborers two shillings and four pence, Indian corn was three shillings and two pence per bushel.

Prices of wheat, corn, and rye.

Prices of pork and cider.

Women
workers.

The women rarely worked for wages during the period now under consideration, but they carded the wool, spun the yarn, and wove the cloth for the manufacture of the homespun clothing of the male members of the family. If they could weave more than was wanted for the consumption of the household they sold the surplus or traded it in barter for the things they needed and which they could not produce. When they worked for wages they received from four to five pounds per annum. In many instances they worked on the land, and they did their share in every way to enable the family not only to secure a livelihood but to build itself upon stable lines.

The work of the colonial period, except in the towns after they got thickly settled or fairly so, was ever the work of pioneers. Their struggle was an arduous one—building log houses and supplying the family, and when they felt crowded by too many neighbors, starting

Spirit of ad-
venture.

out into the wilderness. The spirit of adventure, the spirit of finding what was beyond their own limited horizon, their industry, their willingness to work for what work brought, gave to our forebears everywhere throughout the colonial settlements characters which not only sustained them but which enabled them to build a new nation. Notwithstanding all the vicissitudes and restrictions of petty legislation, the long hours of work, the ceaseless round of toil, they were thrifty and fairly prosperous.

Conditions.

After the first half century it must be admitted that from a purely physical point of view the working-men of the colonial period were fairly comfortable in their conditions. They did not have much intellectual stimulation, nor did they meet the mental friction which belongs to our day. They were without many of the things which are now necessities, but which to them would have been great luxuries, for their wants were few and their expectations of acquiring even simple luxuries restricted. It is difficult, from any philosophical point of view, to say whether they were happier than the workingmen of the present time, but when their struggles are taken into consideration it must be conceded that they were far less favorably situated for the cultivation of those characteristics which make of the workingmen of the present time the basis of social stability. They were hardly factors in the politics of the colonies—at least they were not so to any such degree as he workingmen are now political factors. The old English relation of master and servant prevailed, and the attempts at legislative regulation of wages showed that the influence of the feudal system still exercised considerable power over the minds of leaders. They had but little education as compared with the workingmen of our own day, and their children were inured to the same kind of toil that belonged to their own condition. Could they have foreseen the circumstances and the environment of the workingmen of the present day they would have considered that the dream of the social philosophers of their day was to be realized, for they had none of the amenities of life that are free now on every hand.

Comparison with present time.

The colonists secured one thing which the workingman appreciated. They were free men ; they were not tied to the soil, such servitude which had wrought great evil under the feudal system being utterly forbidden. There was no villeinage nor serfdom, and the condition of the laborer was far in advance of his condition in England or on the Continent, but while the demands for common labor were active, the demands for higher

Freedom of workingmen.

**Scarcity of
money.**

priced master workmen were not so great.   Money was
scarce and men were, in general, seeking an independent
home and the opportunity to better themselves by obtaining land.   As population increased the demand for
laborers by farmers increased, and Indians and negro
slaves came in to complicate matters.   There was always

**Opposition to
arbitrary
wages.**

rebellion among the master workmen and the better class
of common laborers against the arbitrary wages decreed
by courts, and so they preferred to live on their own
land.   This movement of course restricted the supply
of labor and at the same time restricted the opportunities
not only for the diversification of industries but for the
expansion of individual wants.   The colonists were vigorous in their efforts to settle the country and as rigid in
their views as they were vigorous.   Narrow in their con-

AN AMERICAN PLOW OF 1776.

ceptions of life, exclusive in their relations, dogmatic in
their opinions, strangers to pleasure, with the knowledge
now open to all a sealed book to them, it is difficult to
understand that they could have been happier than are
their posterity ; yet there must have been great pleasure
in subduing the hard conditions they met on every
hand and in feeling that they were overcoming obstacles.
Their victory over nature and their constant progress
were their great reward and the source of their con-
tentment.

PART II.

THE EVOLUTION OF INDUSTRY:

1790–1890.

PART II.—THE EVOLUTION OF INDUSTRY:

1790-1890.

CHAPTER X.

THE DEVELOPMENT OF THE FACTORY SYSTEM.

IN TREATING industry and labor in the colonial days, the colonial period for the purposes of this work has been considered as closing March 4, 1789, when the present government of the United States went into operation under the new constitution. Politically speaking, the colonial period ended when the people of the colonies declared themselves free and independent of the government of Great Britain and that the United Colonies should be free and independent states; for at that time, July 4, 1776, the colonies assumed independent positions, and from that time each colony took the name of "state." The date of the Declaration of Independence, therefore, must be considered, from a political standpoint, as the birthday of the nation. Industrially speaking, however, this cannot be so considered, and it is a little difficult to determine, from an industrial point of view, exactly what date to assign for the closing of the colonial period. The states, as they had declared themselves, adopted Articles of Confederation March 1, 1781. The people of the colonies had made the Declaration of Independence, but the Continental Congress which made the declaration was practically a committee of conference, and the Continental Congress under the Articles of Confederation, adopted March 1, 1781, was

Colonial period.

Date of Declaration of Independence from industrial point of view.

but little more. The colonial status existed so far as industry and commerce were concerned, and even after the definitive peace signed at Paris September 3, 1783, when the results of the declaration of 1776 were secured and all the world recognized the new nation, the industrial colonial status still existed, and such condition continued until the adoption of the new constitution in 1787, which went into effect March 4, 1789—in fact, it was largely to relieve the states of the colonial status, industrially and commercially speaking, that the new constitution was framed. Prior to that each state regulated its own commerce and could and did restrict interstate commerce. Duties on foreign commerce varied, according to the views and conditions existing in each state. For these reasons it has been thought proper, in treating of the industries and labor in colonial days in the preceding chapters, to consider the colonial period as ending March 4, 1789.

Colonial status of industry.

Variation in duties.

This is logical, again, from the fact that contemporaneous with the adoption of the constitution new forces came into existence which affected, and vitally, the industrial situation. The commerce of each of the states became the commerce of the United States. The change in the method of manufacturing goods came then, and the birth of the factory system in this country followed the birth of the present constitutional government. The second act under the constitution was passed July 4, 1789, with this preamble :

Change in commercial conditions.

Whereas, it is necessary for the support of the government, for the discharge of the debts of the United States, and for the encouragement and the protection of manufactures, that duties be laid on goods, wares, and merchandise imported :

Be it enacted, etc.

This act, which need not be given, paved the way for

the importation of the factory system of industry, which had already been established in the mother-country. *

When the states had won their political independence they found themselves still dependent industrially upon Great Britain, and largely on account of restrictive legislation. England sought by every means to prevent the introduction of mechanical industry into the United States. This was the uniform course all through the colonial period, and after 1760, when cotton-spinning machinery had been invented and perfected to a practical degree, England sought to retain to herself all the benefits which might accrue from the great inventions that had been made. These inventions consisted of means for spinning and weaving by machinery, and were brought into practical use under the patents of various inventors. Prior to 1767 all yarn used in the manufacture of textiles of all kinds was spun in single threads upon the domestic spinning-wheel, and the weaving had been done on the old cumbersome hand-loom. The principal machines for spinning were perfected by Hargreaves and Arkwright, who broke down the barrier which had long obstructed the advance of the cotton manufacture and practically inaugurated the factory system of the United States, which must date from the time of their inventions. But it took the power-loom, invented by Dr. Edward Cartwright, in 1785, to give the spinning machinery all its power, for prior to his invention all the yarn spun by the power machines had been woven into cloth by the hand-loom weavers. The power-loom, therefore, closed the catalogue of machines essential to the opening of the new era of mechanical supremacy. This

States dependent upon Great Britain.

Power-loom.

---

* This account of the development of the factory system in the United States is taken quite largely from the "Report on the Factory System of the United States," to be found in Vol. II., Reports of the Tenth Census, which the author made to the Superintendent of Census in 1882.

series of inventions was applied during the score of years from 1765 to 1785, and England possessed these inventions and was determined to maintain the sole possession thereof.

Use of steam.

The application of steam aided the rapid development of the new order of things, for on the breaking out of the American war the steam-engine passed beyond its primitive use in draining mines, etc., and was rapidly adopted for all kinds of manufacturing industry. Textile mills had been located upon streams of water, from which power was obtained. With the application of the steam-engine such location was no longer a physical necessity, for mills could be built and run near large towns, whose crowded population could supply their operatives.

It will be seen, therefore, that England, at the close of the Revolution, and even at the time of the adoption of our constitution, held, as she supposed, the key to the industrial world of cotton manufacture ; she certainly held the machinery, without which such manufacture could not be carried on in competition with her own mills. Parliament passed stringent laws prohibiting the exportation of machines, plans, and models of machines. The English policy began to shape itself with regard to trade outside the island, and that policy was to buy as little as possible and sell to everybody, and to use the

English policy toward United States.

colonies, and even the states after they passed into independent condition, as the ever-increasing market for her products. She possessed all the raw material for a large list of products, but cotton was wanting. This she expected to receive from India. The American colonies had been destined for her food-raising department and for an outlet for her surplus manufactures. This had been her expressed policy before the war, and this policy had stimulated her to the long-continued strife which followed.

By 14 Geo. III., c. 71, it was enacted that if any person exported any tools or utensils commonly used in the cotton or linen manufactures, or other goods wherein cotton or linen was used, or any parts of such tools or utensils, he should not only forfeit the same, but also £200. Even the possession of such implements, with a view to exportation, made them liable to seizure and the possessor to arrest. This law was passed in 1774, and related to the inventions of Arkwright and Hargreaves. This legislation on the part of England was contemporaneous with the non-importation resolutions of the American colonies, nearly all of which, prior to the Revolution, took active steps, as has been seen, to encourage manufactures.

Exportation of tools prohibited.

The difficulties, therefore, under which the people of the United States labored in securing the development of their manufactures with the use of the new machinery of England were aggravated by legislation. This country, however, had the natural position which would enable it to develop the textile industry, for here, as well as in England, existed the germ of the textile factory in the fulling and carding-mills which had been erected at convenient localities in nearly all the colonies ; and cotton could be raised in the Southern States, and thus be utilized as nearly at first hands as possible, certainly with an advantage over European competition, for Western Europe was obliged to secure its cotton from India. To secure the factory system there must be the machinery which England was using, and to get this required efforts and struggles which brought out the patriotism and the courage of the manufacturers of the time.

Difficulties of establishing manufactures.

The first attempts to secure the spinning machinery which had come into use in England were made in Philadelphia early in the year 1775, when probably the first

First attempts to secure textile machinery.

spinning-jenny ever seen in America was exhibited in that city. During the war the manufacturers of Philadelphia extended their enterprises, and even built and run mills which writers often call factories, but which can hardly be classed under that term. They were mills rather than factories. Similar efforts, all preliminary to the establishment of the factory system of labor, were made in Worcester, Mass., in 1780. In 1781 the British Parliament, determined that the textile machinery by which the manufactures of England were being rapidly extended, and which the continental producers were anxious to secure, should not be used by the people of America, reënacted and enlarged the scope of the statute of 1774 against its exportation, to which reference has been made. So by 21 Geo. III., c. 37, it was provided that any person who packed or put on board, or caused to be brought to any place in order to be put on any vessel for exportation, any machine, engine, tool, press, paper, utensil, or implement, or any part thereof, which then was or thereafter might be used in the woolen, cotton, linen, or silk manufacture of the kingdom, or goods wherein wool, cotton, linen, or silk was used, or any model or plan of such machinery, tool, engine, press, utensil, or implement, should forfeit every such machine, etc., and all goods packed therewith, and £200, and also suffer imprisonment for one year ; and the next year, 1782, a law was enacted which prohibited, under penalty of £500, the exportation or the attempt to export "blocks, plates, engines, tools, or utensils used in or which are proper for the preparing or finishing of the calico, cotton, muslin, or linen printing manufactures, or any part thereof." The same act prohibited the transportation of tools employed in the iron and steel manufactures. Acts were also passed which interdicted the

Efforts preliminary to factory system.

English laws prohibiting exportation of machines.

emigration of artificers. All these laws were enforced with great vigilance, and were, of course, serious obstacles to the institution of the new system of manufacture in America. So the Americans were compelled either to smuggle or to invent their machinery, and it is simply a matter of history that both methods were practiced until most of the secrets of the manufacture of cotton goods were made available in this country.

The planting of the mechanic arts became a necessity in this country during the War of the Revolution, and afterward the spirit of American enterprise demanded that New England and the Middle States should utilize the water-powers which they possessed, and by such utilization supply the people with home manufactures, and thus secure industrial as well as political independence. It was therefore very natural that when the people of the new nation saw that the treaty of Paris had not brought industrial independence a new form of expression of patriotism should take the place of military service. In obedience to this expression associations were formed the object of which was to discourage the use of British goods, and as the Articles of Confederation, adopted March 1, 1781, did not provide for the regulation of commerce, the legislatures of the several states were besought by the people to protect home manufactures. The constitution of 1789 remedied the defects of the articles in this respect and gave Congress the power to legislate on commercial affairs; and, as already intimated, the constitution was really the outcome of the industrial necessities of the people, because it was largely on account of the difficulties and the irritations growing out of the various commercial regulations of the individual states that a convention of commissioners from the various states was held in Annapolis

Necessity of mechanic arts.

Benefits of constitution of 1789 in developing industry.

in September, 1786, which convention recommended the
one that framed the new or present constitution of the
United States.

Experiments in Massachusetts. The great question then was how to secure textile machinery like that used in England. In 1786 the legis-
lature of Massachusetts offered encouragement for the

WEAVING ROOM IN A COTTON-MILL, LOWELL, MASS.

introduction of machinery for carding and spinning by
granting Robert and Alexander Barr £200 to enable
them to complete a roping machine, and also to "construct such other machines as are necessary for the purpose of carding, roping,* and spinning of sheep's wool,
as well as of cotton-wool," and in all probability the
machinery built by the Barrs was the first in this country
First textile factory. which included the Arkwright devices. The first establishment, however, which can by any interpretation be
considered a textile factory was erected at Beverly,
Mass., in 1787. The legislature aided this enterprise.

---

* ROPING.—The act of drawing out or extending a substance into a filament
or thread.

The factory continued in operation for several years, but its career as a cotton factory was brief, and it did not meet with much success. During the same period other attempts were made in Rhode Island, New York, and Pennsylvania, but chiefly in Rhode Island and in that part of Massachusetts lying contiguous to that state.

Aided by legislature of Massachusetts.

To the states just named belongs the honor of the introduction of power-spinning machines in this country and their early practical use here. Rhode Island and Massachusetts certainly have equal claims, for while in the latter state the first experiments were made in embodying the principles of Arkwright's inventions and in the erection of the primitive cotton factory, Rhode Island is entitled to the credit of erecting the first factory in which perfected machinery, made after the English models, was practically employed. The history of the establishment of this factory is somewhat romantic. It was built by Samuel Slater in 1790, in Pawtucket, R. I.

First factory using English methods.

Samuel Slater.

All efforts at the introduction of the English methods of spinning had failed, but Slater, called by President Jackson "the father of American manufactures," succeeded in introducing them. He was born in Belper, Derbyshire, England, June 9, 1768, and at fourteen years of age was bound as an apprentice to Jedediah Strutt, Esq., a manufacturer of cotton machinery. Mr. Strutt was for several years a partner of Sir Richard Arkwright in the cotton-spinning business ; so Slater had every opportunity to master the details of the construction of the cotton machinery then in use in England, for during the last four or five years of his apprenticeship he served as general overseer, not only in making machinery, but in the manufacturing department of Strutt's factory. Near the close of his term, accidentally seeing a notice in an American paper of the efforts which were being made in the different parts of the United States to secure cotton machinery and of the bounties which were offered to parties who might succeed in so doing, Slater determined to remove to this country. He very well knew the provisions of the English laws, and that under them he could carry neither machines nor models nor plans of machines to the States. He therefore completed his full time with Mr. Strutt, and then continued with him for a period superintending some new works which Mr. Strutt was erecting. He did this that he might perfect his knowledge of the business in every department so thoroughly that he could construct machinery from memory, and thus bring over in his head the knowledge which he could not bring either in plans, models, or specifications ; so Slater embarked at London September 13, 1789, with a most precious cargo, but a cargo that was contained entirely in his own brain. He landed in New York November 17, 1789, and there made connections with parties interested in cotton manufacture ; but not meeting with just the encouragement he expected, he corresponded with Messrs. Brown and Almy, of Providence, R. I., who owned some crude spinning machines, some of which had been brought from the primitive factory at Beverly, Mass. In the following January, 1790, Slater made arrangements with these parties to construct machinery on the English plan. This he succeeded in doing at Pawtucket, making the machinery principally with his own hands, and on the 20th of December, 1790, he started three cards, drawing and roving, together with seventy-two spindles, working entirely on the Arkwright plan, and these were the first of the kind ever operated in America.

South Carolina comes in, and very properly, for some

Slater's plans.

Slater's arrival in New York.

Slater's construction of spinning machinery in America.

of the claims in this respect, although the record is not clear. A writer in the *American Museum*, in July, 1790, refers to a man in that state who had completed and had in operation on the High Hills of the Santee, ginning, carding, and other machines driven by water, and also spinning machines, with eighty-four spindles each, with every necessary article for manufacturing cotton ; and the writer further states that "if this information be correct, the attempt to manufacture by machinery the cotton which they were then beginning to cultivate extensively (in the Southern States) was nearly as early as those of the Northern States." Early cotton machinery in South Carolina

Similar efforts were also made at Philadelphia, as already intimated, by Samuel Wetherell, and his attempts, as were those of the Beverly company in Massachusetts, of the gentleman in South Carolina, and of Brown and Almy in Providence, were all before Slater's coming. While these attempts to introduce spinning by power did not comprehend the English devices and methods in full, they illustrate the difficulty of locating the origin of the factory system. Notwithstanding these efforts, however, it is considered

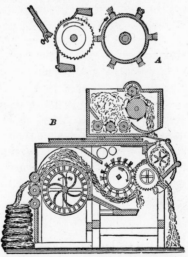

Efforts before Slater's coming.

A. ELI WHITNEY'S ORIGINAL COTTON-GIN.
B. Later form of the same invention.

Slater the first
to erect English
.machinery. safe, historically, to start with Slater as the first to erect cotton machinery on the English plan, and this gives 1790 as the year of the birth of the factory system in the United States.

Another feature came in about this time which encouraged the growth of the factory system, not only in this country, but abroad. This was the invention of a machine for separating the lint from the seed of the cotton plant. This had been done by slow, laborious processes conducted by hand, but in 1794 Eli Whitney, of Massachusetts, who was residing temporarily in Georgia, **The cotton-gin.** invented the cotton-gin,* by which the lint was picked

HULLING COTTON-GIN, WITH FEEDER, BREAKER, AND CONDENSER.

from the seed by means of sawteeth projecting through **Circumstances attending the invention of the cotton-gin.** slits in the side of a chamber in which the seed of the cotton is placed. Mr. Whitney was visiting some friends one day, when mention was made of the difficulties of separating the fleece of the cotton plant from the seed

* COTTON-GIN.—A machine used in separating the seeds from cotton fibers.

which filled it and of the value of some machine, could
the same be invented, for accomplishing this purpose,
and he proceeded at once to elaborate the ideas which
were essential for securing the desired result. By

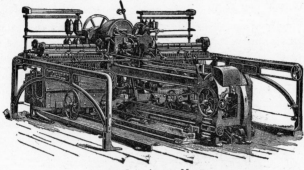

THE SELF-ACTING MULE.

its use cotton became a more thoroughly marketable
article and its production vastly stimulated. The development of cotton-raising in the South, and now of the
cotton manufactures of the South, is due very largely to
this invention.

The cotton-gin
stimulated the
use of cotton.

The factory, however, needed perfection scientifically.
In the old country, where it exists in great perfection, it
did not reach the completed structure at as early a date
as it did in America. The processes of cleaning the fiber
and of spinning the same into yarn were carried on by
one set of works, while the weaving and the finishing
were carried on by others, usually in separate establishments. The perfect factory, the scientific arrangement
of parts for the successive processes necessary for the
manipulation of the raw material till it came out finished
goods, had not been constructed when the system was
established in this country. The power-loom, although
invented in 1785, did not come into use in England until

The perfect
factory.

about 1806, while in this country it was not used at all till after the War of 1812 ; but even after it came into use in England the custom of spinning the yarn under one management and weaving the cloth under another prevailed.

In 1811 Mr. Francis C. Lowell, of Boston, visited

ENGLISH POWER-LOOM FOR WEAVING CALICO.

Efforts of Francis C. Lowell.

England and spent much time in inspecting cotton factories, with the view to the introduction of improved machinery in the United States. His visit was about the time when the power-loom was being introduced in Great Britain, but, as occurred in other respects, its construction was kept very secret. Mr. Lowell, however, learned all he could regarding it and came home with the determination of perfecting it. With the skill of Paul Moody, of Amesbury, Mass., and through the encouragement of Nathan Appleton, a company had been organized for the establishment of a cotton manufactory, to be located in Waltham, Mass., on a water privilege which

Cotton factory at Waltham, Mass.

existed there. The factory was completed in the autumn of 1814, and in it was placed the loom which Mr. Lowell had perfected, having neither plans nor models, and in that year his company set up a full set of machinery for weaving and spinning, there being 1,700 spindles in use. This factory erected at Waltham was the first in the world, so far as any record shows, in which all the processes involved in the manufacture of goods, from the raw material to the finished product, were carried on in one establishment by successive steps, mathematically considered, under one harmonious system. Mr. Lowell, aided by Mr. Patrick T. Jackson, who was associated with him, is unquestionably entitled to the credit of arranging this admirable system. Few changes have been made in the arrangement organized at the Waltham factory.

The scientific factory.

So while England furnished the foundation of the industrial structure known as the factory system of manufacture, America furnished the stone which completed the arch.

CHAPTER XI.

THE DEVELOPMENT OF INDUSTRIES, 1790–1860.

The foundation of our industries. THE impetus was now given in good earnest for the rapid development of the great industries of the country. Their foundations had been laid in colonial days in the constitution of 1789 and in the successful planting of the factory system. Patriotic enthusiasm called into existence many societies all through the states for the protection and encouragement of industrial undertakings. All the great industries, those that are now the great industries, as has been stated, were in existence and so fully recognized, not only by this country, but by England, that they needed only the fostering care of enterprise and the persistent effort of proprietors of capital and of labor to secure rapid development. From the beginning of this century to the present time the expansion has been steady and rapid, although not always constant. There have been periods when adverse conditions resulted in great stagnation here and there, but these conditions have always been overcome and the industries carried along.

Expansion since 1800.

While the story of the development of industries since the organization of the government belongs in a large sense to one grand period, it is naturally divided into two principal periods, one including the years from 1790 to 1860, and the other the years from 1860 to the present time. This division is natural on account of, first, the Civil War, and, second, the renewed and accelerated

Natural periods.

132

stimulation which came from the war, the discovery of greater wealth of resources, and the invention and adaptation of new processes of production. So the story, for the purposes of this work, is divided into these two periods, and the present chapter devoted to that from 1790 to 1860. It is difficult, however, in this comprehensive history, to deal with the extension of the industries of the country in any particular detail, general statements being all that can be allowed.

After the success of the power-loom the cotton manufacture took rapid strides and the hand-loom and the hand-weaver were quickly displaced, although they linger in some parts of the country, especially in North Carolina, Tennessee, and Georgia. Factories sprung up on the streams of New England and the Middle States, and purely factory towns, like Lowell, Lawrence, Holyoke, Fall River, Cohoes, Paterson, and many other thriving places, were erected, and before the close of the war the industry had taken root upon the banks of southern rivers. *Displacement of hand labor.*

The growth of this particular industry well illustrates that of all industries, and its effects are certainly illustrative of the results of the new system. The first facts relative to the cotton industry which are obtainable are for 1810, when the federal government made the first attempt, through the machinery of the decennial census, to ascertain the condition and value of the products of the country ; but it is impossible, from the statements of that census, to ascertain the exact amount of the cotton goods produced, although the value of cotton, wool, flax, hemp, and silk, including stockings, amounted to $39,-497,057. *Cotton industry.*

1810.

In 1831 there were 801 cotton factories in the whole country ; in 1840 there were 1,240 ; in 1850 there were *Cotton factory in 1831.*

1,074, and in 1860 there were 1,091. This decrease in the number of establishments since 1850 is the result of consolidation and the establishment of large works, the smaller factories having closed or united with the larger ones. While the number of factories decreased in the thirty years prior to 1860, the consumption of cotton and the production of goods steadily increased. In

Increased consumption of cotton.

WEAVING ROOM IN A SOUTHERN COTTON-MILL.

1831. 1831 the total number of spindles in this industry was 1,246,703, while in 1860 the number had increased to 5,235,727, and the number of looms arose from 33,433 1860. in 1831 to 126,313 in 1860. The capital invested in the cotton industry in 1831 was $40,612,984, and in 1860 $98,585,269. The value of the products in 1831 cannot be stated. The value of cotton goods in 1860 was $115,-681,774, there being $79,359,900 produced in the New

England States, $26,534,700 in the Middle States, $8,-460,337 in the Southern States, and $1,326,837 in the Western States. In 1831 there was but $290,000 invested in the Southern States in the cotton industry, but in 1860 these states used a capital of $9,840,221. So at the close of our first period the Southern States had demonstrated the fact that the cotton industry could exist there. This great representative industry was on a firm basis at the close of the first period.

Cotton industry in the Southern States.

In the chapters relating to industries in the colonial days but little could be said of the iron industry, because it had not been developed to so great an extent at the close of the colonial period as some other industries; but early in the present century, and in fact during the closing decennial period of the last, the manufacture of iron assumed gratifying proportions. It had an existence in the eastern part of Pennsylvania and in the other colonies, but it had not successfully crossed the Alleghenies, although it had received new impulse east of the mountains after the Revolution. The counties of Chester, Lancaster, and Berks were conspicuous in the development of the great staple manufacturing industry of Pennsylvania in the early part of the period now under consideration. Mr. Swank, in his excellent work, "Iron in All Ages," states that many blast furnaces and forges and a few rolling and slitting-mills were built in these counties before 1800, and that their activity continued after the beginning of the present century. Other iron-producing counties of the eastern half of Pennsylvania joined in the general progress of the industry, giving it a firm foundation which has never been shaken.

Iron industry.

General progress in the iron industry.

Western Pennsylvania was, of course, later in the establishment of the iron industry than the eastern part.

There is a tradition that the first discovery of iron ore
west of the Allegheny Mountains was made by John
Hayden in the winter of 1789–90, on the eve of the new
period. The fact is, however, as testified to by good
authorities, that iron had been discovered at least nine
years before Hayden's alleged discovery ; but whenever
the discovery was made, it was the opening of a wonderfully successful industrial career which has rarely been
equaled in the history of a people, and the development
of the industry in the western counties of Pennsylvania
was rapid and satisfactory.

Of course, some districts were abandoned and others
took their places, but Allegheny County, the great iron-
producing county of western Pennsylvania, began its
operations at a practically recent period, a small furnace
being built by one George Anshutz, who is called the
pioneer of the iron manufactures of Pittsburg, in 1792.
In 1794 it was abandoned for want of ore. It had been
expected that ore could be obtained in the vicinity, but
the expectation was not realized. This enterprise was
very largely devoted to the casting of stoves and grates.
Anshutz removed to Huntingdon County, where, with
others, he built the Huntingdon furnace in 1796.

The first iron foundry at Pittsburg was established in
1803, on the site of the present post-office and the city
hall of that place. From these beginnings Pittsburg in
1829 had grown to the dignity of having eight rolling-
mills, using 6,000 tons of blooms and 1,500 tons of pig-
iron. In the same year there were nine foundries, while
in 1831 two steel furnaces were in operation at Pittsburg. In 1856 there were in Pittsburg and in Allegheny
County twenty-five rolling-mills.

About the year 1840 a revolution was created in the
iron industry of the country by the introduction of bi-

tuminous and anthracite coal in the blast furnace, and since about 1850 the manufacture of charcoal iron in Pennsylvania furnaces has declined.

These two great industries are indicative of the whole expansion, for in nearly all industries the conditions of growth were practically the same. This growth can be clearly understood by stating the results of two accounts of manufactures, one taken in 1810 and the other in 1860. For the first year the marshals employed in taking the census reported the value of goods manufactured by the loom, of cotton, wool, flax, hemp, and silk, with stockings, as stated, at $39,497,057; other goods of these five materials, spun, $2,052,120; instruments and machinery manufactured, $186,650; carding, fulling, and floor-cloth stamping by machinery, $5,957,816; hats of wool, fur, etc., and of mixtures of them, $4,323,-744; manufactures of iron, $14,364,526; manufactures of gold, silver, set work, mixed metals, etc., $2,483,912; manufactures of lead, $325,560; soap, tallow candles, wax, and spermaceti, spring oil and whale oil, $1,766,-292; manufactures of hides and skins, $17,935,477; manufactures from seeds, $858,509; grain, fruit, and case liquors, distilled and fermented, $16,528,207; dry manufactures from grain, exclusively of flour, meal, etc., $75,766; manufactures of wood, $5,554,708; manufactures of essences and oils, of and from wood, $179,150; refined or manufactured sugars, $1,415,724; manufactures of paper, pasteboard, cards, etc., $1,939,285; manufactures of marble, stone, and slate, $462,115; glass manufactures, $1,047,004; earthen manufactures, $259,-720; manufactures of tobacco, $1,260,378; drugs, dye-stuffs, paints, etc., and dyeing, $500,382; cables and cordage, $4,243,168; manufactures of hair, $129,731; various and miscellaneous manufactures, $4,347,601.

Indicative character of textile and iron industries.

Products in 1810.

Mr. Tench Coxe, acting under the directions of the secretary of the treasury, Mr. Albert Gallatin, made a valuable analysis of the manufacturing products of the United States, and the foregoing figures are taken from his statement. His report was completed in May, 1813, and published by Congress. The total value of all the manufactures of the country in 1810, as given by Mr. Coxe, was $127,694,602. By estimating the omitted products Mr. Coxe extended this amount to $172,762,-676, and by adding some doubtful articles, embracing such manufactures as from their nature were nearly allied to agriculture, as, for example, cotton-pressing, flour and meal, productions of grain and sawmills, the manufacture of bricks, tiles, and some other articles, he concluded that the aggregate value of the manufactures of every description in the United States in 1810 was $198,613,474.

The distribution of this vast product over the states shows that Pennsylvania stood at the head, with $33,-691,111, New York coming next with over $25,000,000; then Massachusetts, with nearly $22,000,000 ; Virginia, with $15,250,000, in round numbers ; Maryland, with nearly $11,500,000 ; Connecticut, with over $7,750,000; New Jersey, with over $7,000,000 ; North Carolina, with over $6,500,000 ; Kentucky, with over $6,000,000, while Vermont, New Hampshire, Rhode Island, South Carolina, Georgia, and Maine manufactured products varying from $3,500,000 to $5,500,000, in round numbers.

In 1860 the value of the products of American mechanical industries had reached $1,885,861,676, but the statement by industries for that year cannot be given in detail. The values may be given for some of the principal industries, however. The total value of all kinds of cotton goods was $115,681,774. The value of woolen goods was $61,895,217. Clothing had by this time become a great industry. It had grown up within a few years of the close of the first period, and in all the principal cities had become an industry of magnitude and importance, the value of the product being $73,219,765. The great industry of boots and shoes, which is closely allied to that of clothing, and which was, at the period being considered, beginning to feel the influence of the factory system of labor, represented, in 1860, a product worth $91,891,498.

Growth of clothing industry.

A new industry had come into existence in the form of water-proof goods. There are but few branches showing a more remarkable development than this, for in the space of twenty-five or thirty years rubber had been applied in very many departments of production of the arts and sciences and domestic economy ; yet in 1860 this industry was practically in its infancy, the value of the india rubber goods, however, amounting to $5,768,-450. These figures, which will be brought into comparison in the next period, need not be extended here. They are more emphatic when compared with the results for 1890.

The distribution of the manufactures over the states and territories in 1860 was, of course, far more general than in 1810, not only through the increase in the number of states and the extension of manufactures in consequence, but also over the states that were named for 1810. New York, however, led all the states in 1860, the value of her manufactures for the year being 379 million. Pennsylvania came second, with over 290 million, Massachusetts being third, with over 255 million. These three states are the only ones which passed the 200 million line ; and there was only one state coming

Distribution of manufactures.

between 100 million and 200 million, Ohio, which produced 122 million dollars' worth of goods, while in 1810
her productions were too insignificant for mention. The
states passing the 50 million line were Connecticut, with
nearly 82 million ; New Jersey, with over 76 million ;
California, with over 68 million ; Illinois, with over 57½
million ; Virginia, with over 50½ million. All the other
states came below the 50 million line.

Influences
resulting in
expansion.

The influences which brought about this great expansion of our manufacturing industries prior to 1860 were
referred to in opening this chapter. There had been
fluctuations growing out of the War of 1812, the stagna-
tions of 1837, and the depression of 1857, but from 1830
the course was constant and upward. The influences
which secured this must be considered as permanent and
as not affected materially by periods of depression, artificial stimulation, or the forces of war in either direction.

Patents.

Among these influences the ingenuity of American inventors should not be lost sight of, and the inventions resulting from the exercise of this ingenuity were adopted
with eagerness by the American manufacturers. New
processes, simplifying methods and reducing cost, were
constantly sought for and applied. It is a curious fact,
well known to those familiar with patents, that depressed
periods often result in the stimulation of invention. In
1857 there were 2,900 patents issued, 438 being for agricultural implements and processes. These related to the
invention and improvement of cotton-gins, rice-cleaners,
and fertilizers. The very next year, the year following
the financial crisis, there were 3,710 patents issued, 562
of these relating to agricultural implements and processes,
152 being for improvements in reaping and mowing machines, 42 for improvements in cotton-gins and cotton
presses, 164 for improvements in steam-engines, and 198

for improvements in railroads and railroad cars. Prior to 1849 the number of patents issued had never exceeded 660 annually, but from 1849 to 1860, inclusive, the number never fell below 1,000, except for the years 1850, 1851, and 1853, while for 1860 the number rose to 4,819.

It would be very interesting, and very profitable too, to the student of the evolution of American industries to examine carefully the character of the inventions granted Inventions. during the last twenty or thirty years of the period ending with 1860, and in this period it would be found that there were patented some of the most important inventions of the age, important, at least, in respect to the wants of the people. They related to improvements in looms for producing figured fabrics ; to air-heating stoves, cooking stoves, musical instruments, firearms, sewing machines,

THE SEWING MACHINE.

printing presses, boot and shoe machinery, rubber goods, floor-cloths, and thousands of other inventions tending to raise and improve the standard of the living of the people.

Perhaps the most striking illustration of the influence of inventions is to be found in the manufacture of Boot and shoe-making. boots and shoes, to which reference has already been made. This industry was formerly carried on in little shops, in which a few men, rarely more than four, worked upon the bench, upon stock received from the manufacturer, cut out and ready to be put together. These little shops are closed ; the great shoe factory has taken

their place, and in it is to be seen the perfect adaptation
of the manufacture of goods by successive, harmonious
processes.   To all industries where such successive,
harmonious processes can be applied, that is, where
raw material can be converted into finished goods by
consecutive actions, carried along by a central power,
the factory system of labor has been adapted.   In
all textile manufactures this has been the case, while
outside the textile trades the expansion of the new system has been rapid, until the statistics of industry in the
United States comprehend in large degree the statistics
of manufactures under the factory system.

CHAPTER XII.

THE CIVIL WAR; AN INDUSTRIAL REVOLUTION.

WITH the Civil War there began a new industrial era, not only on account of the expansion of mechanical industries, as related, but on account of the wonderful change in the system of labor which prevailed in a large part of the country. In all that has been said in this work of the development of industry and of labor prior to the Civil War, no mention has been made of the two conflicting systems of labor which existed. Mechanical industry has flourished so far only under the condition of free labor. The development of certain agricultural industries, notably those of cotton and tobacco, was carried on under slave labor. New industrial era.

It is not thoroughly essential that the exact date of the introduction of slave labor into this country should be stated. Historians disagree as to the year, although they agree quite fully as to the month, but from all that can be learned it was in August of 1618, 1619, or 1620. Stith's "History of Virginia" fixes the date in 1618. Certain it is that some time during the three years between 1618 and 1620 slaves were brought to this country and were sold in the colony of Virginia, and slavery existed in some parts of the United States until the emancipation proclamation of President Lincoln, January 1, 1863. Nearly all of the colonies utilized slave labor, some of them, however, having but few slaves, while the system took firm root in the southern colonies. It was Introduction of slave labor. Utilized by nearly all of the colonies.

Mechanical and agricultural labor.

but natural, therefore, that mechanical industry should receive greater attention where free labor predominated, and that agriculture should receive the greatest attention in those parts of the colonies where slave labor was most in vogue. So in any account of the development or evolution of the industries of our country up to the time of the Civil War the chief interest centers in those parts of the country where free labor prevailed.

Most of the Northern States abolished slavery long be-

A VIRGINIA TOBACCO FIELD.

Abolition of slavery in Northern States.

fore the Civil War, but it never played any great part as an obstacle or in any direction in the development of mechanical industry, although it has played a most important part in retarding such development in the South. A distinguished southern financier has treated the retarding influences of slavery from an industrial point of view with great candor, with perfect knowledge of conditions, and keen insight into the influences which led the South to keep her labor employed in certain restricted lines. * According to this writer the destiny of the South was ruled by forces over which her own people had little or no control. Many events occurred outside of her own territory which affected her industrial history. The inventions of Hargreaves, Arkwright, and Crompton, in England, the application of the steam-engine to the manufacture of cotton goods, and the invention of the cotton-gin by Eli Whitney, all contributed to concentrate the attention of the South upon cotton-raising. The cotton-gin made cotton-planting exceedingly profitable, and its rapid extension was stimulated by the English machinery, while the mobility of slave labor added largely to the inducement for its use. The best soils could be taken up rapidly, because labor could be transported from place to place with little difficulty. The introduction of railroads aided in securing this mobility, and this resulted, as Mr. Trenholm remarks, in the population of the original slave states being primarily distributed over an area much too extended for advantageous occupation by so small a number of people.

Uneconomic conditions of slave labor.

Influence of the cotton-gin.

Mobility of slave labor.

Invention, science, and the arts had literally put a new face upon the earth ; the division of labor had augmented the producing capacity of the masses, and multiplied their employments and needs, stimulating trade and diffusing intelligence. The gold of California and Australia, together with the improvements in navigation and inland transportation, produced universal activity in commerce and trade. The whirl and rush of this progress encompassed the South on every side ; she came into contact with it at every point of her extended interests and on every line of her development ; she felt its in-

---

* " The Southern States : Their Social and Industrial History, Condition, and Needs," a paper read before the Social Science Association at Saratoga, N. Y., September 6, 1877, by Hon. W. L. Trenholm, of South Carolina.

fluence upon her industries, and tasted its fruits in her expanding wealth. Yet alone in all the world she stood unmoved by it; in government, in society, in employments, in labor, the states of the South, in 1860, were substantially what they had been in 1810, when the abolition of the slave trade had impressed upon their development the last modification of form of which it seemed susceptible. Not only had the South remained unchanged during all this time, but the flood of immigration which poured over all the rest of the country had passed her by. Millions of men and women from every country of Europe passed along the whole extent of her northern border,

Immigration passed the South.

bringing with them the industrial secrets of every quarter of the globe, and carrying their skill and thrift to the uttermost wilds of the West ; they passed within sight almost of the fertile soil, untenanted lands, and untouched resources of the South, where, besides, the roads, bridges, and railroads were already built, cities and towns already established, churches and schools already existing ; but they would not come in. The conservatism and isolation of the South are the more remarkable because the century was so full of enriching progress, and because the American people have ever taken the lead in exploring new ideas and trying new methods. *

Capitalization of labor.

The result of all these things was the capitalization of labor in the form of slavery, a capital which possessed the power of labor and the ease of transition belonging to capital itself. | It is not strange that immigration passed by the South. It moved along east and west lines and developed the Great Northwest and the West generally ; but the causes were largely industrial. It is probable that immigrants, could they have competed with the mobility of slave labor, would readily have sought the richer states of the South rather than many

Immigrants unable to compete with slave labor.

of the unattractive regions of the West. The immigrant could not compete with the current cost of labor, nor could he gain possession of the rich soils of the South, because if he had attempted it he would have found them

---

* See " The Southern States," by Mr. Trenholm, already quoted.

occupied. Then, again, the raising of cotton required considerable capital, as well as cheap and mobile labor, Necessity of mobile labor. and in this the immigrant found himself largely at a disadvantage. Free labor in itself was too expensive for both laborer and employer; so many of the whites of the South left that part of the country and sought other regions. The census of the United States discloses the facts in this latter respect, for it is found that in 1860 there were 277,000 white persons who had been born in South Carolina still living there, while 193,000 born in that state had found homes in other parts of the country. North Carolina retained 634,000 of her native-born population and 272,000 had left the home state. Virginia showed like conditions, there being 1,000,000 of her native-born whites at home and 400,000 had been separated from the state.

These facts relating to the loss of native population Loss of native population. show of themselves the disinclination of white labor to compete with slave labor; yet it is undoubtedly true that the chief cause preventing the introduction of the mechanical industries in the South is to be found in the great expansion of territory resulting from the desire to increase the cotton and tobacco crops. Manufactures result in concentration of population: agriculture in expansion. The two interests, therefore, were diverse in the elements that relate to population alone. The southern planter, grown up under the conditions which surrounded him, felt the necessity of having large plantations. His dignity, his happiness depended upon it. His wealth was not so much a matter of importance, so long as he could carry on his plantation, as that inborn sentiment which leads a man to adopt certain methods Differing conditions North and South. of living. The manufacturer of the North was an entirely different type; concentration, the handling of de-

,tails, and the adjustment of the elements of mechanical industry were natural to him.   Here, then, were two types of men and two systems of labor that could not be assimilated so long as the types of labor existed sepa-

Antagonism of systems. rately.   The individual types of proprietors alone would not have resulted in antagonism, but together with the different types of labor there could be no diversified in-

A LEAF TOBACCO SALE IN VIRGINIA.

Diversification of industry in the North. dustry in the South, and the manufacturers of the North naturally projected their works along other lines.   So in the North industry became diversified, while in the South the development was always along one line.   As Mr. Trenholm, already quoted, remarks in his valuable article, "industry and society at the North were borne along in the general current of progress; at the South they were fixed in immovable conservatism."

The southern slave laborer's consumption was repre-sented by perhaps forty or fifty cents per week, may be less, while the free white laborer's consumption was represented by four or five times that amount. The individual laborers, therefore, could not have been brought into competition by any legislation, or by any movement of capital, or by any movement of reform. Dr. Franklin wrote an essay on "The Peopling of Countries," in which he said : "It is an ill-grounded opinion that by the labour of slaves, America may possibly vie in cheapness of manufactures with Great Britain. The labour of slaves can never be so cheap here as the labour of the workingmen in Great Britain. Any one may compute it. Reckon, then, the interest of the first purchase of a slave, the insurance or risk on his life, his clothing and diet, expenses in his sickness and loss of time, loss by neglect of business (neglect which is natural to the man who is not to be benefited by his own care or diligence), expense of a driver to keep him at work, and his pilfering from time to time (almost every slave being, from the nature of slavery, a thief), and compare the whole amount with the wages of a manufacturer of iron or wool, in England ; you will see that labour is much cheaper there than it ever can be by negroes here." Very many observers, from Franklin's time on, marked the indifference and extreme slowness of the movements of slaves and made calculations of the cost of slave labor as compared with that of free labor. Mr. Cooper, a former president of the College of South Carolina, computed that a negro, all hazards included and all earnings deducted, would cost, at the age of twenty-one, to the person who raised him, at the very least, $500.* An in-

Consuming power of states.

Dr. Franklin on expense of slave labor.

President Cooper of South Carolina on cost of slave labor.

---

* Cf. "Wages, or the Whip; an Essay on the Comparative Cost and Productiveness of Free and Slave Labour," by Josiah Conder. London, 1833.

Cheapness of
labor under
slavery.

vestment must be made, therefore, in the man before his labor is available; so, while the labor, when it became available, was so cheap that labor under wages could not

STEMMING TOBACCO IN A VIRGINIA FACTORY.

The planter's
disadvantage.

compete with it, the capitalist himself—the planter—was at a disadvantage on account of his great outlay for the labor which he employed.

Mr. Daniel R. Goodloe, a North Carolinian, who has given great attention to the solution of the economic problems connected with slavery and free labor, came to the conclusion more than fifty years ago that capital invested in slaves was wholly unproductive and had the effect only of appropriating the wages due to the slave. He illustrated this proposition in various ways. One instance was that of two farmers, one residing on the south bank of the Ohio River, in Kentucky, and the other on the north bank, in Ohio, each cultivating one hundred acres and employing ten laborers. All their expenses were the same, except as to labor. The Ohio man hired ten freemen and paid them wages, probably out of the products of his crops. The Kentuckian was obliged to invest $10,000 or more in the purchase of ten slaves in addition to all other investments; yet the two farms yielded equal crops. The Kentuckian received more money than the Ohio man, but Kentucky was made no richer by that fact than Ohio was by the distribution of the profits between the farmer and his laborers. Mr. Goodloe has put his illustration into concrete form as follows:[*]

CAPITAL NECESSARY TO GROW COTTON WITH FREE AND WITH SLAVE LABOR.

	Free labor.	Slave labor.
100 acres of land, at $20 per acre	$2,000	$2,000
Value of cattle, horses and farming tools . .	2,000	2,000
Food and clothing of farmer, food of free laborers, and provender for horses, cattle, etc	1,000	
Food and clothing for farmer and his slaves, doctors' bills for latter, and provender for horses, cattle, etc		1,000
Value of ten slaves, at $1,500 each		15,000
Fund for paying wages to free laborers . . .	1,000	
Total investments.	$6,000	$20,000

[*] Cf. "Resources and Industrial Condition of the South," by Mr. Goodloe, in Report of the United States Commissioner of Agriculture for the year 1865. The author is also indebted to Mr. Goodloe personally for furnishing this illustration.

These two things, which appear paradoxical—the cheapness and the cost of labor—of themselves, prevented the introduction of manufactures in the South.

Diversified industry impossible.

Taken in connection with the other features referred to, diversified industry there was an impossibility.

The Civil War found these conditions; with it they all passed away. While the war was organized for political purposes, for the establishment of a new government, it was in reality a great labor movement—not so intended, but so in result; for divested of all political significance, divested even of the conditions under which it was carried on, so far as labor was concerned, it was a war of economic forces, with good or ill results to the

The Civil War a great labor movement.

industrial elements of the nation and particularly the South, for the South had existed under a form of labor entirely antagonistic to that existing at the North and in all other lands where material progress had marked the growth of the people. The South had been waiting, as had the late Count Chambord of France, for the world to turn backward, and to bring with such turning the wealth which comes from the development of natural resources. These resources the South possessed in great

Resources of the South.

abundance. She had rich deposits of iron and other ores, and the coal to work the ores; she had timber, pasture, and arable lands without stint, with waterpowers that might induce mechanics from all lands to settle there; she had a climate to lure the dwellers from inclement zones; she had scenery as varied and as beautiful as can be found in any of the states; and yet, with all these great natural advantages, immigration would not put itself into competition with slave labor. But the war came, the system of labor was changed entirely, and the South as a result has come into industrial competition with the North and with Europe.

The Civil War was an industrial revolution in another sense. The North held the mechanical industries of the country, and naturally, under the stimulus of the war, these industries could be expanded to almost any extent, and they were so expanded, giving to the North every resource of power which mechanics give to great armies. The agricultural South could not compete with the mechanical North. The war, in changing the form of labor

Mechanical resources of the North.

DRYING ROOM IN A SOUTHERN TOBACCO FACTORY.

of the South, forced upon it the adoption of the system existing elsewhere, and therefrom dates the mechanical development of the Southern States. Prior to the war there was little expansion except over areas. The resources of the South were not appreciated, nor were they prospected to any great extent; but with the close of the war attention was turned to the elements which are essential to industrial development. Before the emancipation of slavery very many prominent business

Mechanical development of the South after the war.

men had taken the ground that climatic influences would
prevent the extension of the factory system in the southern portion of the United States, and even within a very
few years public men have insisted that the factory,
workshop, and extensive works using machinery could
not be carried on profitably in the Southern States ; and
yet, with the development since the war, there has come
an extensive factory system there, and to such a degree

PICKING COTTON.

as to show clearly that no climatic influence can stay its
further development.

The statistics of the growth of the South disprove the
old views and confirm the wisdom of the men who have
put their energy and their capital into southern enterprises. The South soon found that besides the capacity
to raise cotton and tobacco for domestic and foreign consumption, crops which constituted her chief source of
wealth, another great source was hidden beneath the
surface, consisting in the mineral deposits of the country.

This wealth is vast, indeed, and the statements relative to it show the basis of the whole southern development since the war.* The Southern Appalachian region, while it does not cover all the iron and coal resources of the Southern States, probably contains the great bulk of minerals of the very best quality. It embraces a strip of Iron and coal
resources. elevated mountainous country seven hundred miles long, with an average width of one hundred and fifty miles, and extends from the Pennsylvania line, the great iron region of the North, southwestwardly through Maryland, the Virginias, Kentucky, Tennessee, the Carolinas, and into Alabama and Georgia. It is an unbroken coal-field of more than thirty-nine thousand square miles, its surface being a combination of mountain and plateau. The vastness of this coal area of the Southern Appalachian field is more readily comprehended when brought into comparison with the coal areas of other countries. It is estimated that it contains forty times the amount of coal, accessible to economical production and distribution, that was contained in the coal-field of Great Britain before a pick was struck. Great Britain has not begun to exhaust her supply, even now, and with the Southern Appalachian field, containing forty times the wealth of Great Britain, the South may well feel that she has another natural source of wealth—her mineral deposits —that is inexhaustible and that makes her a power in the industrial world.

The fear that came after the war that what the southern people considered their great and natural staple, cotton, would not be raised in as great quantities as under the system of slave labor, has been entirely removed by the Cotton crops. development of that particular industry. The largest

* The author is indebted to statements made by Col. Geo. B. Cowlam, of Knoxville, Tenn., and by Major Goldsmith B. West, of Tredegar, Ala.

cotton crop in the Southern States prior to the war was in
the year before it commenced, 1860, when 4,669,770
bales were produced. This quantity was not reached
again until 1871, when it was 4,352,317 bales ; but as

"Cotton Day" at Marietta, Georgia.

early as 1876 the product equaled the proportions of that
of 1860, and since 1876 there has been no year when the
crop has not been greater than at any time prior to the
war, while in 1894 the production reached the vast
amount of 9,500,000 bales.

While formerly the South exported nearly all of her
cotton crop, she is now consuming a very large percentage of it, 700,000 bales having been consumed last year
in southern cotton-mills. But these statements belong
now to the development of the whole country since 1860.

They are brought out here simply as specific illustrations of the truth of the statement that the Civil War was a great industrial revolution, not only in light of the fact that it changed the labor system of the South, but that it changed the economic conditions of the South as well relative to her material prosperity. When the industrial status of millions of people is changed to a directly opposite system, whatever action brings about the change must be considered an industrial revolution, and while it is clearly true, in the light of all the history we now have, that the ultimate effects of slavery were harmful to the

Slavery harmful to industrial interests.

SHIPPING COTTON, CHARLESTON, SOUTH CAROLINA.

best interests of the country, the immediate influence was in an economic way advantageous. Slavery enabled the clear-headed and vigorous early settlers to hasten the work of subjugating the wilderness of eastern North

Its immediate influence an economic advantage.

America in a measure which would have been impossible if there had been no such servile labor at their command.* Whatever service it had to perform in such directions, however, had been completed, and the evolution of industry in the United States required a change, and such change being effected by the Civil War, makes it the appropriate subject of a chapter on the industrial history of the country.

Evolution of industry required a change.

---

* " The United States of America," edited by N. S. Shaler.

CHAPTER XIII.

THE DEVELOPMENT OF INDUSTRIES, 1860–1890.

THE growth of the manufacturing industries of the United States since 1860 has been so extensive and varied that it is difficult to select the industry or group of industries that forms the most striking feature of the period. The United States Census of 1860 reported the capital invested in mechanical and manufacturing industries as $1,009,855,715 and the product as $1,885,-861,676. The establishments were scattered throughout thirty-nine states and territories, but the center of industry was in the New England and Middle States, these states contributing sixty-seven per cent of the total product. New industries have been constantly appearing, while well-established household or neighborhood industries have been rapidly developing and passing under the factory system.

The enumeration of industrial statistics has been confined to those industries that were conducted by distinct establishments. For instance, the making of bread is reported as an

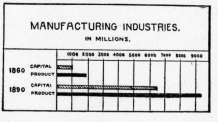

industry ; the total, however, includes only the manufacture of bread as conducted in bakeries, and not the

159

making of bread in private families, nor is cognizance
taken of any establishment whose yearly product does
not amount to $500. The total, therefore, should not
be considered as an exact statement of the output for
all industries. Considering new enterprises and industries that have passed from the household to the factory
system as legitimate elements of increase, the total capital invested in mechanical and manufacturing industries
advanced to $6,525,156,486 and the value of products
to $9,372,437,283 in 1890, an increase of 546 per cent
in capital and of 397 per cent in product.

Per capita
value of
products.

The per capita value of products for 1890 amounted
to $149. If to the manufacturing we add the products
of mining, amounting to $587,230,662, agricultural

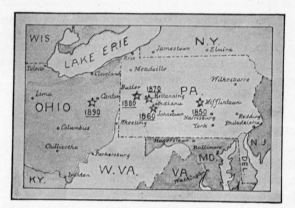

CENTER OF MANUFACTURING, 1850–1890.

Improvement
in processes of
manufacture.

products valued at $2,460,107,454, and fishery products
amounting to $44,277,514, we have a grand aggregate
of $12,464,052,913, or $198 per capita. The application of science and invention to manufacturing processes
has extended to all classes of industry, stimulating the

production and resulting in a more highly finished and cheaper product. New enterprises have been established in regions remote from the established centers of industry in 1860, causing a more equal distribution of the product. Following upon the rapid advance in the population of the Western States, large and diversified manufacturing enterprises have been established, and the center of the manufacturing industries of the country has moved slowly toward the west. In 1890 the center was about eight and one half miles south of Canton, Ohio, while in 1850 it was near Mifflintown, Pa.

Distribution and center of production.

The principal industries in 1860 were the textiles, clothing, lumber, iron and steel, leather, boots and shoes, flour and meal, sugar, paper, printing and publishing, carriages and wagons, foundry and machine-shop products, and liquors, distilled and malt ; the product for these industries forming over sixty per cent of the total product for all industries. The increase in the principal industries has been in keeping with the increase in all industries.

Principal industries.

The total capital invested in the several branches of the textile manufacture, for instance, increased from $150,080,852 in 1860 to $739,-973,661 in 1890, or 393 per cent, while

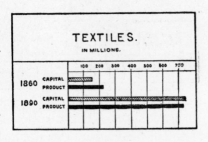

the value of product increased from $214,740,614 to $721,949,262, or 236 per cent. The textile industries are concentrated largely in the New England and Middle States, those states producing 89.37 per cent of the total value of textile products during 1890, the New England States alone contributing 50.64 per cent

Textiles.

and the Middle States 38.73 per cent. Massachusetts is the leading textile manufacturing state of the Union, and produced 25.62 per cent of the entire

Importance of textile manufacture.

product of the country for 1890. The importance of the textiles in the value and quantity of product, as well as the variety and importance of the uses to which the product is put, excels that of any other single industry in the United States.

Cotton.

Of the different branches of the industry cotton stands first. There were 1,091 establishments engaged in the manufacture of cotton in 1860, with an average product of $106,033 and an average of 4,799 spindles per establishment. In 1890 there were 905 establishments, with an average product of $296,112 and an average of 15,677 spindles, an increase of 179 per cent in the product and of 227 per cent in the number of spindles per establishment. During the

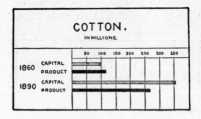

same period the aggregate capital invested in the industry increased from $98,585,269 to $354,020,843, or 259 per cent, and the value of product from $115,681,774 to $267,981,724, or 132 per cent. The decrease in the number of establishments and increase in the value of product, as well as the increase in the size of the average establishment, indicate the extent to which the industry

Concentration of cotton manufacture.

has been concentrated in fewer and larger establishments. While phenomenal increases appear for all branches of the textile industry since 1860, the concentration is not so marked in the other branches as it is in the cotton manufacture.

The capital invested in the different branches of wool manufacture increased from \$38,814,422 to \$245,-886,743, or 533 per cent, and the product from \$73,-454,000 to \$270,527,511, or 268 per cent, and the number of looms and spindles from 16,075 and 639,700 to 69,658 and 2,793,147, respectively. The average value of product per establishment in 1860 was \$49,-766, and in 1890 \$159,792. During the same period Woolens.

HAND-LOOM NOW IN USE IN NORTH CAROLINA.

there was an increase of 217 in the number of establishments and of thirty looms and 1,217 spindles per establishment. The application of inventions to textile machinery, especially to that employed in the wool manufacture, has resulted in a greater variety of the more highly finished products, and has so increased the productive capacity of the establishments and caused a resulting decrease in values that the quantity rather than the value of product should be used in ascertaining the

The application of inventions.

percentage of increase. Unfortunately, the constant variations which occur in the characteristics of the finished product destroy any general standard of quantity for comparison.

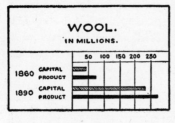

The manufacture of carpets is one of the most characteristic branches of the textile industry in the United States, and one in which great advances have been made since

Carpets.

1860. There were two hundred and thirteen establishments engaged in the manufacture of carpets in 1860, with a capital of $4,721,768 and a product valued at $7,857,636. In 1890 the number of establishments had decreased to one hundred and seventy-three, while the capital increased to $38,208,842 and the product to $47,770,193. The total number of running yards of carpet increased from 39,282,633 in 1880 to 74,770,910 in 1890, or ninety per cent. The industry is largely concentrated in Philadelphia, where one hundred and thirty-

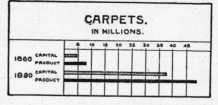

three mills are located, the product for the city being forty-six per cent of the total output for the entire country.

Silk.

While the silk manufacture is one of the oldest industries in the United States, the total capital invested in 1860 amounted to only $2,926,980 and the value of products to $6,607,771, being about thirteen per cent of the entire consumption for that year. In 1890 the home factories produced fifty-five per cent of the total consumption, the product being valued at $87,298,454, while the capital invested in the industry had increased to $51,007,537. The foundation of silk manufacture in the United States lay in the making of sewing silk. The adaptation of silk thread or twist for use on the sewing machine occurred in 1852 and created a new classification of "machine twist," and gave impetus to this branch of the industry, un-

Foundation of silk manufacture.

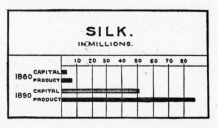

til the production of sewing silk and machine twist amounted to 1,119,825 pounds in 1890. The constant changes in fashions have caused frequent alterations and improvements in the machinery used in silk manufac-

Effect of changes in fashion.

A FAMILY TEASING WOOL.

ture ; this has resulted in great improvement and increased beauty and variety of design in the finished

product. The principal classes of product in 1890 were "ribbons," valued at $17,081,447, and "dress goods, figured and plain," valued at $15,183,134 ; the classification of the product of the mills, however, is practically without limit. The recognized seats of the industry in 1860 were in Connecticut, Massachusetts, New York, and Pennsylvania. The manufacture has spread and large establishments are now located in fifteen states and territories. In 1860 the product for New Jersey was valued at $969,700 ; in 1890 it had increased to $30,760,371.

Another branch of the textile industry worthy of consideration is the dyeing and finishing, as done by establishments especially equipped and engaged exclusively in this industry. In 1860 there were one hundred

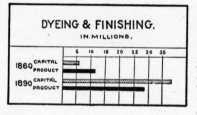

and twenty-four establishments engaged in dyeing and finishing, with a capital of $5,718,671 and a product of $11,716,-463. In 1890 the capital had advanced to $38,450,800 and the value of products to $28,900,-560. While the industry has increased rapidly and still retains its importance as a distinct, integral part of the textile manufacture, the textile mills have engaged extensively in the dyeing and finishing of their own products, chemicals and dye-stuffs to the value of $11,278,970 being used for this purpose by the mills during the year 1890.

The revolution in the tailoring industry that followed

upon the invention of the sewing machine, resulting in the combination of the small shops and the organization of large establishments for the manufacture of wearing apparel, for sale ready-made, was practically complete by 1860. Unfortunately, no authoritative statistics are available for the manufacture as distinct from the custom tailoring of that date. There were 3,968 establishments reported in 1860 as engaged in the manufacture of women's and men's clothing, with a capital of $26,386,-443 and a product of $80,758,344. The number of establishments had increased to 19,882 in 1890, the capital to $203,812,466, and the value of product to $446,-186, 834. The rapidly increasing demand for men's and boys' ready-made clothing stimulated the manufacture to such an extent that it was recognized as a distinct industry in 1890, when 5,067 establishments were reported, with a product of $251,-803,664. In 1860 the four cities of

Tailoring.

Ready-made clothing.

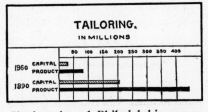

Boston, New York, Cincinnati, and Philadelphia manufactured more than one half of the men's clothing of the entire country. While the centers of the industry necessarily remain in the large cities, the total for the one hundred and sixty-five principal cities forming ninety-seven per cent of the total product in 1890, the manufacture has become greatly scattered, establishments being reported for almost every state and territory.

The manufacture of clothing and articles of personal adornment, exclusive of jewelry and foot-wear, has assumed enormous proportions, the product for such in-

Clothing.

dustries aggregating over $700,000,000 for the last census year.   One of the most important of the specialties into which the industry is divided is the manufacture of

Men's furnishings. shirts, collars and cuffs, and men's furnishings.   Two hundred and nineteen establishments were engaged in the manufacture of these articles in 1860, with a product valued at $7,218,790, which advanced to $63,509,539 in 1890, the number of establishments being 1,455.   The manufacture is confined almost entirely to the large cities, the cities with a population of 20,000 and over controlling eighty-nine per cent of the output.

The manufacture of ladies' ready-made clothing, exclusive of corsets, hoop-skirts, and knit goods, was con-

fined to ninety-six establishments in 1860, with a capital of $473,400 and a product of $2,261,546, the product being restricted almost entirely to the manufacture of

Ladies' ready-made clothing. cloaks and mantillas.   The demand for ladies' ready-made undergarments, exclusive of the product of the knitting mills, has become general and has greatly increased the manufacture.   There were 1,224 establishments engaged in the industry in 1890, with a capital of $21,259,528 and a product valued at $68,164,019.

Foot-wear. The manufacture of foot-wear, next to clothing, is the industry that is the greatest promoter of personal comfort and is among the manufactures that were firmly established in 1860, there being a larger number of persons

SHOEMAKER AT THE BENCH.

engaged in it at that time than in any other industry save that of agriculture, the operatives forming more than one twelfth of those employed in all classes of manufacture. There were 12,487 establishments reported

Importance of the shoe industry.

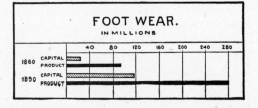

in 1860, with a capital of $23,358,527 and a product of $91,891,498. These figures, however, include the operations of the small custom shops. Data for the

Number of establishments.

factory industry in the entire country were collected in

1880, when 1,959 factories were reported, with a capital of $42,994,028 and a product of $166,050,354, the total number of boots and shoes of all classes manufactured during the year amounting to 125,478,511 pairs.

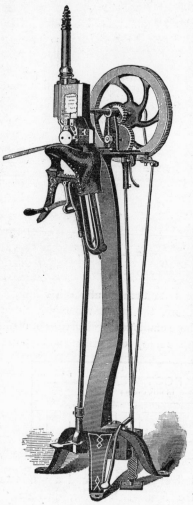

"THE CHAMPION" PEGGER.

The industry has now become greatly specialized, separate factories being engaged exclusively in the manufacture of boot and shoe cut stock and uppers, also in the making of stiffenings, heels, insoles, linings, tips, clasps, strings, staples, and various other articles coming under the classification of "boot and shoe findings." All branches of the industry, including the small custom shops, aggregated

Value of product.

Specialized features.

23,684 establishments in 1890, with a capital of $117,-923,375 and a product of $280,215,185. The factory industry proper was represented by 2,082 establishments, with a capital of $95,282,311 and a product valued at $220,649,358, being an increase of thirty-three per cent in the value of product during the ten years from 1880 to 1890. The total number of boots and shoes made in 1890 was reported as 179,409,388 pairs, an increase of forty-three per cent over 1880. The oldest seat of the industry is in Massachusetts, and the greatest production remains in that state, the product being fifty-three per cent of the total for the country in 1890.

Oldest seat of shoe industry.

Among the industries that contribute to the personal wants, the manufacture of food products ranks next in importance to the textiles and the making of clothing. According to the United States Census of 1860, there were 16,956 establishments, with a capital of $104,927,-586 and a yearly product valued at $323,023,598, engaged in the manu-facture of various forms of food prod-ucts. The manu-facture of butter was not reported as an industry dis-

Food products.

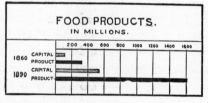

tinct from the farm product, nor did slaughtering and meat-packing appear except as the product of the retail butcher. The manufacture of canned goods, in which 1,328 establishments, with a capital of $24,522,581 and a product of $49,886,305, were reported in 1890, did not appear as a distinct industry in 1860, and the product of that year was exceedingly limited, it being almost entirely a household industry.

Canned goods.

The different varieties of food products are now practically unlimited, new forms of tasty preparations constantly appearing in the market. The growing demand for such articles has increased the production, and the grand aggregate for 1890 was 41,608 establishments, with a capital of $524,669,429 and a product of $1,647,-477,291. The annual product for each of the four principal branches of the industry, viz.: bread, crackers, and other bakery products; flouring and grist-mill products; slaughtering and meat-packing; and sugar and molasses refining, exceeds $100,000,000.

The manufacture of bread, crackers, and other forms of bakery products, as conducted by distinct establishments, conveys no definite idea of the magnitude of the industry. The total product reported for 1860 amounted to $16,980,012, and for 1890 to $128,421,535; both of these amounts, however, fall far below the true value of the product, since the industry exists not only in every state and territory, but in every city and town of any importance.

The increase in the production of flour, meal, and other products of the grist-mills in the United States has been in keeping with the increase in population and agri-

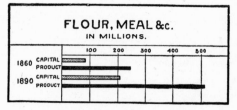

culture. The capital invested in the industry in 1860 amounted to $84,585,004 and the product to $248,580,-365. In 1890 the capital was $208,473,500 and the product $513,971,474, being an increase of 146 per cent in capital and 107 per cent in the value of product.

While the number of mills in operation in 1890 shows an increase over 1860 of 4,602, the tendency during recent years has been to centralize the manufacture in fewer and larger establishments. The number of mills decreased from 24,338 in 1880 to 18,470 in 1890, while the average product per establishment increased from $20,757 to $27,827, and the daily capacity from 194 to 298 bushels. As these figures include all the small custom mills, they convey no idea of the size of the average merchant flour-mill. A number of the large mills are congregated at Minneapolis, Minn., the yearly output for the city in 1890 being valued at $30,707,998. The average capital invested by each establishment was $431,490 and the average product $1,228,320. Owing to the decrease in the value of flour and meal and the large increase in the daily capacity of the mills, which has advanced from 4,730,106 bushels in 1880 to 5,495,-562 bushels in 1890, the increase of 107 per cent given above as the increase in value of product does not convey a correct idea of the actual increase during the thirty years.

Flour-mills.

CHAPTER XIV.

THE DEVELOPMENT OF INDUSTRIES, 1860–1890

(*Concluded*).

Meat-packing and slaughtering.

AUTHENTIC data concerning meat-packing and slaughtering were first gathered at the census of 1870, the first appearance of the industry, as conducted by distinct establishments producing for the trade, being in the decade of years from 1860 to 1870. In 1870 there were 259 establishments reported, with a capital of $22,124,787 and a product of $62,140,439. The number of establish-

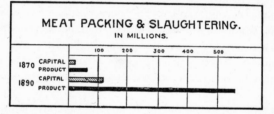

ments had increased to 1,118 in 1890, the capital to $116,887,504, and the product to $561,611,668. The principal seats of the industry are in Chicago, Ill., and Kansas City, Kan., the product for the two cities forming forty-three per cent of the product for the United States.

Cheese.

As previously stated, the manufacture of butter did not appear as a distinct industry from the agricultural products prior to 1860. The manufacture of cheese as a distinct industry appears also to have been insignificant during 1860. The total quantity of cheese and butter made as a dairy product during that year was 103,663,-927 and 459,681,372 pounds, respectively. The manufacture of cheese in factories increased rapidly during the ten years from 1860 to 1870, as in the latter year 1,313 cheese factories were reported, with an annual product valued at $16,771,665, and producing 109,435,-229 pounds of cheese ; there were other products of the factories, in which there was considerable butter, all valued at $16,096. There were 4,552 factories reported as engaged in the manufacture of cheese, butter, and condensed milk in 1890, with a product valued at $60,-635,705. The total quantity of cheese was reported as 238,035,065 pounds and of butter 181,284,916 pounds. Combining these totals with the dairy or farm product gives a grand aggregate of 256,761,883 pounds of cheese and 1,205,508,384 pounds of butter made in the United States during 1890. The manufacture of condensed milk is a branch of the industry that has developed almost entirely since 1860, the product for that year amounting to less than $50,000. The product is now of an entirely different character from that prevailing in 1860, and is sold in various forms. The manufacture prevails in the states of Illinois, Massachusetts, Michigan, and New York, the total production for 1890 being 37,926,821 pounds, valued at $3,586,927.

Butter and cheese now factory products.

The manufacture of oleomargarine and butterine appears first during the decade of years from 1870 to 1880, following upon the establishment of the slaughtering and meat-packing as a distinct industry, the materials used in the manufacture of oleomargarine being obtained largely from the slaughtering houses. The industry has flourished and the total production for 1894 amounted to 69,622,246 pounds. The total production from No-

Oleomargarine.

vember 1, 1886, to June 30, 1894, aggregated 353,611,-
320 pounds.

Iron and steel
industry.

In no class of industry in which the raw material is
of the same substance has there been such a growth,
specialization, and improvement in the form, character,
and diversity of the finished products during the past
thirty years as in the iron and steel industry.   The manipulation of the crude and finished forms of the products

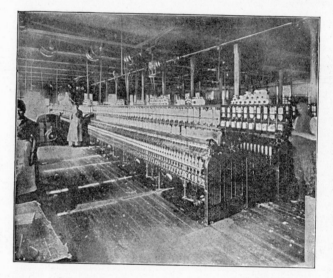

SPINNING ROOM IN A SOUTHERN COTTON FACTORY.

of the blast furnace, rolling-mill, steel works, and forge
is unlimited, ranging from the heaviest structural iron
and ordnance to the finest surgical instrument.

Number of
establishments
engaged.

The manufacture of iron and steel was among the
industries of first magnitude in 1860, there being 652
establishments, according to the United States census,
engaged in the manufacture of pig and blooms and rolled

iron and steel during that year. Since 1860 the rapidly increasing demand for all forms of iron and steel has greatly accelerated the manufacture, the capital increasing from \$48,372,897 to \$414,044,844 in 1890, and the value of products from \$57,160,243 to \$478,687,519. The tendency of the industry has been to concentrate special branches in larger and better equipped plants, where the latest improvements in machinery can be readily adopted, and where the furnace and mill practice can be brought to the highest perfection. The increase in the size of the establishments appears from the fact that in 1870 the average product per establishment was \$256,446 and had increased to \$665,768 in 1890. This tendency has stimulated the reduction in the selling price

Tendency to concentrate.

of the finished products and has greatly increased the quantity of the iron and steel manufactured. The value of products increased from \$207,208,696 in 1870 to \$296,557,685 in 1880, or forty-three per cent, while the quantity of products increased ninety-nine per cent. During the ten years from 1880 to 1890 the value of products increased from \$296,557,685 to \$478,687,519, or sixty-one per cent, and the tons of products increased one hundred and fifty-one per cent. The introduction of the Bessemer and the Siemens-Martin, or open-hearth, processes for the manufacture of steel, and the substitution of coke for coal and charcoal in the making of pig-iron, are the principal improvements in the process of manufacture. The introduction of modern processes for the manufacture of steel and the increased demand

Introduction of new processes.

for this class of product have resulted in a greater production of steel than of iron. The total production of steel in 1860 amounted to 11,838 gross tons, and in 1890 to 5,049,693 gross tons. Notwithstanding the large increase in steel, the manufacture of iron has not declined except relatively, the products of the puddling furnaces amounting to 2,353,248 tons in 1880 and to 3,225,140 tons in 1890, an increase of thirty-seven per cent.

Bessemer steel was first manufactured in any considerable quantities in the United States in 1867, there being about 2,679 tons of ingots produced during that year. Open-hearth steel first appeared in 1869, when 893 tons of ingots were produced. So rapid has been the advance in the steel manufacture that the production in 1890 out-distanced that of Great Britain by 1,370,650 tons, the product for the United States being 5,049,693 gross tons, while that of Great Britain was 3,679,043 gross tons. The principal cause of the development of the iron manufacture has been the rapid expansion of our railroad system, stimulating the development of the steel-rail industry. In 1880 there were 33,680 miles of steel and 81,967 miles of iron railroad track in the United States. In 1890 the miles of steel rails had increased to 167,606, while the miles of iron rails had decreased to 40,697, there being eighty-one per cent of the total mileage laid in steel rails.

Among the other important products of this industry that have appeared since 1860 is the wire nail. The wire nail first appeared in considerable quantities in 1884. So constant and increasing has been the demand for this form of nail that the production in 1890 amounted to 2,893,316 kegs of one hundred pounds, as compared with 2,139,086 kegs of iron-cut nails and 3,717,944 kegs of steel-cut nails, the total production of nails for the year being 8,750,346 kegs of one hundred pounds.

In contrast with the prosperity of the iron and steel industries, as a whole, has been the decline in the production of blooms and hammered bar-iron direct from the ore. This industry had reached considerable magnitude in 1860, the yearly product being about 30,000 net tons, but in 1890 the product did not exceed 8,000 tons.

Decline in production of blooms and hammered bar-iron.

While various industries in which iron or steel, in some form, enters as the principal material have appeared for the first time during the past thirty years, it is probable that none have attracted more notice than the manufacture of typewriters and bicycles and tricy-

THE DORRANCE "BREAKER," NEAR WILKES BARRE, PENNSYLVANIA.

cles. The typewriting machine, in its present form, dates from 1873, the first machine having been manufactured at Ilion, New York. There were thirty factories reported in 1890 as engaged in the manufacture of typewriters and typewriter supplies, with a capital of $1,421,783 and a yearly product valued at $3,630,126.

Manufacture of typewriting machines.

The manufacture of the modern form of bicycle dates from 1875, the first machines being manufactured at Hartford, Conn. The industry has become specialized, and data that correctly represent the manufacture in all its phases are not available. In 1890, however, twenty-seven establishments, with a capital of $2,058,072 and a product of $2,568,326, are reported as engaged in the manufacture of the machines proper, while eighty-three shops, with a product of $301,709, were engaged in repair work exclusively.

One of the principal assistants to the rapid increase in the iron and steel industries has been the production of coke. Exclusive of the product of gas works, the

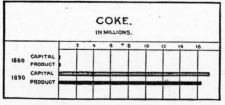

manufacture of coke in 1860 was confined almost entirely to Allegheny, Cambria, Clarion, and Fayette Counties, Pennsylvania. There were twenty-one establishments reported, with a capital of $62,300 and a product of $189,844. The rapid increase in the iron and steel industries and the consequent demand of the blast

furnaces stimulated the production of coke, and in 1889 there were 218 establishments, located in eighteen different states and territories, and reporting an aggregate capital of $17,462,729, with a product valued at $16,-498,345. The capital invested increased 266.11 per cent and the product 207.83 per cent during the ten years from 1880 to 1890 ; during the same period the number of ovens, pits, or mounds increased from 10,116

to 33,906, or 235.17 per cent. There were 2,752,475 tons of coke manufactured in 1880, of which the blast furnaces consumed 77.32 per cent. In 1890 there were 10,- 008,169 tons manufactured, of which the blast furnaces consumed 92.30 per cent. The use of coke in the manu- Consumption of coke.

WILKES BARRE "BREAKER BOYS."

facture of pig-iron is rapidly superseding charcoal. Consumption of charcoal. During 1890 there were only 664,711 tons of charcoal pig-iron produced, being but seven per cent of the total quantity of pig-iron manufactured during that year.

Increase in the use of coke.
The greater care taken in the preparation of the coal, the use of better ovens, and the introduction of more economical methods of working, have gradually increased the percentage of the yield of coal in coke, until in 1889 the general average for the United States was 63.36 per cent, the average for Pennsylvania being 65.03 per cent. Pennsylvania has uniformly held first place in this industry, its product amounting to 73.67 per cent of the total production for 1889.

Petroleum.
One of the industries that have appeared and assumed enormous proportions since 1860 is the production and refining of petroleum. The production of petroleum in commercial quantities in the United States dates from the drilling of a well by Mr. Drake (called Colonel Drake), near Titusville, Pa., in August, 1859. In June, 1860, however, the daily product of all the wells probably did not exceed 200 gallons, but in the fall of 1861 the daily production had reached 6,000 or 7,000 barrels. Petroleum has been found in almost every state and territory, but the large producing districts, those from which it has been obtained in paying quantities, are confined to Pennsylvania, New York, West Virginia, Ohio, Indiana, Colorado, and California.

Yearly production of petroleum.
The yearly production has increased with varying intensity, the highest point being reached in 1891, when it amounted to 54,291,980 barrels. The total production since 1859 amounts to about 607,000,000 barrels, and it is estimated that the product of the United States constitutes fifty-seven per cent of the production of the world.

Following upon the production of petroleum in large quantities, companies were formed for the refining of the crude product, but statistics concerning this branch of the industry were not collected until 1880, when eighty-six establishments were reported, with a capital of $27,-325,746 and a product valued at $43,705,218. In 1889 the number of establishments had increased to ninety-four, the capital to $77,416,296, and the value of product to $85,001,198, there being one hundred and six separate refineries, located in nine different states. The states of New York, New Jersey, and Pennsylvania,

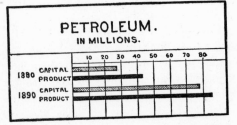

however, produced seventy-six per cent of the total product for the year, the industry being practically controlled by a few large corporations. The products of the refineries of chief value are illuminating oils and naphtha ; about 17,000,000 barrels of illuminating oils and over 3,000,000 barrels of naphtha were refined during 1889.

We have considered the contribution of some of the principal textile, clothing, food, and metal industries to the industrial development of the country. Other industries of vital importance to material prosperity have taken an important part in the great increases shown ; ranking among the first of these are lumber and the manufacture of brick and tile. The product of lumber and planing-mills and the cutting and hewing of timber in 1860 amounted to $108,946,393, and had increased to $621,638,934 in 1890. The three leading states in the

Petroleum statistics for 1889.

Product of lumber and planing-mills.

industry in 1860 were Maine, New York, and Pennsylvania.   The center of the industry in 1890 was in the

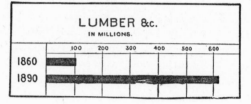

"Lake group" of states, comprising Michigan, Minnesota, and Wisconsin, the product for these three states aggregating $190,410,409, or $81,464,016 more than the total product for the United States in 1860.

There were 1,678 establishments in 1860 reported as engaged in the manufacture of brick and tile, with a

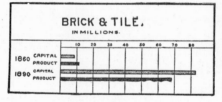

capital of $7,-994,428 and a product of $11,-263,147. In 1890 there were 5,828 establishments reported, with a capital of $82,578,566 and a product of $67,770,695, being an increase of 502 per cent in the value of product.

In 1860 twenty-nine establishments were reported as engaged in the manufacture of articles from caoutchouc, or india rubber and gutta-percha, with a capital of $3,634,000 and a product valued at $5,768,450.   The industry was largely confined to Connecticut, New York, and New Jersey, these three states reporting 82 per cent of the entire product.   By 1890 the number of establishments had increased to 168, and the capital to $36,804,261, an advance of 913 per cent, while the product was reported at $42,887,017, an increase of

643 per cent. The product of Massachusetts alone amounted to $19,492,831, or more than three times the entire value shown for 1860, while Connecticut, Massachusetts, Rhode Island, and New Jersey returned 87 per cent of the total product for the United States. The importation of crude india rubber advanced from 2,125,561 pounds in 1863 to 42,962,554 pounds in 1893.

Use of crude india rubber.

The only remaining industry that we shall consider as showing the industrial development since 1860 is printing and publishing. The development of the printing and auxiliary industries is a true index to the progress of civilization and the advance in all arts and manufactures. The increase in the printing and publishing industry of the United States is far in advance of that of any other country, and has been in keeping with the rapid increase in population, wealth, and intelligence. In 1860 printing and publishing, including newspapers, periodicals, books, and job printing, were reported by 1,666 establishments, with a capital of $19,622,318 and a product of $31,063,898. In 1890 there were 16,566 establishments re-

Printing and publishing.

PRINTING & PUBLISHING.
IN MILLIONS.

	50	100	150	200	250
1860 CAPITAL					
1860 PRODUCT					
1890 CAPITAL					
1890 PRODUCT					

ported for the same industry, with a capital of $195,387,445 and a product of $275,452,515. Seventeen thousand six hundred and sixteen publications are reported as being in existence during 1890, of which 14,901 reported as to circulation, the combined circulation per issue for this number being 69,138,934 and the aggregate number of copies printed during the year 4,681,113,530.

Number of publications.

It should be remembered that in all statements of the value of total product, whether for one census period or another, the values given relate solely to the value of the goods at the manufactory, as a rule; that is to say, the value of the raw material, the aggregate wages paid, and all the expenses of production, together with reasonable interest and profit to the producer, constitute the valuation given. No calculation has been made in any case which would eliminate the raw material; so there is a constant duplication, and sometimes a reduplication, of values in the value of product, because the raw material of one manufacturer is the finished product of another. To illustrate specifically, the producer of nails purchases his pig-iron, of which nails are made, of the manufacturer of pig-iron, who makes it from the ore. The manufacturer of pig-iron has returned his product with the cost of his raw material, which is chiefly the ore. The manufacturer of nails returns the value of his nails and his raw material, which raw material he purchased of the producer of pig-iron. The manufacturer who uses nails in the construction of woodwork, or in any other way, returns the value of his finished product, his raw material, to a certain degree, being the nails or other hardware, the value of which has already been returned by the manufacturer of such hardware as his finished product, the latter's raw material having been returned by the producer of pig-iron. This simple illustration shows the difficulty of arriving at the exact value of product in any one year, and also shows the limitations of the statistical method in securing such value; but as these duplications and reduplications appear in all statements relating to the value of product for the various years, the general comparison of the trend is fairly legitimate. Bearing these things in

Analysis of manufactures.

Illustration of use of raw material.

mind, when it is stated that the total productions of the United States, during the constitutional period, covering one hundred years of census-taking, have been extended from twenty millions of dollars, as estimated for the first census year (1790), to $9,372,437,283 in 1890, it does not matter much on what basis the accounts are taken so long as the account is fairly uniform in its methods through all the periods.

Growth of
manufactures
in one hundred
years.

The distribution of this vast product for 1890 among the states shows that those which were in the lead in 1860 are now in the lead, New York coming first, with a product of $1,711,577,671. Pennsylvania is second in line, with a product of $1,331,794,901. Then comes Illinois, her product being $908,640,280. Massachusetts, which was third in 1860, is now the fourth state in productive power, the value of her manufactured goods in 1890 being $888,160,403. Ohio takes fifth place, her product being $641,688,064. These are the only states whose product is over half a billion dollars each. There are several ranging from one million to a quarter of a billion or more, and these states are New Jersey and Missouri, with over three hundred million ; Wisconsin, Connecticut, Indiana, and Michigan, with about one quarter of a billion each.

Distribution in
1890.

The center of the manufacturing interests of the country at different periods has been shown in the diagram given in the preceding chapter. The influence of inventions in this wonderful expansion has been greater, even, since 1860 than during the period ending with that year, but these inventions are altogether too numerous to warrant any specific mention thereof, especially as the influence of some of the most important of them is shown in Chapter XXVIII., relating to the influence of machinery on labor.

Influence of
inventions.

Civil War stimulated manufactures.

Manufactures were also stimulated in a vast degree by the Civil War. The necessity of supplying great armies resulted in driving our manufactories to the utmost capacity. The wonderful development of natural resources ; the discovery and development of new sources of supply of the metals ; the ambition to supply the home demand, ever increasing through immigration, and to send our manufactured goods to foreign markets —all these have made the past generation one of great industrial expansion. The stimulation given through various tariff movements has also had its effect; but all these influences must be taken together when considering the evolution of the industries of our country. This evolution, however, has carried along with it other movements having a deeper social and ethical significance than the mere accumulation of wealth, and attention will now be turned to such matters.

Evolution leads to other considerations.

CHAPTER XV.

THE NUMBER OF PERSONS EMPLOYED AND THEIR TOTAL
WAGES.

THE first authentic statistics concerning the total number and wages of persons employed in establishments of manufacturing and mechanical industry of the United States are contained in the reports of the seventh census, being for the year 1850. The attempt was then made to ascertain the average number of men and women, respectively, employed during the year, with the total amount paid in wages for the same period. The average number reported was 957,059.

At the sixth census, covering the year 1840, the number of employees was shown for a large variety of industries, the total aggregating 564,617. The total of wages, however, was not reported, and the number cannot be accepted as a trustworthy index to the actual number engaged in establishments of productive industry during that year. The fact that an attempt was made to secure statistics on this subject, and that the number of workmen reported by the establishments that responded to the call for information constituted three per cent of the total population, establishes the importance of the inquiry at that early date.

Number employed, 1840.

While prior to 1850 machinery was extensively employed in many lines of industry, the rapid development of our present system of manufactures may be considered as dating from that year. The proportion that the num-

Proportion of population engaged in manufactures.

ber actually employed by establishments was of the entire
population in 1850 and at subsequent periods is as follows: 1850, 4.13 per cent; 1860, 4.17 per cent; 1870, 5.33
per cent; 1880, 5.45 per cent; and 1890, 7.53 per cent.
The figures for 1870, 1880, and 1890 do not include the
number engaged in mining, quarries, or fisheries, but,
notwithstanding this fact, the proportion has steadily increased. The numbers of employees on which these
percentages are based are the average numbers reported
by establishments as having been employed during the
year. If the number of persons having occupations
that fall in the different mechanical and manufacturing
pursuits, irrespective of whether they are employed by
establishments, work independently at odd jobs, or are

idle, is considered, it will be found that the proportion
they form of the total population at the different census periods is as follows: 1860, 5.91 per cent; 1870,
6.36 per cent; 1880, 6.81 per cent; and 1890, 8.13
per cent. The total population is used in computing
these percentages; therefore they should not be considered as indicating the proportion that those actually
engaged in such occupations are of the total number
who could so engage. If the percentage for 1890 is
based on the population of fifteen years of age and over,
it will be found that those having mechanical or manufacturing occupations amount to 12.61 per cent of the
total.

While data concerning actual and average wages of
all classes of mechanics have been collected and are discussed in a subsequent chapter, the facts presenting the
aggregate amounts expended in wages have been confined to the operations of establishments of productive
industry. In other words, no attempt has been made to
ascertain the grand total of the earnings of all persons

engaged in mechanical and manufacturing industries.

The increase in the number of employees and in the total and average wages, the decrease in the proportion of the product of manufactures assigned to labor, and the increase in the productive capacity of employees, are the three principal effects that the development of the factory system has had on employees and wages.

Proportion of employees to product.

As an indication of the increase in the number and wages, it appears that in 1850 the average number of employees was reported at 957,059 and the total wages as $236,755,464. In 1890 the

Total wages, 1850–1890.

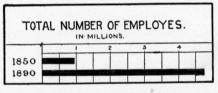

TOTAL NUMBER OF EMPLOYES.
IN MILLIONS.

1850
1890

number is reported as 4,712,622 and the wages as $2,283,216,529. Owing to improved statistical methods, the totals for 1890 include certain elements not reported, or not fully reported, for previous years. Reducing the figures, as far as possible, to a comparable basis, the number appears as 4,286,523 and the total wages $1,911,137,838, an increase of 3,329,464, or 347.88 per cent, in number, and of $1,674,382,374, or 707.22 per cent, in total wages, over 1850. During the same period the average annual earnings per employee increased from $247.38 to $445.85, being an increase of $198.47, or 80.22 per cent.

Average earnings.

In contrast with the increase in the bulk and average wages is the decrease in the proportion of the net value of product assigned to labor. The net value of product is the value remaining after deducting the cost of materials, and may be considered as the value added to the cost of the raw materials by the combined operation of capital and labor. The total for all industries in the

Increased bulk and decreased value of product.

United States shows that in 1850 fifty-one per cent of the net value was assigned to labor and in 1890 forty-five per cent.   The decrease in the proportional amount assigned to labor is offset, to a considerable extent, by the increase in interest account, which is also payable

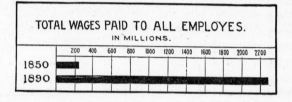

out of the net product, as the average amount of capital required for a product valued at \$100 increased from \$52.32 in 1850 to \$69.62 in 1890.

Of the numerous causes that combined to produce the general increase in the number of employees and in wages and the decrease in the proportion of the value of the finished product assigned to labor, the adoption of machinery and labor-saving devices is at once the most important and the most easy of practical demonstration.

The cost of materials is generally the principal item of expense in manufacturing, and as this cost is included in the gross value of product, the industries that apparently produce the greatest value do not necessarily engage the greatest number of employees.   Excluding the mechanical trades, such as masonry, blacksmithing, and carpentering, we find that the manufactures reporting the greatest number of employees are those in which machinery is largely employed, such as the textiles, boots and shoes, clothing, and various metal and woodworking industries.

As illustrative of this fact, it appears that in 1850 the

New England States and New York, Pennsylvania, and New Jersey reported seventy-three per cent of all the employees and seventy per cent of the gross value of product. The wide application of the factory system that has occurred since 1850 has not been sufficient to counterbalance this disproportion, the percentages in 1890 standing fifty-four and fifty-two, respectively. During the same period the increase in the number of employees in these states was 233 per cent, and in the value of product 584 per cent. While the percentage of increase in the United States, exclusive of the states named, has been greater, the increase in employees being 643 per cent and in the value of product 1,376 per cent, the disproportion in the increase in the value of product and employees is also greater. In other words, the increase of employees in old established manufacturing centers has been more in keeping with the increase in the value of product than in comparatively newly developed districts.

Wide application of the factory system.

Increase in number of employees and value of product.

It requires 1.12 employees on an average to produce a net product valued at $1,000, as obtained from the total for the New England States, New York, Pennsylvania, and New Jersey, while the totals for the Western States indicate that a net product of the same value requires, on an average, .9 of one employee. In the New England States fifty-seven per cent of the net product was assigned to labor, as compared with fifty-two per cent in the rest of the country, the proportion going as low as fifty-one per cent in the South Central States, the wages, in each instance, including the salaries of officers and clerks. It must not be inferred from these percentages that the introduction of machinery in any particular industry has been invariably followed by the employment of a larger number of persons to a product of a

Persons to each $1,000 worth of product.

given value.   They do show that in the sections of the country where machinery is extensively used and where the products, as a whole, are of a more highly finished character, more persons are required to produce a given value than in sections where these features do not predominate.

The increase in the number and wages of employees in the manufacture of textiles and of boots and shoes, two industries in which machinery has reached the greatest perfection, is as follows : The manufacture of textiles reported 194,082 employees in 1860, receiving $40,353,-462 in wages, as compared with 501,718, excluding officers, firm members, and clerks, and $163,516,593 in wages for 1890.   The average annual earnings per employee in 1860 were $207.92, and in 1890 $325.91, the increase during the thirty years being 56.75 per cent.

In the manufacture of boots and shoes the number of employees increased 53,843, the total wages $49,563,-342, and the average annual earnings $242.01, or 117.81 per cent, during the forty years from 1850 to 1890.

The extensive application of machinery in the manufacture of boots and shoes dates from the decade of 1850–1860.   During this period the proportion of the net product assigned to labor decreased from seventy-two per cent to sixty-three per cent; the average annual earnings increased from $205.43 to $251.48; the net product increased sixty-three per cent, and the capital required for one dollar of net product increased from forty-three to forty-eight cents.   In the thirty years from 1860 to 1890 the proportion of net product assigned to labor decreased to fifty-three per cent ; the annual earnings increased to $447.44; the net product increased 171 per cent, and the capital required for one dollar of net product to eighty-eight cents.

As illustrative of the increase in the productive capacity of employees, we find that in 1830 one operative was required for every 25.02 spindles in the cotton manufacture, but owing to perfected machinery, improved processes, and the development of industrial skill, the number of spindles operated by one employee had increased to 64.82 in 1890.

Not only has the expansion of our manufacturing interests followed upon the adoption of machinery, but the number and productive capacity of the operatives have increased, while there has been an increase in the wages and a reduction in working time. The cost of manufacture and the proportion of the product assigned to labor have decreased, while the capital and interest account have materially increased.

Accepting these general conclusions to be the results of the various changes that have occurred in the status of employees during the development of our factory system, a brief consideration of the employees and wages as reported at the United States Census of 1890 will be profitable.

The figures substantiate the theory that wages are highest in the Western States, where the cost of living is relatively higher. Wyoming leads, with an average annual wage for male operatives, including skilled and unskilled but not pieceworkers, of $806, and is followed by Colorado, with an average of $685. The industry reporting the highest average wages for the same class of employees is the manufacture of paper patterns, the average being $773. Comparatively few establishments and employees are reported for the states and industries showing the very highest wages. These averages, therefore, cannot be accepted as a true indication of the general average for the United States.

The concentration of the principal industries in fewer
and larger establishments has resulted in a comparatively
few establishments controlling a large proportion of the
total employees. Nine hundred and five cotton factories, for instance, report 221,585 employees, on an average, each day of the year, while eleven establishments
manufacturing rubber boots and shoes report over 9,000
employees, or 842 per establishment, being the largest
number reported for the average establishment in any
industry during the year 1890. The general concentration of manufactures in cities is shown by the fact
that the cities with a population of 20,000 and over,

while contributing twenty-four per cent of the population, gave employment to sixty-two per cent of the
employees reported by establishments of productive
industry.

The reports disclose that 418,081 male and 42,928
female officers, firm members, and clerks were actively
engaged in manufacturing or in supervision, to whom
$391,988,208 was credited as salaries, or an average an-
nual earnings of $850.28 as compared with $444.83 for
all other employees. There appears, on an average,

one clerk, officer, or firm member to every 9.22 employees, the office force constituting about one tenth of
the total number.

The constantly increasing intricacy of manufactures,
and the necessity for close and accurate calculations on
the total cost, and the different elements of cost that
enter into each of the different stages of process, as
well as the never-ceasing changes in fashion, demanding
new and tasteful designs, tend to increase the im-

portance of the office force. The highest skill and
scientific knowledge, combined with practical experience, are demanded. Probably in no industry is this

more emphasized than in the manufacture of chemicals, as at present conducted. Chemical engineering forms the important factor in the adjustment of the costly machinery and the direction of the numerous operations that produce the unlimited variety of products from this industry, while the laboratory, with its corps of careful workers, forms the pulse of the entire establishment. With the concentration of industries and the increase in the size of the establishments, the number and importance of the office force will increase.

The tendency in all industries is to regulate the pay of pieceworkers to conform to the pay of operatives engaged in the same line of work, and the totals of all classes of manufactures during 1890 show that while the annual earnings of male operatives of all classes were $498, those of pieceworkers amounted to $500. The average annual earnings of female operatives amounted to $276, and of pieceworkers to $255. The pieceworkers constitute sixteen per cent of the total employees, there being about one to every 4.6 operatives. Pieceworkers are employed to the greatest extent in the manufacture of clothing, their numbers, in some branches of the industry, exceeding the number of regular operatives. Much of the work in this industry can be readily performed at the homes of the workers. One manufacturer frequently engages a number of independent contractors, who in turn employ numerous hands to work by the piece. The ramifications of the industry render it practically impossible to obtain the exact number of pieceworkers actually employed. The average number is reported at 145,640, as compared with 159,392 operatives, but the actual number is somewhat in excess of this total.

The greatest number of employees in the establish-

Pieceworkers and their earnings.

Pieceworkers and operatives compared.

ments engaged in the mechanical and manufacturing industries are reported as skilled and unskilled operatives. The average number of men, women, and children of this class employed during each day of 1890 was 3,492,029, receiving $1,590,516,997 as wages, the number being seventy-four per cent of all employees and the wages seventy per cent of the total wages. The men numbered 2,881,795, receiving $1,436,482,387 as wages; the women numbered 505,712, receiving $139,329,719 as wages; and the children numbered 104,522, receiving $14,704,891 as wages.

The development of the factory system in almost every line of industry tends to a concentration of the labor in the factory building. While the introduction of machinery and the improved skill of the operatives have greatly increased the quantity and reduced the cost of the product, the growing competition in all lines causes a constant pressure for a greater quantity at less cost, and the employment of pieceworkers at the works, under factory regulations and discipline, is conducive to this result. It stimulates to greater exertions, while guarding against overwork by regulating the hours of labor, and gives the workman the advantage of good sanitary surroundings. The number of pieceworkers so engaged

is rapidly increasing, and they are so closely identified with the operative receiving pay according to time that in a general report for the entire establishment there is apt to be no distinction made between the two classes. Therefore, the number of operatives cannot be considered as consisting entirely of employees receiving pay according to time. The class, however, represents the mass of the workingmen in these industries, and their wages are the true criterion of the actual earnings. The average annual earnings for men of this class were $498, for

women $276, and for children $141. The earnings for
this class in 1890, as obtained from the totals for the 165
cities that had a population of 20,000 and over, were for
men $567.54, for women $291.80, and for children
$159.23. In the districts outside of the cities the aver-
ages were for men $401.34, for women $239.88, and for
children $120.87. The excess of the general average
for the cities over that for the United States or for the
districts outside of the cities is due to numerous causes,
the most important of which is the excess in living expenses.

Earnings of
men, women,
and children.

CHAPTER XVI.

WOMEN AND CHILDREN IN INDUSTRY.

Not in demand in early period.

IT CANNOT be said that women and children constituted an economic factor during the colonial days. Their labor was not in demand, except in a domestic sense, to any great extent. To be sure, the spinning and weaving that were carried on in the homes were done by women, but it would be incorrect to say that they entered into the mechanical industries of the times, for they were not hired to do these things as a rule, but did them as a part of their household duties, although near the close of the colonial period women and children had been introduced into some works, particularly in the setting of wire teeth in the wool and cotton-cards that were used for the hand-combing of the fiber. The manufacture of cards had become quite extensive by 1784, one factory alone, it is alleged, employing about one thousand and two hundred hands, chiefly women and children. In the early days of this particular industry the women worked at setting the teeth very much as they did at knitting, taking the board and teeth home with them, and even carrying them out when they went to spend an afternoon with a neighbor.

Mr. Hamilton's report.

Mr. Hamilton, in his report on manufactures made to Congress in 1791, which has been referred to, speaks of the "vast scene of household manufacturing which contributes more largely to the supply of the community than could be imagined without having it made an object of particular inquiry.

Great quantities of coarse cloths, coatings, serges, and flannels, linsey-woolseys, hosiery of wool, cotton, and thread, coarse fustians, jeans and muslins, checked and striped cotton and linen goods, bedticks, coverlets, and counterpanes, tow linens, coarse shirtings, sheetings, toweling and table linen, and various mixtures of wool and cotton, and of cotton and flax, are made in the household way, and, in many instances, to an extent not only sufficient for a supply of the families in which they are made, but for sale, and even in some cases for exportation. It is computed in a number of districts that two thirds, three fourths, and even four fifths of all the clothing of the inhabitants are made by themselves.'' So it appears from these brief historical references that by 1790 the never-ceasing industry of the women was the principal factor in the development of a manufacture that was probably contributing more directly to the personal comfort and prosperity of the people than any other then in existence. Important as the industry was, the large majority of the women engaged in it considered it an adjunct to their household duties, as has been stated, and not as a gainful occupation—that is, one for which they were to receive particular remuneration—for the larger portion of the product of their work was consumed by the family in which it was produced.

Early manufactures.

Adjuncts to household duties.

With the establishment of the factory system the employment of women and children became more common; yet there was a prejudice against women taking places at the looms and the spinning machines of the textile factories. After the invention of spinning and weaving machinery in England, and the textile factory there became a fixed element in industry, women were brought into it from the rural districts, and the labor of children taken from the almshouses was absorbed. By these

Demand came with factory.

methods the manufacturers were enabled to secure their employees at very low compensation. On this account, when the factory was established in America, and the

services of women and children were sought, there was a great prejudice against it, and for the first ten or twenty years after the permanent establishment of the factory system proprietors were obliged to offer extra inducements for women to enter their service.

By 1815 the textile industry had practically passed into the factory system, and by 1830 the old household industry was rapidly disappearing. Prior to 1815 women and children, to some extent, were engaged in occupations for which they received money or its equivalent as compensation for their services. Their more extended employment and the establishment of their

position as independent wage-workers date practically from the period between 1815 and 1830. They followed the textile industries into the factories, and the consolidation of industries in large establishments instead of small, individual shops broadened the field and gave women opportunities of entering independently into the gainful pursuits, which they gladly embraced; yet they were employed in but few occupations even then. Harriet Martineau, an English lady, who visited America

in 1840, related that she found but seven employments open to women—teaching, needle-work, keeping boarders, working in cotton-mills, type-setting, working in book-binderies, and household service. A study of the industrial conditions of the present time convinces one that now there are but few lines of remunerative employment not occupied to some extent by women. They

are found in nearly all departments of governmental work, and there is hardly a single field where women are not employed. This general entrance into the industrial field was assured when the factory system of labor displaced the hand-labor system, for the factory system was concretely the result of the universal tendency to association inherent in our nature, and under the development of which every advance in human improvement and human happiness has been made.

The age of invention must be held accountable for this entrance of woman into spheres entirely strange and unknown to her prior to that age, for under the hand-labor system she was used to home duties, to field drudgery, and to the work necessary for the assistance of her husband or father in the hand labor which he performed, and under that system she lived a narrow, contracted, unwholesome life in the lower walks of industry, and she was not known or recognized in the higher. As an economic factor, either in art or literature or industry, she was hardly recognizable ; but with the establishment of the new system, the attraction to women to earn more than they could earn as domestic servants or in some fields of agricultural labor, or to earn something where before they had earned nothing, constituted them an economic force, the result of which has been that women have assumed the position and are obliged therefore to submit to all the conditions of a new economic factor. It can hardly be said, however, that in the lower forms of labor in industrial pursuits women have superseded men. On the contrary, they have supplemented the work of men, and the necessities of the people which could be supplied under the new system of labor made it possible for them to supplement the services of men. Women were paid a lower rate of wage than men, although subsequent to their introduction as economic factors men were obliged sometimes to take practically the same wage when performing

Invention largely accountable for employment of women.

Woman an economic force.

Women have supplemented work of men.

Women paid lower rate of wage than men.

the same duty as women, but the wages that were paid were not so much lower as it is often supposed they were, when the same lines of duty are considered.

Higher grades open.

There has been a constant change from lower to higher forms of employment. From factory operatives women have entered higher grades, as teachers, book-keepers, telegraph operators, etc., and as their expertness has been recognized the demand for skilled and well-equipped employees of course increased ; but with this demand there has been a corresponding and a compensating absorption of the labor of men in the great developing enterprises of America.*

Meager statistics back of 1870.

It is unfortunate, in the treatment of this particular subject, that statistics as to the actual number of women and children employed in all remunerative occupations in the country are not obtainable back of 1870. Facts as to their wages are quite fully given back to 1831. It is interesting to note the change of conditions as indicated by numbers, and the information as to the number generally employed can be ascertained for all the decennial periods since and including 1850, at which time there were, according to the census of that year, 225,298

Number in manufactories in 1850.

female and 741,671 male employees in the manufacturing industries of the country. This gives 1 female to every 3.29 males. In many industries that developed rapidly, however, heavy manual labor and physical endurance, rather than skill, were required of the employees. In such industries women could not engage ; therefore the proportionate number of women in the total for all industries existing in 1850 cannot be considered excessively small. In those industries in which women could and did engage from the inception of the factory system they had

---

* Cf. "Why Women are Paid Less than Men," by the author : *The Forum,* July, 1892.

held their own, in numbers at least. In the wool manufacture, for instance, there was 1 female to every 1.4 males, and in the cotton and hosiery manufacture there was 1 male to every 1.8, or about every 2, females. In industries such as tailoring, the manufacture of hats and caps, gloves, india rubber goods, millinery, umbrellas, and others where a rapidity of movement and a delicacy of touch which could not be supplied by mechanical devices were required, the number of females exceeded the males.

Women formed 23.30 per cent of all employees engaged in manufacturing establishments in 1850. The proportionate number, however, has been constantly decreasing, women furnishing but 17.21 per cent of the total number of employees in manufacturing industries in 1890. The actual number has increased in a ratio somewhat in excess of the decrease in the relative number. During the forty years from 1850 to 1890 the actual number of women employed in manufacturing industries increased 531,765, or 235 per cent. The num- ber of children employed in manufactures was first ascertained in 1870, when 114,628, including both sexes, were reported, this number being 5.58 per cent of all employees. As in the case of women, the proportionate number of children has steadily decreased, till in

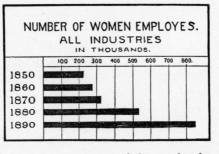

NUMBER OF WOMEN EMPLOYES.
ALL INDUSTRIES
IN THOUSANDS.

	100	200	300	400	500	600	700	800
1850								
1860								
1870								
1880								
1890								

1890 they formed but 2.57 per cent of the total; the decrease in the number of children has been not only relative, but actual, which decrease is due primarily to legislation in the several states, prohibiting the employment of children under a certain age in any manufacturing, mechanical, or mercantile establishment. The laws relating to this particular subject have been outlined in the chapters on labor legislation.

Increase, 1870 to 1880.During the decade of years from 1870 to 1880 there occurred the greatest increase in the number of women and children employed, the actual increase being 58.21 per cent for women and 54.39 per cent for children, while during the following decade of years the children decreased 34.09 per cent. The women, however, increased 47.91 per cent, as we have seen. These percentages indicate the extent of the increase in the number of women and the decrease in the number of children employed in mechanical and manufacturing establishments in the United States, considering the total for all branches of industry, and including those in which women are not likely to engage, at least to any extent.

In 1890.In actual numbers there were 3,745,123 men, 846,614 women, and 120,885 children, on an average, employed in the mechanical and manufacturing industries during 1890, there being 1 woman to every 4.4 men and 1 child to every 7 women. The number of women and children employed in manufactures in any locality is controlled by the character of the predominating industries and the proportion their number is of the total population. The women form a larger percentage of the total Large percentage of women in New England and Middle States.population of the New England and Middle States than they do of other sections, and the predominating industries are of the character in which they can engage. We therefore find that the proportionate number of women employed is greater there than in any other section. On the other hand, the laws against the employment of children are generally more stringent in New England than elsewhere, and the number of children employed is proportionately less than in other states. The figures support this theory in the following manner:

Laws regulating their employment.

The women employed in the New England and Middle States in 1890 were 69 per cent of the total for the United States, while the children were but 52 per cent of all children; there were 3.3 men to each woman and 9.2 women to each child employed. In the United States exclusive of the New England and Middle States there were 7.0 men to each woman and 4.6 women to each child. Almost three fourths of the women and but little over one half of the children employed in the mechanical and manufacturing industries of the United States are engaged in the factories of the New England and Middle States. There are more than twice

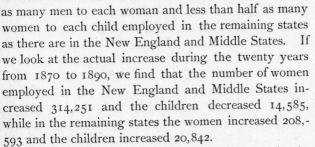

as many men to each woman and less than half as many women to each child employed in the remaining states as there are in the New England and Middle States. If we look at the actual increase during the twenty years from 1870 to 1890, we find that the number of women employed in the New England and Middle States increased 314,251 and the children decreased 14,585, while in the remaining states the women increased 208,-593 and the children increased 20,842.

Decrease in number of children employed.

For similar reasons the employment of women in the manufactures of cities is more general, and the children proportionately less, than in the rural districts. In the principal cities the females constituted 20.49 per cent of

More general in cities.

the total employees in 1890 and in the districts outside the cities 13.89 per cent, the proportionate number in the cities being 6.60 per cent greater. The children form 2.10 per cent of the total employees in the cities and 3.31 per cent in the country.

The textiles and the manufacture of boots and shoes are among the oldest factory industries in the United States, and the increase in the number of women employed in them can be considered as indicating the rate of increase in all industries in which women are likely to engage to any extent. Taking the total for wool, hosiery, and cotton factories, we find that in 1850 the women formed 57 per cent of the total employees, there being 1 man to every 1.3 women. In 1890 the women formed 48 per cent of the total, there being 1 man to every 1.1 women. During the forty years the men increased 129,366, or 214 per cent, and the women 133,-

177, or 168 per cent. In 1890 the women formed 41 per cent of the total employees in wool manufacture, 67 per cent in hosiery, and 48 per cent in cotton. There were 32,949 women and 72,305 men reported as employed by establishments engaged in the manufacture of boots and shoes during 1850, which probably included the employees of a large number of small custom shops. In 1890 the factory industry alone reported 96,233 men, 43,213 women, and 2,839 children, the women forming 30 per cent of the total, as compared with 31 per cent in 1850, there being about two men to every woman at both periods, but during the forty years the men increased 33 and the women 31 per cent.

The initiatory employment of women in these two industries was in many respects different; women were engaged extensively in the textile industries when the manufacture entered the factory system, and they necessarily passed into the employment of the factories. Women were not so extensively engaged in the manufacture of boots and shoes, and when the manufacture became a factory industry it opened to them almost an entirely new field. The statistics show that while the percentage of increase in the number of women employed in the textiles is much larger than in the manufacture of boots and shoes, due to the larger number employed, the proportionate number has decreased much more rapidly than in the boot and shoe industry. In other words, the extent to which women can displace the labor of men in the textiles having been more nearly attained at some period between 1850 and 1890 than in the boot and shoe industry, the proportionate number began to diminish.

While the number of women employed in industries in which they were engaged at the inception of the factory system has been increasing, it is interesting to notice, as illustrative of their engaging in new pursuits, that during the decade of years from 1880 to 1890 not only the largest percentages of increase are shown for the industries and states reporting a relatively small number of women in 1880, but also that the relative number of women employed in such sections and industries has also increased.

Number of women employed increases.

All the industries in the United States, and their variety is practically unlimited, were assigned to one of three hundred and sixty-nine general groups at the census of 1890. An examination of the totals of these groups discloses the fact that in only nine of them are no women or children employed. Their employment, therefore, either as clerks, operatives, or apprentices, may be considered as universal. The apparent number of vocations in which women cannot engage is constantly diminishing, and is now relatively very small.

Classification of industries in 1890.

The subject of the actual and relative wages of women
increases in importance with the increase in the number
employed in the mechanical and manufacturing industries, and with the extent to which they displace the
labor of men. The rapid increase in the number of
women employed in certain lines of industry, the decrease in the number of children, and the normal increase
in the number of men employed in the same industry,
indicate that the women are, to some extent, supplying
the places of the children and engaging in the cheaper
classes of labor. Notwithstanding this fact, the greatest
percentage of gain in average wages in the cotton industry is in favor of the female employees. The average

weekly earnings for women in the cotton factories of
New England in 1831 ranged from $2.20 to $2.60, and
for men from $4.50 to $7.00, while the average for children was from $1.50 to $2.00. In 1880 the average for
women ranged as high as $6.37, for men $9.05, and for
children $3.30. Between 1831 and 1880 men's wages
had increased 38 per cent, women's wages 149 per cent,
and children's 115 per cent. These averages, being for
the five leading cotton manufacturing states, are a true
indication of the general relative increase for the industry in the entire country. In 1890 the average in the
same industry for the entire United States for women was
$5.53, ranging from $3.21 to $6.42, and for men $7.75,
ranging from $5.17 to $10.44, the average for children
being $2.65. The highest averages for all classes were
reported for the New England and Middle States and
the lowest for the Southern States.

The average annual earnings for women clerks during
1890, as obtained from the total for all industries, was
$462, and for men $890. The women operatives received $276, as compared with $498 for men, the aver-

age for children in the same class being $141. The dis-proportion between the wages of the sexes is further emphasized by the fact that the men formed 82.53 per cent of the total operatives and received 90.32 per cent of the total wages of operatives, while the women formed 14.48 per cent of the number and received but 8.76 per cent of the wages. The proportion of wages in the case of men exceeds the number by 7.79 per cent, and in the case of women falls short of the number by 5.72 per cent. A careful examination of the actual earnings of women discloses the fact that in many industries their average earnings equal or exceed the earnings of the men. This is especially true of the pieceworkers.

Disproportion in wages of the sexes.

It should be remembered that as men have stepped up into higher occupations, those which have come up as new callings in life, they have received comparatively higher compensation than women in the old occupations. The latter have occupied the positions of book-keepers, telegraphers, and many of what might be called semi-professional callings ; and as women have occupied them, men have entered higher callings—engineering, electrical and mechanical, and other spheres of life that were not known when women first stepped into the industrial field. As women have progressed from entire want of employment to employment which pays a few dollars per week, men, too, have pro-gressed in their employments and occupied entirely new fields not known before. So the facts certainly indicate that women, instead of crowding upon the men to as great an extent as is generally supposed, are rapidly taking the places of boys and girls and doing the work which they formerly did in our factories. The con-stantly increasing proportion of men indicates this, but supplemented by the constantly decreasing number of

Men take higher em-ployments.

Women largely take the places of boys and girls.

children, the fact becomes apparent. It is to be hoped
that the legislation of the different states will progress to
such an extent as to keep children under fourteen or
fifteen years of age entirely out of manufacturing establishments. Many of the states do this, practically prohibiting children under ten years of age from working in
mechanical and manufacturing pursuits, and it is gratifying to know that the proportion of children has not only
fallen during the last ten or fifteen years but is constantly
and rapidly falling.

The employment of women in mechanical pursuits
opens many questions for ethical study, one of the chief
being the employment of married women. There are no
very general or very trustworthy statistics on this subject, but so far as investigation shows it may be estimated with a fair degree of accuracy that about ten per
cent of the women employed in the manufacturing industries of the country are married.

Another interesting subject which their employment
suggests is the reasons why women are paid less than
men, when that is the case, and, except as already pointed
out, it is usually so. The chief reasons why she receives
a lower compensation are largely economic. She has
stepped out of industrial subjection and come into the
industrial system as an entirely new economic factor.
If there were no other reasons, this alone would be sufficient to keep her wages low and prevent their very
rapid increase ; but there are other reasons which, with
that just stated, keep her at work at low compensation.
She occupies a lower standard, caused to some extent by
a lower standard of life, both in physical features and
in mental demands. She is also the victim of the influence of the assistance which she receives in a large
proportion of cases from her family and friends. This

Legislation as
to children.

Number of
married
women.

Reasons for
lower pay.

works positively to lower her economic standard, keeps her industrial productivity at a low grade, and actually compels her to stand on a lower plane than do men. The quantity and the quality of the work which she per- *Discussion as to low pay.* forms are influenced by this reason. Then, again, she rarely enters industrial pursuits with a sufficient equip- ment for life-work. This is not the result of any incapacity of mind or lack of skill, but is due largely to the hope that the permanence of work will be in- terrupted by matrimony. She suffers also from a lack of technical training, and does not feel warranted in spending years in equipping herself for the best service. While competition has had a great deal to do with bring- ing about the present industrial condition of woman as a recognized fact, it has also had much to do in keeping her compensation at a low point, for as she has come into industry as a new economic factor, the pressure to secure positions has created an artificial supply altogether out of proportion to the demand ; so every position she might occupy is sought by many, the result being that her remuneration is within the power of the employer.*

It is gratifying to learn, from the facts that can be ex- amined, that woman's condition is constantly being *Woman's con- dition improv- ing.* bettered. Certainly women workers, as a class, are be- ginning to understand the power and the force which come from organization. Working girls' clubs are being formed everywhere, and through these clubs there will come a removal of some of the injustice which has been done women in mechanical and manufacturing pursuits. Their social and economic powers will be extended and recognized through the power of asso- ciation. The work of their organizations is very

---

* For a fuller discussion of this feature of the employment of women, see the article in *The Forum* for July, 1892, already referred to.

largely ethical. Women are not making war upon capital or forcing their demands for higher pay as the broad result of organization, but through an association of interests and the bringing of their condition to public attention, they are securing the gradual recognition of their value as an economic factor. The influence of their organization will be felt in many directions. Their employment has become more and more the subject of legal restriction. They have heretofore been classed with children, and legislatures have felt it incumbent upon them to regulate their employment so far as hours and conditions were concerned. Men have been benefited by legislative interference in the employment of women, for although it has never yet been deemed wise to interfere with the employment of men, yet they have found their work regulated to a certain degree through the regulation of the work of women and children. It is a significant fact that without law the hours of labor of men were long ago lessened, while the hours of labor of women and children were reduced only by means of positive legislative enactments. Now, with the rational presentation of their conditions by themselves, legislative restrictions will take on more and more of the rational elements. As the facts relative to the employment of women become more and better known the public can more fully comprehend the whole ethical, social, and political effect of their employment in manufacturing establishments.

Women not making war upon capital.

Their employment the subject of legal restriction.

CHAPTER XVII.

LABOR AND RATES OF WAGES, 1790–1890.*

A STATEMENT of the actual or average wages for any period or locality, especially when used for purposes of comparison, is not complete unless accompanied by information as to the hours of labor, regulations as to extra earnings, division of earnings among underhands, and other methods peculiar to the period or locality. Information as to cost of living and prices of commodities should also be considered, since it is not the amount of money wages that most nearly concerns the workman, but the amount of subsistence obtainable at a given period for a given expenditure. This chapter, however, is confined chiefly to a presentation of wages, prices being incidentally treated. The rates selected are either actual wages or the average for a number of establishments in different localities, and it is believed they fairly represent the wages for the different classes of labor. While the rate of wages for the same class of employees in different establishments within a given district may vary, the tendency is to equality. Statements of wages must be accompanied by other information.

In giving wages and prices for the past one hundred years, especially for the first half of the century, recourse has been chiefly to Eastern and Middle State conditions. This has been necessitated by the lack of data for other portions of the country, but it is believed that the facts given are fairly representative relatively of Statements chiefly for Eastern and Middle States.

* The graphic cards in this chapter illustrate the course of wages in various industries from 1840 to 1890.

variations in all manufacturing districts of the country taken as a whole, notwithstanding the great variations occurring between one part of the country and another.

At the beginning of the constitutional period, as stated in the chapter on wages in colonial days, not much change had been experienced in the rates of wages paid in different trades, but between 1790 and 1830, when the factory system was in fair and general operation and labor of every character commanded higher wages, it being in greater demand, there was a fair advance, carpenters in 1790 being paid less than 60 cents a day ; in 1800 something over 70 cents ; in 1810, $1.09 on the average ; in 1820, $1.13 ; in 1830, about $1.13, reaching, however, in the northern parts of our country an average of $1.40 a day during the period from 1830 to 1840. After this there was not much change for carpenters until 1860. Taking laborers, on the other hand, as fairly representative of general conditions, it is found that they were paid, in 1790, about 43 cents a day, on the average ; in 1800, 62½ cents a day ; from 1800 to 1810, about 82 cents a day ; from 1810 to 1820, something over 90 cents a day, while from 1840 to 1860 they varied from 87½ cents to $1 a day. Printers were receiving, at the beginning of the century, about $1.00 a day, and their wages had increased to $1.75 by 1860. Shoemakers were paid 73⅓ cents a day, on the average, during the decennial period 1790 to 1800, while they averaged from 1820 to 1830 $1.06 a day, reaching $1.70 in 1860. Looking to cotton-mill operatives, whose wages are not quoted much prior to 1820, we find that they were paid 44 cents a day, on the average, between 1820 and 1830, nearly 90 cents a day from 1830 to 1840. This wage held, with slight increase, to 1850, while during the next decade of years their average pay was $1.03

Margin notes:

Wages in 1790, 1810, 1830, 1840, 1860.

Cotton-mill operatives.

a day. Woolen-mill operatives did somewhat better, being paid in the earlier part of the factory period, that is, the decade of years prior to 1830, $1.12 ; they rarely reached this high wage again before 1880.

The record of wages after 1830 is far more complete, and the course of their rise or fall can be more clearly stated.   In 1831 daily wages for agricultural laborers ranged from 57.5 cents to $1.00 ; blacksmiths received from $1.00 to $1.25 per day. The daily average for carpenters was $1.07, but ranged as high as $1.50, while masons received $1.26.   Since 1873 wages in these staple occupations had more than doubled, but the segregation of mechanics and labor of all kinds into classes had made rapid progress, and an average wage for such a broad grouping conveys no idea of the rates of wages for the different classes.   The average daily wages for paper-mill operatives in 1831 was 66.6 cents, printers $1.25, shoemakers $1.06, cotton-mill operatives 88.6 cents, woolen-mill operatives 94.6 cents, glassmakers $1.13, and millwrights $1.21. *Wages after 1830.*

During the thirty years from 1830 to 1860 two violent commercial convulsions occurred, one in 1837 and one in 1857. Excessive importations, speculation, and the abuse of the credit system were the principal causes of both these business depressions ; both had the effect of *From 1830 to 1860.*

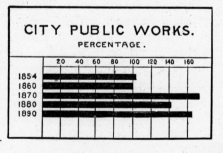

temporarily reducing wages in certain industries. Wages had not fully recovered from the panic of 1857 by 1860.

The averages for the decade ending that year, however, show a decided advance over 1830. An average for the ten years ending with 1860 gives agricultural laborers $1.01 per day, blacksmiths $1.69, carpenters $2.03, and masons $1.53 ; paper-mill operatives received $1.17, printers $1.75, shoemakers $1.70, cotton-mill operatives $1.03, woolen-mill operatives 87.3 cents, glassmakers $2.96, and millwrights $1.66. The wages in all of these occupations, with

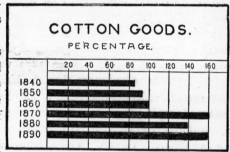

the exception of woolen-mill operatives, show an advance over 1830. The percentage of increase ranges from 16.3 for cotton-mill operatives to 161.9 for glassmakers. On making a similar comparison of wages for twenty different occupations, it is found that but one shows an increase in average daily wages.

Increase in wages.

Without considering the effect that the war, the fluctuation in currency, or the financial crisis of 1873 may have had on wages during the twenty years from 1860 to 1880, we will compare the averages for 1860 with similar averages for 1880. Agricultural laborers in 1880 received $1.31 per day, blacksmiths $2.28, carpenters $2.42, masons $2.79, paper-mill operatives $2.79, printers $2.18, shoemakers $1.76, cotton-mill operatives $1.40, woolen-mill operatives $1.24, and glassmakers $1.79. These average wages for leading industries indicate the general increase in wages in all occupations during the fifty years from 1830 to 1880. But a general

Average for
leading
industries.

average wage for operatives in cotton, woolen, or any other branch of industry in which there are numerous classes of employees, each class being graded and receiving pay in proportion to the importance in the general result and the degree of skill and care required of the operative, does not convey a satisfactory idea of the actual wages. For instance, the daily wages of overseers in the carding department of a repre-

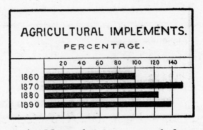

General averages unsatisfactory.

sentative cotton factory in Massachusetts ranged from $2.00, with thirteen hours of labor, in 1842 to $5.00, with ten hours of labor, in 1891. The pay for overseers in the weaving department of the same establishment advanced from $1.75 in 1843 to $5.00 in 1891. Considering the lower class of labor in the same factory, we find that the average daily wages of pickers and section-hands increased

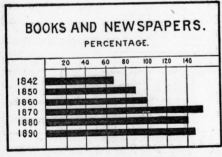

from 71.5 and 69.5 cents, respectively, in 1842 to $1.03 and $1.64 in 1891, while the hours of work decreased from thirteen to ten.

Carrying this comparison of actual wages for distinct classes into the building trades, a representative establishment in New York reports the pay for carpenters

Representative establishments.

in 1843 as $1.50 per day, and in 1891 $3.50, with the
hours of work reduced from ten to eight. The pay of
bricklayers and their helpers increased from $1.75 and
$1.00, respectively, in 1851 to
$4.00 and $2.50,
respectively, in
1891, with a de-
crease of two hours
in working time.
The daily wages of
draughtsmen and

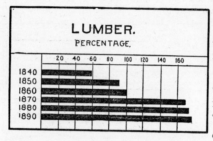

foremen blacksmiths, two widely separated yet dependent classes of labor, as reported by an establishment
engaged in manufacturing metals and metallic goods in
New York, increased from $1.75 and $2.50, respectively, in 1848 to $5.31 and $5.83 in 1891. Making
a similar comparison for an entirely different class
of wage-earners, that
of railroad employees,
we find the pay of
locomotive engineers
and firemen increas-
ing from $2.14 and
$1.06 in 1840 to $3.77
and $1.96, respec-
tively, in 1891; dur-

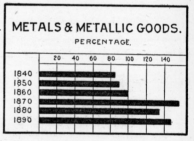

ing the same period the pay of passenger car conductors
increased from $2.11 to $3.84.

The wages just given are taken from the pay-rolls of
representative establishments and indicate the increase
in the actual wages for given occupations, but considered
by themselves they convey a wrong impression of the
average wages. While the pay of overseers in the

carding and weaving departmant of a cotton factory
ranged as high as $5.00 per day in 1891, we find by the
examination of sixty-four cotton and woolen factories,
scattered throughout twenty states and employing 31,-

657 hands, that
21,338 employ-
ees, or 67 per
cent of the total,
received between
41 cents and
$1.20 per day,
while only 24 em-

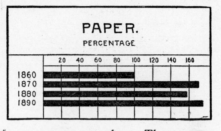

ployees received $5.00 or more per day. The average
daily wages for the industry, then, is nearer $1.00 than
$5.00. For the same reason, the daily wages in the
manufacture of iron and steel is between $1.00 and
$2.00, although the rates ranged from 41 cents to
$19.40 per day. Grouping a number of representative
establishments of the principal manufacturing industries
which employed a total of 59,784 hands, it is found that

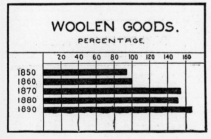

20,969, or 35 per
cent of the em-
ployees, received
from $1.00 to $1.60
per day. There-
fore, the average
daily wages for all
classes of mechan-
ics and operatives

in factories may be considered as having been between
$1.00 and $2.00, although the proportionate number receiving more than $2.00 per day was somewhat larger
than the proportion receiving less than $1.00 per day.

Considering the wages for the great mass of wage-

earners, the common and agricultural laborers, during
the entire period since 1633, the daily wages for the best
laborers advanced from 25 cents to 33.3 cents immediately before the Revolution, to 42.5 cents immedi-

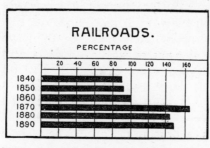

ately after, and
during June of
1891 the wages of
common laborers
ranged from $2.50
in Montana to 75
cents in the Caro-
linas and $1.25 in
New York. Farm
laborers received, during June, 1891, from $30 to $40
per month, with board and lodging, in Montana and
California, to $9 and $10 in the Carolinas and Virginia,
and $15 to $20 in New York. Masons (master workmen) received 33.3 cents per day in 1633 and $1.00 in
1790, while during the busy season of 1891 their wages
ranged from $4.50 to $5.00 in California and Colorado,
$2.50 in North Carolina, and $2.50 and $3.36 in Penn-
sylvania and New
York.

The wages
paid in numerous

occupations can
be compared, and
in each instance
the same, or a

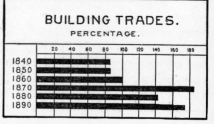

similar, advance is shown. The three classes given,
however, are sufficient with data given in Chapter IX.,
to convey an idea of the great increase in the money
wages of all classes of workmen during the two hundred
and fifty-eight years. While the number actually em-

ployed increases or diminishes with business prosperity or depression, their employment or idleness appears to have had but little effect on the rate of pay. Wages during almost the entire period have had an upward tendency, decreases being the exception and generally only of temporary duration.

Turning from the specific wages paid in some of the leading occupations, it is interesting to study the relative percentage of increase of wages in general. This can be done by assuming that at a certain period wages can be represented by 100, or par, and then calculating the increase or decrease from par in accordance with the facts. * Whatever wages were in 1860, they are quoted at 100. Starting from this basic point, it has been found that, taking the wages (which were taken from actual pay-rolls) in twenty-two industries and from nearly one hundred distinct establishments, and making a simple average, the percentages stood at 87.7 in 1840, as compared with 100 in 1860 ; that in 1866 they stood

Increase in general.

at 152.4, and in 1891 at 160.7. But it might be objected that a simple average does not indicate the general per- centage of in- crease or de- crease ; so the

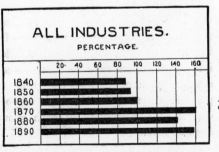

ALL INDUSTRIES.
PERCENTAGE.

All industries combined.

figures have been averaged according to their importance, each industry relative to all industries, as represented by the number employed in each. On this basis, taking 1860

* This method was adopted by the Senate Committee on Finance in its re- port on "Wholesale Prices and Wages," being Senate Report No. 1394, Fifty- second Congress, second session.

as represented by 100 again, it is found that the general average of wages in 1840 is represented by 82.5, in 1866 by 155.6, and in 1891 by 168.6 ; that is to say, on this basis wages have increased since 1860, as is shown by percentages, to the extent of 68.6 per cent ; and this figure shows the course of wages in this country since that year. On the basis of 100 in 1860, the increase has been from 82.5 in 1840 to 168.6 in 1891, the close of the period discussed.

Prices.

It is difficult always to make a statement concerning the course of prices for any considerable period of time

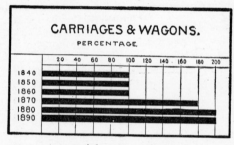

that will be satisfactory to all students. The actual price of different articles does not alone indicate such course, because one article enters into the consumption of the people in slight degree, the price of such article having a wide range, while another article, entering largely into consumption, may be represented by a price quite steady ; so there is always contention as to whether the price represented by the basis of consumption or the degree of consumption of each group of articles has risen or fallen.

1830 to 1860.

In the Sixteenth Annual Report of the Massachusetts Bureau of Statistics of Labor there are very extensive quotations of the prices of commodities covering the period from 1752 to 1883 and general comparisons from 1830 to 1860. Without going into the details of these comparisons, it appears that from 1830 to 1860 agricultural products advanced in price 62.8 per cent; burning oils and fluids, 29 per cent; candles and soap, 42.6 per cent; dairy products, 38.8 per cent; fish, 9.8 per cent; flour and meal, 26 per cent; fuel, meaning by this wood only, 55.4 per cent; meats, which included turkey in this particular comparison, 53 per cent. On the other hand, prices declined for boots and shoes 38.9 per cent; clothing and dress goods, 24.7 per cent; dry goods, 30.9 per cent; food preparations, 17.5 per cent; letter paper, 35.1 per cent; spices and condiments, 36.5 per cent.

By a consolidation of the percentages showing either an advance or decline in prices for the fourteen classes of articles just cited, the general percentage of increase in prices is found to be 9.6 per cent. If, on the other hand, the averages for the same classes of articles be considered, and not the percentages obtained for each class, it is found that the general average increase in prices was 15.7 per cent. The mean of these two percentages is 12.7, and this more probably indicates the correct position of the fourteen classes of articles just named in their general tendency between 1830 and 1860.

Decline in prices.

If, however, wages for the same period, as given for the various occupations named in the report cited above, be consolidated and averaged, the general average increase shown for the period ending with 1860, as compared with that ending with 1830, is 52.3 per cent. These facts clearly indicate that for that thirty years wages advanced to a much greater degree than prices.

It is fortunate that the public can now have recourse to the report of the Senate Committee on Finance, which has been referred to. Wholesale prices are given in this report for 223 leading articles of consumption from 1840 to 1890, and taking the prices of these articles as a whole, and considering them on the same basis as

Prices, 1840 to 1890.

that on which wages were considered, that is, assuming the quotations for 1860 to be 100, or par, it is found that the percentages are, for 1840, 97.7 per cent relatively to 100 in 1860, 187.7 for 1866, and 94.4 for 1891 ; or, in other words, prices generally, so far as the 223 leading articles are concerned, fell from 100 in 1860 to 94.4 in 1891.

Placing wages and prices in juxtaposition in a general

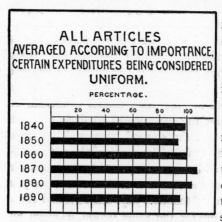

comparison, it is found that wages, considered relatively to the importance of one industry to all industries, stood at 168.6 in 1891 relatively to 100 in 1860, and that the prices of 223 commodities entering into consumption, on the basis of the importance of each article in proportion to the importance of all, fell from 100 in 1860 to 94.4 in 1891. The conclusion, therefore, must be positive and absolute that, while the percentage of increase in prices rose in 1866 to a point far beyond the increase in wages, prices had, by 1891, fallen to a point lower, on the whole, than they were in 1840, and wages had risen even above the high point they reached in 1866.

It should be stated that in these percentages the

prices of rents have not been considered. Rents have increased greatly, but taking the rise in rents into consideration, as well as the rise in food products and some other things, and drawing a general conclusion relative to real wages, the statements just made must hold as practically and generally established.

These few illustrations—and they are all that can be given comprehensively in this work—show quite clearly the real wages as against the nominal wages of the working people, and they lead to the statement that whenever prices of commodities rise they rise higher, relatively, than does the price of labor, and that when prices

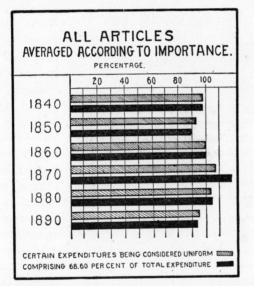

All articles averaged.

go down they go down much lower, relatively, than does the price of labor, which remains ordinarily very nearly at its inflated price ; for, as a matter of fact, the wages of 1890 and 1891 were very nearly as high, and in many instances quite as high, as they were in the inflated period from 1860 to 1870. This statement is further illustrated by the fact that a carpenter receiving $3.50 per day in

Comparison with inflated prices.

1866, in the inflated currency of that year, received the same face pay, that is, $3.50, in 1891, on a gold basis ; so, too, in prices one could buy, in 1840, calico at 12 cents a yard, while in 1866 the same goods, in the inflated currency of that year, sold for 21 cents a yard, and in 1891 they could be bought for 6 cents a yard, on a gold basis. It has not been worth while, therefore, in any of the comparisons which have been given in this chapter to reduce values to a gold basis.

PART III.

THE LABOR MOVEMENT.

PART III.—THE LABOR MOVEMENT.

CHAPTER XVIII.

THE INCEPTION OF THE LABOR MOVEMENT.

IN THIS part the story of what is commonly called
"the labor movement" is told. This movement comprehends the attempts of labor to secure its demands and
its efforts at organization, labor legislation, strikes, lockouts, and boycotts. The labor question has been present
always in the development of the world. In ancient times
there were guilds, societies, and various organizations for
one purpose or another ; but since industry has become
organized and the factory system a fixture the labor movement has assumed entirely new features, and its proportions cover a vast range of questions involving economics
and ethics. The labor movement is the labor question,
and the labor question, concretely stated, is the effort of
wage-workers to secure a higher standard of living. It
is their struggle upward. How to secure the ends for
which the struggle is instituted is probably the great
question of the day. Contemporaneous with the development of the industries of the United States the
movement referred to has taken place, and the speed of
the movement has been accelerated as the development
has grown. The industrial evolution of the United
States, therefore, involves the labor movement in its en-
tirety, and the account of its various features and of the
complications resulting from the continued struggle becomes legitimate in any account of the evolution.

*Labor's
attempts to
secure its
demands.*

*Labor question
defined.*

Prior to the establishment of the factory system there was little organization. The southern colonies, having the slave system for the prosecution of their industries, did not offer any fertile field for the wage-worker to agitate the questions which interested him. The northern colonies, while having a different system of labor, offered but little field for such agitations, because industry was primitive in its nature, land was plenty, laborers were in demand, and habits and wants were simple ; and yet the labor movement of the country, in the broadest sense, had its birth in both Virginia and Plymouth, for the two represented antagonistic systems of labor, the results being of vast importance to the welfare of the country, the antagonism culminating in 1861 in the great Civil War.

The two systems of labor had their effect in various directions, both in the economics of production and in the relation of the laborer to society. The comparison of free with slave labor has been treated in its appropriate chapter, but the very conditions of slave labor prevented organization, and so no traces of any labor movement prior to the Civil War can be found in the South. Free labor, however, offered opportunities for movements in various directions, and yet, on account of the conditions already cited, history does not reveal any concerted action of any consequence during the colonial period, except, it may be, in the early days in Massachusetts, when the ship calkers, who were politicians, organized what was known as the "Calkers' Club," the purpose of which was "to lay plans for introducing certain persons into places of trust and power." Samuel Adams's father, at a date as early as 1724, took an active part in this club, and it is from its name, it is said, that the term "caucus" was derived. But the elements of organization were wanting, for such organization comes through

Little organization prior to factory system.

Ship calkers.

the aggregation of laborers in industrial centers. Association is the life principle of industry as well as of all efforts at progress, and so in all probability there were societies of tradesmen of different classes having various motives in forming their associations. The domestic system of labor, which kept workers in individual workshops and in their homes, stood in the way of extensive organization ; thus it was not until the opening of the present century that labor unions began to have any influence in the shaping of affairs. They, however, exercised but little influence until after the first quarter of the century had passed.

The tailors, who have always been active participants in political matters, established a trades union as far back as 1806. This association probably grew from the influence exerted by members of the craft coming from England, who preserved their loyalty to the Journeymen Tailors' Unions of the old country. There were like organizations of hatters in 1819, and the shipwrights and calkers established their order in 1822, under the name of the "Columbian Charitable Society of Shipwrights and Calkers of Boston and Charlestown," and in 1823 the legislature of Massachusetts granted the society a charter. April 3, 1803, there was incorporated in the city of New York an association called the "New York Society of Journeymen Shipwrights," while another society was created in 1806, known as the "House Carpenters of the City of New York." The compositors of the latter city were also probably organized in the early years of the present century, for history shows that Thurlow Weed was elected a member as early as 1817. Their society was known as the "New York Typographical Society," Peter Force being its president. Curiously enough, although Mr. Weed's residence in Albany

Tailors' unions.

Hatters.

Shipwrights. House carpenters.

Compositors.

enabled him to secure the incorporation of the society, there was a strike in Mr. Weed's office in 1821, which grew out of the fact that one of his compositors was a "rat," that is, a non-union man.

Movements after 1825.

With the year 1825 new elements and purposes appeared, and the way was opened for the development of the labor movement. It would be difficult to assign any single ruling cause for the new spirit which arose after that year, yet many reasons may be assigned for it. The demand for less hours of labor and for higher wages and experiments in coöperation may have had much to do with the inauguration of the movement. The spirit of association was rapidly developed through the influence of the altruistic preachings of Robert Owen, who came to this country in 1824. Owen had

Coming of Robert Owen.

established one of the most prominent experiments in the Old World for the amelioration of bad conditions in labor communities. This was at New Lanark in Scotland. His chief experience there was in the year 1819, but he carried his experiments to such a success that he gained respect and renown everywhere.

The main cause of his success began with the practical improvement of the working people under his superintendence as manager and afterward as owner of the cotton-mills at New Lanark. He found himself surrounded by squalor and poverty, intemperance and crime. He erected healthy dwellings with adjacent gardens, and let them at cost price to his people. He built stores where goods of proper quality might be purchased at wholesale prices, and so aided in removing the pernicious effects of what is known as the "truck system." He established the first infant school in Great Britain, and he excluded all under ten years from his workshops and made the physical and moral training of the young his

special care. He adopted measures to put down drunkenness and to encourage the savings of the people. As
a natural consequence, the employees became attached
to their employer, taking a personal interest in the success of the business, and laboring ably and conscien-
tiously to make the mills of New Lanark a great financial success. An American traveler, Mr. Griscom,
visited Owen's mills in 1819, and in making a report
upon them used the following language :

Measures adopted by Owen.

> There is not, I apprehend, to be found in any part of the
> world a manufacturing village in which so much order, good
> government, tranquillity, and rational happiness prevail. It af-
> fords an eminent and instructive example of the good that may
> be effected by well-directed efforts to promote the real com-
> fort, and, I may add, the morality of the laboring classes.

And Kaufmann, in his work on socialism, speaks of
New Lanark as one of the romantic valleys of the Clyde
which have been invested with the charm of poetry by
Sir Walter Scott, and as having also been rendered the
scene of an earthly paradise, from a social point of view,
by Robert Owen. It is not strange, therefore, that
when Owen came to America in 1824 his fame came
with him and the laborers caught a new spirit and a new
enthusiasm in relation to their surroundings. He received great attention from the American people, and it
is probable that he laid the basis for the rapid extension
of Fourierism over the whole country, probably more
than two hundred communistic villages having been
founded in the United States as the result of the doctrines taught by Charles Fourier.* Some of these villages still exist, but their prosperity, such as came to
them, was due largely to the fact that they traded with
the world and the world was not communistic. It is not

Owen's fame preceded his coming.

---

* For an account of these communities see "History of American So-
cialisms," by John Humphrey Noyes.

necessary here to discuss their peculiarities and characteristics, but it is well, perhaps, to remark that Horace Greeley, Albert Brisbane, Charles A. Dana, and others equally well known, were interested in the movement and helped to establish some of the most celebrated Fourieristic societies, the most notable of which was that at Brook Farm, in Massachusetts. Most of these attempts died after a few years of feverish existence, and yet they had an immense influence, extending over twenty or thirty years, in calling attention to socialistic and even communistic attempts.

Period of reform movements.

The period from 1825 to 1850 may well be called the period of reform movements, many of them having but brief existence, others being firmly established in the minds of the people and extending in their influence beyond the associations which promulgated reform doctrines, and which are, many of them, felt even at the present day and will be felt for generations to come.

Another reason, perhaps, for the concentration of effort by working people is found in the rapidly developing factory system, the very essence of which is the principle of association. The concentration of population in industrial centers, as already remarked, fostered organization. These, and it may be other reasons, sufficiently account for the extension of the labor movement after the year 1825. Certain it is that unions began to be formed everywhere in the Northern States and the agitation for legislation for workingmen specifically carried on. Boston and New York were the most prominent localities in these movements. Labor

Early labor literature.

literature began to appear as the result, and as early as 1825 the *Working Man's Advocate* was published in New York City. Dr. Richard T. Ely, in his excellent work on ''The Labor Movement in America,'' thinks it probable that this was the first appearance of a representative labor press in the United States. This publication was followed by the *Daily Sentinel* and *Young America*, all published by two Englishmen, George Henry Evans and Frederick W. Evans, who came to this country in 1820. The former was a land reformer. More than six hundred papers in the country indorsed the demands which these men made through their papers. These demands comprehended the right of man to the soil, the breaking up of monopolies, the freedom of public lands, the inalienability of homesteads, and called for the abolition of all laws for the collection of debts and for the adoption of a general bankrupt law. They also demanded a lien for the laborer upon his own work for his wages, the abolition of imprisonment for debt, equal rights for women with men in all respects, and the abolition of chattel slavery and of wages slavery.

From Thurlow Weed's autobiography it is learned that a "Workingman's Convention" was held at Syracuse, in the state of New York, in 1830, at which Ezekiel Williams was nominated for governor. In the election which followed less than three thousand votes, however, were cast for Mr. Williams, but the next year the movers, under the name of the "Workingmen's Party," united with the Whigs and succeeded in electing three or four members of the legislature. It was from this movement that the Loco-Foco party originated.

A great convention was held in Boston on the 16th of February, 1831, consisting of farmers, mechanics, and other workingmen. * From this grew a delegate convention which was held in the subsequent year, on the 6th of September, in Boston. Many of the men after-

Publications of the Evans brothers.

Boston convention of 1831.

---

* See First Annual Report of Massachusetts Bureau of Statistics of Labor, 1870.

ward prominent in politics and in business were members of this convention. It discussed landed interests, taxation, and coöperative trading. Ten points were considered by it. These were the organization of a central committee for each state ; the institutions of lyceums or institutes ; reform in the militia system ; the expediency of calling a national convention of workingmen ; the ten-hour system ; the effect of banking institutions and other monopolies upon the condition of the laboring classes ; the improvement of the system of education, including the recommendation of such legislative enactments in relation to the internal economies of factories as would insure to the operatives a competent degree of instruction ; the abolition of imprisonment for debt ; the adoption of a national bankrupt law ; the extension of the right of suffrage, and lien laws. These points were similar in many respects to the demands already referred to as announced by the Evans brothers. The Hon. Edward Everett commended the organization of the Workingmen's party in a lecture which he delivered before the Charlestown Lyceum in Massachusetts. Other meetings were held in the city of Boston, at which it was recommended that the mechanics of all branches should hold meetings by themselves for the purpose of consulting together and of doing all possible to come to a mutual agreement upon the system of working hours. At various meetings and by various conventions questions which to-day are being discussed by labor organizations were carefully considered, the relation of employers to employees, the question of whether the ten-hour system is a benefit, and such matters, being the prominent subjects of consideration. The right of laborers to organize for the purpose of securing and protecting their interests and the question as to whether a

Various points considered by the convention.

Similar meetings and their discussions.

general trades union would diminish strikes and lockouts were also prominent in the discussions. Following the meetings of 1831 and 1832 in Boston, "The General Trades Unions of the City of New York" were active in discussing the questions cited. This is the first attempt, so far as any accounts go to establish the fact, to unite workingmen of different trades in one organization. In later years this has been the rule.

General Trades Unions of New York.

The movement during the succeeding years took various forms, the employers taking a part in the matter from their point of view. The merchants and ship-owners of Boston, at a meeting held in the Exchange Coffee Rooms on the 15th of May, 1832, voted to "discountenance and check the unlawful combination formed to control the freedom of individuals as to the hours of labor, and to thwart and embarrass those by whom they are employed and liberally paid." The report of this meeting also sets forth "the pernicious and demoralizing tendency of these combinations, and the unreasonableness of the attempt, in particular where mechanics are held in so high estimation and their skill in labor so liberally rewarded." The members of that meeting held that labor ought always to be left free to regulate itself, and that neither the employee nor the employer should have the power to control the other ; and they looked with deep regret upon the course pursued by their fellow-citizens, the journeymen, in the adoption and maintenance of a system of measures designed to coerce individuals of their craft and to prescribe the time and manner of their labor. The employers claimed that labor organization would drive the trade from the city, and in their conclusions they resolved : "We will neither employ any journeyman who at the time belongs to such combinations, nor will we give work to any master mechanic

Action of merchants and ship-owners.

Their views as to employees.

who shall employ them while they continue thus pledged to each other and refuse to work the hours which it has been and is now customary for mechanics to work." The resolutions were signed by the representatives of one hundred and six firms.

Failure of ten-hour movement.

The movement for ten hours was a failure, so far as success at the time it was originated was concerned, but it is probably true that it resulted in increasing the membership of organizations and in intensifying the agitation. The men were not destitute of influential friends, however. In Massachusetts such men as William Ellery Channing, Robert Rantoul, Horace Mann, and James G. Carter, advocated their claims. Education, and all that education means, was preached as the surest method of reaching the aims of the labor organizations. It was the whole burden of Channing's lectures on self-culture and the laboring classes. He had great confidence in them, believed in their wisdom and integrity, and that they were perfectly competent to so develop their mental and moral powers as to enable them to meet the great questions of the time.

Brief story of labor organization.

But the story of labor organization, its course, its successes, its failures, the philosophy underlying it, the influence it has exerted in many directions, would fill volumes in itself. It is sufficient here to say that, no matter what the opposition of any particular period was or the character it assumed, no matter what antagonisms within disturbed their order, no matter how defections reduced their ranks at times and jealousies prevented their immediate success, labor organizations from 1825 continued through success and failure, their propaganda extending first to all great cities and ultimately to all parts of the land.

CHAPTER XIX.

LABOR ORGANIZATIONS.

THE history of organizations constitutes an integral part of the history of the country, and their growth to the present time an influential feature of industrial development. Their relation to strikes, their advocacy of all educational methods, their conservative action at times offset the radicalism which has at the same time led them into injudicious action. Through the years between 1825 and the present time their history is a progressive one, and its details would bring into prominence almost every industry in the country. Out of them there have grown some great associations or organizations, developing power and bringing to the attention of the country conditions which need reforming and relations which call for the highest ethical influence to secure proper adjustment.*

History of organized labor part of industrial history.

In this progress events in Europe have had more or less influence, those of 1848 in France contributing largely to the renewal of the agitation of American socialism and labor reform. The exodus from Ireland following the famine and increasing the volume of immigration to the United States contributed to the agitation. The pressure in our own country also helped the movement. One of the chief and most annoying questions

Contributing causes to agitation.

---

* For an excellent account of special organizations and details of their growth, demands, and doctrines, see " The Labor Movement: The Problem of To-Day," edited by George E. McNeill: Boston, 1887; " The Story of Manual Labor," by John Cameron Simonds: Chicago, 1886; " Thirty Years of Labor," by T. V. Powderly: Columbus, O.; " The Labor Movement in America," by Richard T. Ely, Ph.D.: New York, 1886.

was that of the hours of labor. They were excessively

Long hours of
labor cause of
discussion.

long. Twelve, thirteen, and fourteen hours a day were
not uncommon in textile factories and in some other
lines, and at times even sixteen hours constituted a normal working day. The wage-earners protested against
this, and the protests were made at an early day, so
early that the agitation for ten hours can be said to be
contemporaneous with the beginning of the labor movement. It now constitutes an important element in labor
agitations, notwithstanding that in many places the purpose of organization in this respect has been accomplished. When the agitation was strong and yet an
issue undecided, one of the presidents of the United
States, Mr. Van Buren, issued a proclamation or a

President Van
Buren's procla-
mation.

general order, April 10, 1840, introducing the ten-hour
system into the navy yard at Washington, D. C., and
in "all public establishments." The ten-hour day had
received sanction in the city of Baltimore some time
before President Van Buren interceded. The laborers
in that city proclaimed to the world that ten hours
should constitute a day's labor. They won in the
conflict, and ever since ten hours a day has been the rule
in that city. In 1845 the agitation was stimulated in
Massachusetts throughout the textile industry, but it was

Ten-hour
agitation in
Massachusetts.

not until 1874 that a law was passed making ten hours
the normal day in that state for women and children.
William Claflin, one of the governors of the state, later
on openly advocated the ten-hour system. To-day that
system prevails almost everywhere in the country, and in
some states law has established, under certain conditions,
even a shorter day. This will be referred to more fully
under "Labor Legislation."

This account of labor organizations, general and brief
as it has been necessarily, should not be closed without

mention of the leading unions now in existence and exerting an influence in the affairs of the country. One of the
most important of these is the International Typographical Union. Nearly every state and territory is now represented at its annual sessions. This union has had many
distinguished friends, notably the late George W. Childs,
of *The Public Ledger*, of Philadelphia ; Mr. Anthony
J. Drexel, one of the great bankers of that city;
and others who have passed away, and many prominent
men, statesmen, and business men still living. So far
as the writer can ascertain, this union traces its origin to
1850, when a "National Convention of Journeymen
Printers" met in New York. The next year a meeting
was held in Baltimore, but a permanent organization was
not effected until 1852, when delegates met in Cincinnati.
The title "National Typographical Union" was at that
time adopted, but this name was changed to "International Typographical Union" at the annual meeting in
Albany, N. Y., in 1869. The word "international"
was introduced in order to bring into the organization
Canadian printers. Dr. Ely, in his work already quoted,
asserts that "international" as a part of the title of
American trades unions is intended to include members
from the United States and Canada, few of them including Europeans. The International Typographical
Union is the oldest existing American trades union. In
this respect the American labor movement resembles the
labor movement elsewhere, for generally we find the
printers among the pioneers in the organization of labor.
This is true of Italy, France, and Germany, the printers' unions being among the oldest and strongest of
existing labor organizations.*

Following the Printers' Union, the hatters established

---

* "The Labor Movement in America," by Richard T. Ely.

Hatters' unions.   their great organization.   This was in 1854, the " National Trade Association of Hat Finishers of the United States of America" being organized in that year.   In 1868, however, it divided, one branch keeping the old name and the other taking the name of the "Silk and Fur Hat Finishers' Trade Association of the United States of America."

Iron-molders.

A noted trades union is the " Iron-Molders' Union of North America," founded July 5, 1859, and the " Machinists' and Blacksmiths' Union of North America," founded in the same year, and incorporated at that time by Congress, was once a powerful and influential body. It does not now, however, exert any influence, and it is doubtful if it exists.   The Brotherhood of Locomotive

Locomotive engineers.

Engineers started as the " Brotherhood of the Foot-Board, at Detroit," August 17, 1863, but on the same date in the next year it reorganized under the name and title of the " Grand International Brotherhood of Locomotive Engineers."   The " Cigar-Makers' National

Cigar-makers. Bricklayers.

Union," born in 1864 ; the " Bricklayers' and Masons' International Union," instituted October 17, 1865 ; the

Conductors.

" Order of Railway Conductors," organized as the " Conductors' Brotherhood" in 1868 ; the "United States Wool Hat Finishers' Association," organized in 1869 ; the " Brotherhood of Locomotive Firemen," organized the same year ; the " National Union of Horseshoers of

Iron and steel workers.

the United States," dating from 1875 ; the " Amalgamated Association of Iron and Steel Workers," one of the strongest trades unions in the United States, starting

Granite cutters.

in 1876 ; the " Granite Cutters' National Union of the

Carpenters and joiners.

United States," organized in 1877 ; the "Brotherhood of Carpenters and Joiners," organized in 1881 ; the "Rail-

Bakers.

road Brakemen," in 1884 ; the " Journeymen Bakers' National Union," in 1886, etc., etc., constitute the leading trades unions of the country. Many of these unions have weekly newspapers of more or less influence.

The three great orders which to-day exert the most general influence in this country are the Knights of Labor, American Federation of Labor, and American Railway Union, and their prominence warrants a statement of some of the leading facts connected with their history and principles. These three great orders are founded on two separate but fundamental ideas, the Knights of Labor and the American Railway Union upon one idea, and the American Federation of Labor upon the other. The distinctive features of these two ideas are, first, the organization of members of a single vocation. The underlying principle of such associations is that men who think alike should act together. This has been the fundamental principle or basis of all organization, civil and political as well as industrial and professional. Trades-unionism in England and in this country is based upon this idea, and it seems to be the stronger basis, so far as the experience of labor organizations is concerned.

The principle which underlies the second idea is that which ignores vocation and seeks to harmonize all individual or separate interests in the interests of the whole. This is the basis of society, but it has not been applied to labor organizations to any extent until within the past fifty or sixty years. Since 1830 there have been several attempts in France, and in some other continental countries, to bring all workingmen, whether of one nation or of many, into harmonious association, each member everywhere seeking the good of the whole. The principal instance of a labor organization based upon this broad principle was the International Association of Workingmen, popularly known as the "International," organized in London in 1864. This association sought to

Three great orders.

Fundamental ideas of associations.

The "International."

bring workingmen, wherever manufacturing had gained
any notable foothold, into one society ; and it grew for
a while, but never at any time had it a membership exceeding one hundred thousand. It did not extend to the
United States with sufficient force to involve any large
number of workingmen in this country, and not until
1870 or 1871 were there any branches of it organized
here. The part which the "International" played in
the struggles in Paris in 1871 killed it for America, and
practically killed the society itself. It had a stormy existence, and was wrecked finally by its being taken under
the control of the radical socialists of Europe. It sowed
some seed, principally through its broad foundation, and
not through its practices.

The second great attempt to organize labor on this
broad basis, that is, as broad as society itself, in which all
parts should be recognized, was the Noble Order of
Knights of Labor, which organization was born on
Thanksgiving Day, 1869, in the city of Philadelphia,
and was the result of the efforts of Uriah S. Stephens, as
the leader, and six associates. They were all garment-
cutters. For several years previous to this date the gar-
ment-cutters of Philadelphia had been organized as a
trades union, but had failed to obtain satisfactory rates of
wages in their trade. Dissatisfaction prevailed, and in
the fall of 1869 the union was disbanded ; but Stephens,
foreseeing this result, had, by himself, prepared the out-
line of a plan for an organization which should embrace
all branches of honorable toil, and which, based upon
education, through coöperation and an intelligent use of
the ballot, should gradually abolish the present wage
system. Mr. Stephens was a Free Mason, and he
brought into the ritual of the new order many Masonic
features, especially those relating to forms and cere-

Knights of Labor.

Uriah S. Stephens the founder, 1869.

monies. The obligations were in the nature of oaths, taken with all solemnity upon the Bible. The members were sworn to the strictest secrecy. The name of the order was not to be divulged, and it was for a long time referred to in the literature of the Knights of Labor, in their circulars, meetings, reports, and conversation, as "Five Stars," five stars being used in all printing and writing to designate the name of the order. Many classical expressions were taken from the Greek and introduced into the ritual. The instructions given to every person admitted to the order are as follows :

Knights of Labor known as "Five Stars."

Instructions on initiation.

Labor is noble and holy. To defend it from degradation ; to divest it of the evils to body, mind, and estate which ignorance and greed have imposed ; to rescue the toiler from the grasp of the selfish—is a work worthy of the noblest and best of our race. In all the multifarious branches of trade, capital has its combinations ; and, whether intended or not, they crush the manly hopes of labor, and trample poor humanity in the dust. We mean no conflict with legitimate enterprise, no antagonism to necessary capital ; but men, in their haste and greed, blinded by self-interests, overlook the interests of others, and sometimes violate the rights of those they deem helpless. We mean to uphold the dignity of labor, to affirm the nobility of all who earn their bread by the sweat of their brows. We mean to create a healthy public opinion on the subject of labor (the only creator of values), and the justice of its receiving a full, just share of the values or capital it has created. We shall, with all our strength, support laws made to harmonize the interests of labor and capital, and also those laws which tend to lighten the exhaustiveness of toil. To pause in his toil, to devote to his own interests (*sic*), to gather a knowledge of the world's commerce, to unite, combine, and coöperate in the great army of peace and industry, to nourish and cherish, build and develop, the temple he lives in, is the highest and noblest duty of man to himself, to his fellow-man, and to his Creator.

No details or general laws for the government of the order appear to have been adopted until the formation of

No general laws at first.

the first Local Assembly in 1873 ; but the plan presented at the meeting in November, 1869, was heartily approved, and adopted by Mr. Stephens' associates.

Local assemblies began to increase and the order grew apace, and although by the first quarterly report it is shown that it had a membership of but twenty-eight, it numbered at one time nearly one million members. The order consists of Local and District Assemblies and a General Convention of Delegates. The history of the order in its details is an interesting one, and shows the usual ups and downs of labor organizations. Religious prejudices grew in it, and finally its work was modified. The degree work as it was patterned after the Masonic ritual is not now known in the Knights of Labor, there being no degrees, in the sense of secret organization.

The growth of the order was exceedingly rapid, so rapid that the Executive Board felt constrained at one time to call a halt in the initiation of new members. Its accessions were nearly 400,000 in one year. Mr. Powderly, in his testimony before the Strike Investigating Committee of Congress April 21, 1886, stated as follows :

"Our present membership does not exceed 500,000, although we have been credited with 5,000,000." From various causes it has, during the last three or four years, suffered a decrease in membership, and now its membership is estimated at about 150,000. The order is represented in nearly every state by its local and district assemblies.

The intellectual history of the order is of far more importance to the public than its material history, and is to be found in its declaration of principles, its constitution, and its legislation. Prior to 1878 no declaration of principles had been made. The unwritten law of the order was observed, the membership being small and the local and district assemblies few ; but as it grew in numbers and its influence extended over vast areas, written laws and written declarations became not only essential for the welfare of the order, but a necessity for its working. Prior to the abandonment of the secrecy of the workings of the order—that is, in 1881, when the oath-bound obligations were abolished and the simple pledge took its place—a declaration of principles had been adopted. This declaration of principles was adopted at the meeting of the General Assembly, in Reading, Pa., January, 1878. Various additions have been made to this declaration from time to time, so that the Knights of Labor now stand upon a declaration of principles which, with a preamble, contains the basis of the working of the order. In the preamble, after referring to what is called "the alarming development and aggressiveness of the power of money and corporations under the present industrial and political systems," and that such development "will inevitably lead to the hopeless degradation of the people," the Knights declare that their body is not a political party, but that it is more, for in it are crystallized sentiments and measures for the benefit of the whole body politic. The declaration of principles calls upon all who believe in securing the greatest good to the greatest number to join in helping the Knights of Labor to make industrial and moral worth, not wealth, the true standard of individual and national greatness.

Declaration of principles of the Knights of Labor.

Their aim is to secure to the workers of society the fullest enjoyment of the wealth they create ; leisure for the development of their intellectual, moral, and social faculties, and all the benefits, recreations, and pleasures of association—in a word, they declare themselves ready to join in any movement which will enable them to share in the gains and honor of advancing civilization. In or-

General aim.

der to secure these results they demand at the hands of the lawmaking power of municipality, state, and nation the establishment of the Referendum in the making of laws ; the creation of bureaus of labor for the collection of information ; that the land, including all the natural sources of wealth, being the heritage of all the people, should not be subject to speculative traffic ; that taxes upon land should be levied upon its full value for use, exclusive of improvements, and that the community should be entitled to all unearned increment ; the abrogation of all laws that do not bear equally upon capitalists and laborers, and the adoption of measures providing for the health and safety of those engaged in mining, manufacturing, and building industries. They also declare that there should be proper indemnification for injuries received through lack of the necessary safeguards. The incorporation of labor organizations should, in the opinion of the order, be recognized, and laws should be enacted providing for weekly payment of wages. They also take up the old and earliest claim under the labor movement in this country, that mechanics and laborers should have a first lien upon the product of their labor to the extent of their full wages.

The order is opposed to the contract system on national, state, and municipal work, and in favor of the enactment of laws providing for arbitration between employers and employed and the enforcement of the decision of the arbitrators. In their conventions, however, the arguments have been, in many instances, against this declaration. They also favor the compulsory attendance at school of children between the ages of seven and fifteen years and the furnishing of text-books by the state free of charge. They also favor a graduated tax on incomes and inheritances. They are opposed to the hiring out of convict labor. They have a financial

plank demanding the establishment of a national mone-
tary system, in which a circulating medium in necessary
quantity shall issue directly to the people, without the
intervention of banks ; they are opposed to interest- Measures opposed by the order.
bearing bonds, bills of credit or notes, but would pro-
vide that, when need arises, the emergency shall be met
by the issue of legal-tender, non-interest-bearing money ;
they are also opposed to the importation of foreign labor
under contract ; they are in favor of a postal savings
bank, and they go to the extent of declaring that the
government ought to obtain possession, under the right
of eminent domain, of all telegraphs, telephones, and
railroads. In closing their declaration, they pledge
themselves to associate their labors in establishing co-
operative institutions, such as will tend to supersede the
wage system ; to secure for both sexes equal rights ; to
gain some of the benefits of labor-saving machinery by
a gradual reduction of the hours of labor to eight hours
per day ; to persuade employers to agree to arbitrate all
differences which may arise between them and their employees, in order, as they state in closing, that the bonds
of sympathy between them may be strengthened and
that strikes may be rendered unnecessary.

The order has a systematic and methodical constitu- Constitution.
tion, which consists of thirteen articles and is much like
the constitutions of all organizations, except that it is
quite elaborate. The motto of the order is, " That is
the most perfect government in which an injury to one
is the concern of all."

From the formation of the General Assembly (which Attitude of the Knights of Labor as to strikes.
consists of delegates from district assemblies) in 1878
up to 1883 there was a strong element in the order in
favor of supporting strikes, and strike funds were raised
by a tax on the members. At the same time, the more

advanced thinkers in the order were trying to educate the members to use every means for the settlement of difficulties, and so far succeeded that at the Cincinnati session, in 1883, the strike laws of the order were made so rigid that they practically amounted to a prohibition of strikes, so far as the support of the order was concerned. The laws now in force do not permit the support of a strike by the whole order.

The literature of the Knights of Labor is not extensive. The *Journal of the Knights of Labor* is the official organ of the order. The first number of this journal, under the name of the *Journal of United Labor,* was issued May 15, 1880, and was published monthly. It is now a weekly journal.

The real growth of the order may be said to date from the Detroit session of 1881, when the strict secrecy of the order was abolished and it was declared that its name and objects should henceforth be made public.*

Literature of the order.

---

* For an extended historical sketch of the Knights of Labor, see *Quarterly Journal of Economics* for January, 1887, article by the author.

CHAPTER XX.

LABOR ORGANIZATIONS (*Concluded*).

THE "American Federation of Labor" is, as its name signifies, a federation of minor bodies or organizations. It grew out of a call, issued conjointly by the "Knights of Industry" and a society known as the "Amalgamated Labor Union" (the latter being an offshoot of the Knights of Labor and composed of members of that order who had become somewhat dissatisfied with it), for a convention to meet August 2, 1881, at Terre Haute, Ind. The Knights of Industry was a society whose membership was from the states of Illinois and Missouri. The membership of the Amalgamated Labor Union, which was organized in 1878, was from Indiana and Ohio. The object of the convention was to supplant, with a new and secret order, the Knights of Labor. The largest constituency of this preliminary convention was, however, trades union in its character, and they were opposed to increasing the number of labor societies then existing ; so the suggested secret organization was not effected. Another call was made, however, and a convention was held in the city of Pittsburg November 19, 1881. The call for this convention had in it the following statement :

American Federation of Labor.

Date of its organization.

We have numberless trades unions, trades assemblies, or councils, Knights of Labor, and various other local, national, and international labor unions, all engaged in the noble task of elevating and improving the condition of the working classes. But great as has been the work done by these bodies, there is vastly more that can be done by a combination of all these organizations in a federation of trades and labor unions.

The convention represented 262,000 workingmen, who sent to it 107 delegates, the result of their deliberations being a permanent organization under the name and style of the "Federation of Organized Trades and Labor Unions of the United States and Canada." *

Date of organization under present name.

The American Federation of Labor, under its present name and in its present form, was organized December 8, 1886, at Columbus, O. Two years later it was decided that as the American Federation of Labor was the direct outgrowth of and the successor to the federation formed in 1881 at Pittsburg, the conventions of the American Federation should date from that year.

Preliminary steps.

The Terre Haute convention was the preliminary step, however, which led to the organization. Prior to 1881 there had been several attempts to organize a national union which should represent, in a federated form, the various trades unions, national and international, existing in the United States, the first of these attempts taking place early in the year 1866, when the trades assemblies of New York City and Baltimore issued a call for a national labor congress, which resulted in a convention of one hundred delegates, representing some sixty open and secret organizations, the delegates coming from all parts of the Union. The convention met August 20. A second convention was held in Chicago

Its general aim.

the following year. The aim was to imitate the Trades-Union Congress of England, in which local bodies, not allowed to discuss politics in their meetings, could send delegates to the central body and there deal with ques-

---

* For an extended account of the organization of the American Federation of Labor, its history and aims, see chapter by P. J. McGuire in pamphlet entitled " Trades Unions," by William Trant, published by the American Federation of Labor, New York, 1888.

tions of a political nature, and thus influence national legislation in favor of the working classes.*

In 1868 the National Labor Union held two conventions, one in May and the other in September, and in 1869 it held a meeting in Chicago. In 1870 it met in Boston, in 1871 in Philadelphia, and in 1872 at Columbus, O. The latter was the last convention of the National Labor Union.

National Labor Union, 1868.

Many trades unions went under in 1873, owing to the industrial depression. There was nothing in them particularly to hold members together.

Effects of depression of 1873.

Several of the leading trades-unionists of the country called an "Industrial Congress" to meet in Rochester in April, 1874, and on the 14th of that month a convention was held, representing a secret organization then known as the "Sovereigns of Industry." The intention was to take up the old work of the National Labor Union. The "Industrial Brotherhood of the United States," another secret order, partaking largely of the character of the Knights of Labor, took part in this convention. The natural consequence was that the two interests, that is to say, the two ideas, that on which the Knights of Labor was organized and the trades-union idea, as already described, became antagonistic; yet a platform which adopted most of the declaration of principles of the Knights of Labor was framed. The intention of the convention was not carried out, however, the movement ending with the Rochester meeting. Other attempts were made in 1875 and 1876, but they were largely political, and having engaged in their political work, the temporary orders were very naturally disbanded. The other years prior to 1881, when the Federation of Organized Trades and Labor Unions of the

Further attempts at federation.

* Chapter by P. J. McGuire, already referred to.

United States and Canada was created, witnessed attempts at federation, but they were ephemeral in their nature.

The permanent organization effected at Pittsburg November 19, 1881, under the call which has been cited, adopted a platform more comprehensive than that of the Knights of Labor, although not essentially differing therefrom.   It demanded eight hours as a day's work ; called for national and state incorporation of trades unions ; favored obligatory education of all children and the prohibition of their employment under the age of fourteen ; also favored the enactment of uniform apprentice laws ; opposed bitterly all contract convict labor and the truck system for payment of wages ; demanded laws giving to workingmen a first lien on property upon which their labor had been expended; insisted upon the abrogation of all so-called conspiracy laws ; advocated the establishment of a national bureau of labor statistics ; urged the prohibition of the importation of foreign labor ; opposed government contracts on public work ; favored the adoption by states of an employers' liability act, and urged all labor bodies to vote only for labor legislators.

With the first convention at Pittsburg the new order seemed to take on life and vigorously prosecuted its work. At its second convention, which was held in Cleveland, O., November 21, 1882, the organization took steps to prevent the recurrence of the fate of its predecessors and issued a manifesto discountenancing political action, taking the ground that the federation had been organized as a purely industrial body and should so continue.   This manifesto is worthy of preservation in any history of the labor movement, and is as follows :

We favor this federation because it is the most natural and assimilative form of bringing the trades and labor unions together. It preserves the industrial autonomy and distinctive character of each trade and labor union, and, without doing violence to their faith or traditions, blends them all in one harmonious whole—a "federation of trades and labor unions." Such a body looks to the organization of the working classes as workers, and not as "soldiers" (in the present deprecatory sense) or politicians. It makes the qualities of a man as a worker the only test of fitness, and sets up no political or religious test of membership. It strives for the unification of all labor, not by straining at an enforced union of diverse thought and widely separated methods, not by prescribing a uniform plan of organization, regardless of their experience or interests ; not by antagonizing or destroying existing organizations, but by preserving all that is integral or good in them and by widening their scope so that each, without destroying their individual character, may act together in all that concerns them. The open trades unions, national and international, can and ought to work side by side with the Knights of Labor, and this would be the case were it not for men either overzealous or ambitious, who busy themselves in attempting the destruction of existing unions to serve their own whims and mad iconoclasm. This should cease and each should understand its proper place and work in that sphere, and if they desire to come under one head or affiliate their affairs, then let all trades and labor societies, secret or public, be represented in the Federation of Trades and Labor Unions.

During the next few years the new order had many ugly questions to deal with. At an early date considerable friction was created between the federation and the Knights of Labor, and the attempts to include socialism and the doctrines of anarchists occupied a good deal of its attention and thought.

Friction between the federation and Knights of Labor.

The order had a constitution from the start, but at its convention in Baltimore, December 16, 1887, it adopted a revised constitution, under the name of the American Federation of Labor, by which it is now known. The preamble of that constitution is as follows :

Adoption of constitutions of the American Federation of Labor.

Whereas, A struggle is going on in all the nations of the civilized world, between the oppressors and the oppressed of all countries, a struggle between the capitalist and the laborer, which grows in intensity from year to year, and will work disastrous results to the toiling millions, if they are not combined for mutual protection and benefit.

It therefore behooves the representatives of the trades and labor unions of America, in convention assembled, to adopt such measures and disseminate such principles among the mechanics and laborers of our country as will permanently unite them, to secure the recognition of the rights to which they are justly entitled.

We therefore declare ourselves in favor of the formation of a thorough federation, embracing every trade and labor organization in America, under the trades-union system of organization.

Federation not a secret order. The federation is in no sense a secret order, nor is it an order which claims the individual allegiance of members, its membership consisting of national and international trades unions or societies represented in it. It is therefore a purely democratic and representative organization. It is a federation composed of the leading **Affiliated orders.** trades unions of the country. Affiliated with it are the older and more influential bodies, such as the International Typographical Union, the Amalgamated Association of Iron and Steel Workers, the United Mine Workers, the Cigar-Makers' International Union of America, the Brotherhood of Carpenters and Joiners, etc., etc.*

---

* The register of the principal national trades unions of the United States comprises the following orders: American Agents' Association, Journeymen Bakers' National Union, Journeymen Barbers' International Union of America, Blacksmiths' National Union, Boiler-makers and Iron Ship-builders, International Brotherhood of Brass Workers, Brewery Workmen's National Union, International Bricklayers and Stonemasons' Union, International Broommakers' Union, Butchers' National Protective Association, Brotherhood of Carpenters and Joiners of America, Amalgamated Society of Carpenters and Joiners, Carriage and Wagonworkers' International Union, Cigarmakers' International Union of America, United Mine Workers of America, Coopers' International Union of North America, Orders of Railway Conductors, National Brotherhood of Electrical Workers, Brotherhood of Locomotive Engineers, Brotherhood of Stationary Engineers, United Order of Engineers, Brotherhood of Locomotive Firemen, International Furniture Workers' Union of America, Furriers' Union of United States of America and Canada, United Garment Workers of America, Glass Employees' Association of America, The United Green Glass Workers of United States and Canada, Table Knife Grind-

As the constitution of the federation provides, its object is the encouragement and formation of local trades and labor unions and the closer federation of such societies, through the organization of central trades and labor unions, in every state, and the further combination of such bodies into state, territorial, or provincial organizations, to the end that legislation in the interests of the working masses may be secured. The Knights of Labor, it will be remembered, is an order composed of local and district assemblies of its own, and while the local assemblies may and do represent different trades and callings in life, they are nevertheless bound by one uniform system of laws and regulations, their ritual and proceedings being the same throughout the country; while the

Objects of the federation.

Differs from Knights of Labor in organization.

ers' National Union, Pen and Pocket Knife Grinders and Finishers' National Union, Granite Cutters' National Union, Hat Finishers' International Association of North America, Hatmakers' International Union of North America, Silk Hatters' Association of North America, Wool Hatters' Association, Saddle and Harness Makers' National Union, International Journeymen Horseshoers of United States and Canada, Horse-collar Makers' National Union, Ironmolders' Union of North America, Sheet Iron and Cornice Workers' International Union, Amalgamated Association of Iron and Steel Workers, Spring Knife Makers' National Protective Union of America, Building Laborers' International Protective Union of North America, National Longshoremen's Association of the United States, Machinists International Union, International Association of Machinists, Musicians' Mutual League, National Patternmakers' League, Brotherhood of Painters and Decorators of America, United Piano-makers, Operative Plasterers' International Association, Journeymen Plumbers and Gas and Steam Fitters of United States, Metal Polishers, Buffers and Platers' Union of North America, Potters' National Union, United Brotherhood of Paper-makers, International Typographical Union, German-American Typographia, Quarrymen's National Union of America, Steam Railroadmen's Union, Amalgamated Association of Street Railway Employees of America, Brotherhood of Railway Shopmen, Retail Clerks' National Protective Association, National Seamen's Union of America, Lasters' Protective Union, Boot and Shoe Workers' International Union, National Federation of Silk Workers, National Cotton Mule Spinners' Association of America, Journeymen Stone Cutters, Stove Mounters' International Union, Switchmen's Mutual Aid Association, Brotherhood of Railroad Trainmen, Tack-makers' Protective Union of United States and Canada, Journeymen Tailors' Union of America, United Brotherhood of Tanners and Curriers of America, Mosaic and Encaustic Tilelayers' National Union, Railway Telegraphers, Commercial Telegraphers, National Union of Textile Workers of America, Brotherhood of Railroad Trackmen, Hardwood Furniture and Piano Varnishers' International Union of America, Hotel and Restaurant Employees' National Alliance, Elastic Web Weavers' Amalgamated Association, Machine Woodworkers' International Union of America, Woodcarvers' National Union of North America. This list does not include 1,500 local unions affiliated with the American Federation of Labor, and several thousand other unaffiliated local unions, all of which have no national head. A few of these unions are not yet formerly affiliated with the Federation of Labor, yet all are united by virtue of a common polity. See *Tribune Almanac,* January, 1895.

American Federation of Labor is a federation of various orders dissimilar in their methods of organization and having no common constitution or laws.   The General Assembly of the Knights of Labor is composed of delegates from its subordinate branches, and the annual national convention of the American Federation of Labor consists of delegates from its affiliated societies.   Each affiliated society, however, has its own government, distinct from the government of the national convention.   It has no power to order strikes, such matters being left to its affiliated societies.   It is advisory in such matters, but not conclusive in its action.   Its prestige comes both from itself and from the character and standing of some of its most important affiliations.   The order has grown, numbering over 500,000 members at the present time, and is in a flourishing condition.

The American Railway Union is the latest organization where the founders have sought to bring into one order a large body of employees.   It was organized in Chicago June 20, 1893, and now numbers, as alleged, about 150,000 members.   It differs materially from the Knights of Labor and the American Federation of Labor, so far as its integral elements are concerned.   It includes all railway employees born of white parents, and its declaration of principles adopts the motto, " In union there is strength," and declares that conversely without union weakness prevails.   The union was organized for the protection of members in all matters relating to wages and their rights as employees, and affirms that railway employees are entitled to a voice in fixing wages and in determining conditions of employment.   In its organization it provided for various departments designed to promote the welfare of the membership in a practical way and by practical methods.   Among other things, it was the design to establish an employment department, in which the name of every member out of employment could be registered; also a department of education, contemplating lectures upon subjects relating to economics, such as wages, expenses, the relations of employer to employee, strikes, their moral and financial aspects, etc. The declaration also provides for a department to promote legislation in the interest of labor and for a department of insurance.

The American Railway Union is composed of a general union consisting of a board of directors and local unions instituted under the jurisdiction of the general order. The order, while pledged to conservative methods, undertakes to protect the humblest of its members in every right ; but while it pledges itself that the rights of its members will be sacredly guarded, no intemperate demand or unreasonable propositions will be entertained. It started with the belief that all differences may be satisfactorily adjusted and harmonious relations established and maintained, and that the service may be incalculably improved, and that the necessity for strike and lockout, boycott and blacklist, which the declaration of principles declares to be alike disastrous to employer and employee and a perpetual menace to the welfare of the public, ought forever to disappear. Its general convention consists of representatives from the local unions, and it is the policy of the general union not to declare strikes of its own motion, but to refer such matters to the particular class affected. Its distinctive feature is the organization of all railway employees under one jurisdiction. It was the first attempt to accomplish this. The Knights of Labor admits all classes of wage-workers, but it cannot in any sense be considered as an organization of railway employees, nor have any great number of such employees, compared with the whole number, ever been connected

Composition of the American Railway Union.

Distinctive features.

with the Knights of Labor.   The American Federation of Labor and the Knights of Labor have many railway employees connected with them, but neither has ever attempted to secure a national, compact organization of all classes of railway employees.   There have been attempts at times to federate certain railway organizations, but at no time did the scope of the federation proposed or effected extend beyond the employees engaged in the train service.

Lack in all constitutions.   In the constitutions of all organizations, so far as they have been examined, there appears to be a great lack in this, that while they do not countenance riots, violence, intimidations, etc., they do not provide for the discipline of their members when guilty of such acts.

Extent of organized labor.   The question may be asked : "To what extent is the labor of the country organized?"   This question can be fairly well answered.   The Knights of Labor, with 150,000 members in round numbers ; the American Federation of Labor, representing 500,000, and the American Railway Union, representing 150,000, make a total membership of 800,000.   There are, according to the best estimates, probably 600,000 more connected with various local organizations not affiliated with the American Federation of Labor nor in any way connected with any of its subordinate orders, the Knights of Labor, or the American Railway Union.   This makes a total of 1,400,000 members in the labor organizations of the country, and these are to be found mostly in the manufacturing and mechanical industries.   In such industries 4,712,622 persons were employed in 1890.   The regular membership, therefore, of the labor unions of the country constitutes 29.71 per cent of the whole number engaged in manufacturing and mechanical industries.   These statements should not be accepted as accurate, because there are so many societies of workingmen and women not known as trades unions in any sense, societies which have for their object chiefly some beneficial result and those organized for social and educational purposes, taking no part in the great labor movement. They are, however, in a sense, labor organizations, but do not undertake to influence legislation or attempt the regulation of wages and conditions of employment.

Organizations not affiliated with large orders.

Labor organizations have had much to do with the development of industry, the legislation which relates to labor, and the establishment of some very deep and vital principles affecting not only labor itself, but the general welfare of the public. A brief account of labor legislation, therefore, very naturally follows the account of labor organizations.

CHAPTER XXI.

THE BASIS OF LABOR LEGISLATION.

Not of like importance in all states.

Regulation in colonial days.

THE history of labor legislation in the United States cannot well be told in a connected form. Some states have quite elaborate codes ; others have followed in some respects and have ignored all legislation in other directions, while some of our states, in which no great number of mechanical industries have been established, have not felt the necessity of placing upon their statute books any laws regulating or protecting labor. In the colonial days labor was regulated even to its price, and the constant attempt to fix the price of commodities was a part of the general system of colonial legislation, following therein the methods of the mother-country. Trade was subjected to the most stringent regulations. Since colonial days the removal of restrictions upon the interchange of commodities has been the rule, yet, curiously enough, the same period has witnessed much governmental regulation in like directions. There seems to be an antagonism in these statements, yet they are true. The establishment of new industries, the ramifications reaching in various directions, the congregation of labor in industrial centers—all these things have necessitated interference on the part of the government with individual and corporate action, while a truer knowledge of economics has convinced states that they cannot regulate price by law. So the apparent contradiction is true in fact. As one class of restrictions has been removed and the interchange of commodities made freer, other restrictions have been placed upon labor and the conditions surrounding it. But the restrictions of colonial days cannot, in a modern sense, be considered labor legislation, nor, in fact, can such restrictions be classed as labor legislation generally. Of course, away back in olden times the laws relating to apprentices, etc., were strictly labor legislation, and some English regulations were projected into the legislation of the colonies ; but the legislation which particularly belongs to the development of industry only is that which needs to be dealt with at the present time.

Such restrictions not "labor legislation" in the modern sense.

In order to give the best idea of the growth of what may be properly termed "labor legislation," its development in various directions, and its effect, the experience of a single state will suffice, and a better idea of the development of labor laws will be given the reader by such a connected history of one state's actions ; for this purpose the labor legislation of the commonwealth of Massachusetts offers the best illustration of what has been accomplished.

Growth of labor legislation.

The establishment of the factory system, the story of which is told in other chapters, brought with it some of the conditions which entered into the factory industry of England when the system became fixed there, and in 1802 England inaugurated a system of laws which has had its influence in all countries where the factory system has taken root. The English factory brought into it large numbers of laborers from agricultural sections. There were also employed many women and children. These employees were mostly of an ignorant class, but their ignorance had not attracted attention because of its diffusion. The concentration of this ignorant class in industrial centers, however, brought attention to condi-

Conditions which came with factory system.

tions and enlisted the interest and the sympathy of some of the leading English statesmen, among the rest, Sir Robert Peel, a member of Parliament and a great textile manufacturer. Through his exertions a crude factory act was passed in 1802, and from that day to the present the principles involved in that law have kept the English lawmaking power actively employed, until statutory regulations and restrictions have been extended over nearly every trade of the kingdom.

Crude English act of 1802.

When the consequences of congregated labor, working under the influence of simply natural forces, without the restrictions of positive legislation, were observed the great questions began to be asked, Has the nation any right to interfere? Shall society suffer that individuals may profit? Shall the next and succeeding generations be weakened morally and intellectually that estates may be enlarged? *

Questions which followed congregated labor.

Sir Robert Peel was the first man to ask such questions of Parliament. His efforts dealt simply with the regulation of the employment of apprentices. Under its provisions the employer was compelled to clothe his apprentice, whose work was limited to twelve hours a day. Night work was prohibited, and every apprentice was to receive daily instruction throughout the first four years of his time, and his school attendance was to be reckoned as his working time. There were many other regulations relating to instruction on Sundays, and useful sanitary clauses were contained in the law. It proved inoperative in a great measure, but the principle was established. The arguments against the enactment of Sir Robert Peel's bill have been repeated in England during all subsequent movements, and they have been heard in debate in every session of every legislature in the United

First factory act largely inoperative.

* " Reign of Law," Duke of Argyle, page 348.

States every time any proposition has been made to protect labor.

There has never been any necessity for enacting the elaborate factory code of England as it now stands on her statute books, because the conditions surrounding factory labor in this country were not those experienced in England ; yet the long hours of labor in the earlier days of the textile factories of New England came to be considered a burden upon the operatives, and so it was very natural that the first attempts to secure legislative restriction related to working hours. Conditions here not the same as in England.

A careful examination of the whole subject discloses no particular attempt to secure any enactments in this country prior to 1831. In that year a special commission appointed by Governor Lincoln of Massachusetts reported upon certain features of bankruptcy laws, proposing the abolition of imprisonment for debt, and in 1834 an act abolishing imprisonment for debt was approved. In 1836 Massachusetts specifically regulated the instruction of youths employed in manufacturing establishments, and from that date until 1863 labor legislation was practically confined to the subjects of education of children employed in factories, imprisonment for debts, liens, and various special acts incorporating mechanics' institutes, etc., etc. In 1832 the subject of regulating the hours of labor by legislation was frequently agitated and was the subject of reports by various commissions and legislative committees, but, strangely enough, no definite action was taken until 1874, when what is known as the ten-hour law was passed. This law established the hours of labor for women and for children under eighteen years of age at sixty per week. The hours of labor of children under twelve had been limited to ten per day as early as 1842, and the Honorable Horace No attempts in the United States prior to 1831. Efforts in Massachusetts.

Horace Mann's
views.
Mann, in his report on education for 1840, took very
strong ground relative to the necessity of limiting in
some way the actions of employers and of "unnatural
parents" in securing the employment of children in
textile factories. In all probability the efforts of Mr.
Mann led to the legislation of 1842, regulating the hours
of labor of children under twelve.

Reduction
of hours.
The agitation for reduction of hours of labor also led to
the ten-hour plan on a voluntary basis in most of the shipbuilding trades in the commonwealth, for they were employed on that basis in 1844, while as early as 1853 many
of the trades were working but ten hours. As stated in
an earlier chapter on the labor movement, President Van
Buren issued his well-known order April 10, 1840, "that
all public establishments will hereafter be regulated, as to
working hours, by the ten-hour system." However, it
cannot be said that the movement for the reduction of the
hours of labor progressed with any persistency, so far as
time was concerned, yet it gained strength from year to
year, fitful as it was. The thread is wanting to make a
history of labor legislation thoroughly harmonious.

Agitation of
1845.
The aggressive agitation may be said to have commenced in 1845, when petitions were introduced to the
legislature (Massachusetts is meant in this part of the history) praying for reduction of hours of labor in corporations, eleven hours being the fixed time desired in that
year ; but the legislative committee to which the petitions
were referred reported against the petitioners. The reasons given were that it would be unjust to regulate hours
for corporations, when private individuals would be free
from the operations of such a law ; and the committee
stated its belief that factory labor was no more injurious
than other kinds ; that wages would necessarily have to be
reduced if such a law was passed, and that other states

would distance Massachusetts in the markets of the world.
To use the exact words of the committee, such law would
"close the gate of every mill in the state." The question
of hours then remained dormant, so far as the legislature
was concerned, until 1850, when a legislative committee
that had been instructed to consider the subject ascertained that mills in Lowell were running twelve hours
daily, or fourteen hours more per week than English mills ;
yet the majority of the committee considered legislation
inexpedient, the minority reporting a bill establishing
eleven hours as the legal day on and after September 1,
1850, and ten hours on and after July 1, 1851.   The bill
was defeated.   Two years elapsed before the subject came
up again, when, in 1852, an attempt was made to have
ten hours made the legal day, in the absence of any special contract, and providing that children under fifteen
should not work more than ten hours.   The bill providing for this measure failed.

*Failure of legis-
lation.*

Nothing of any consequence occurred relative to attempts to secure labor legislation until 1865, when an un-
paid commission of five was appointed to collect information
and statistics in regard to the hours of labor and the condition and prospects of the industrial class.   This was
the first step in the world toward the establishment of
bureaus of statistics of labor.   Governor Bullock, in his
address for 1866, called attention to the report of this
commission.   He stated that the question of the hours of
labor was not merely one of sanitary connections, but one
which related to the social condition of the state.   He said
he had no hesitation as to the rightful authority of the
legislature over the subject, and believed that a concession
to the wishes of those who sought for a thorough inquiry
would be productive of a better understanding, not only
of the specific question itself, but of the intimate and mu-

tually beneficial relations which all classes sustained to each other. In response to this the legislature passed, in 1866, an act in relation to the employment of children in manufacturing establishments, and this act is worthy of consideration at this point. It reads as follows :

Act of 1866 relating to employment of children.

AN ACT

IN RELATION TO THE EMPLOYMENT OF CHILDREN IN MANUFACTURING ESTABLISHMENTS.

SECTION 1.   No child under the age of ten years shall be employed in any manufacturing establishment within this commonwealth, and no child between the age of ten and fourteen years shall be so employed, unless he has attended some public or private school under teachers approved by the school committee of the place in which such school is kept, at least six months during the year next preceding such employment ; nor shall such employment continue unless such child shall attend school at least six months in each and every year.

SECTION 2.   The owner, agent, or superintendent of any manufacturing establishment, who knowingly employs a child in violation of the preceding section, shall forfeit a sum not exceeding fifty dollars for each offense.

SECTION 3.   No child under the age of fourteen years shall be employed in any manufacturing establishment within this commonwealth more than eight hours in any one day.

SECTION 4.   Any parent or guardian who allows or consents to the employment of a child, in violation of the first section of this act, shall forfeit a sum not exceeding fifty dollars for each offense.

SECTION 5.   The governor, with the advice and consent of the council, may, at his discretion, instruct the constable of the commonwealth and his deputies to enforce the provisions of chapter forty-two of the General Statutes, and all other laws regulating the employment of children in manufacturing establishments, and to prosecute all violations of the same.

Massachusetts commission to make investigations.

The same legislature, that of 1866, authorized the appointment of a commission of three persons to investigate the subject of the hours of labor in its relation to the social, educational, and sanitary condition of the working classes. This language is very significant. It is found in nearly every act creating a bureau of statistics of labor in the United States.

The next year, 1867, the legislature regulated the schooling and hours of labor of children employed in manufacturing and mechanical establishments, and this act has been considered fundamental in its provisions, and it belongs to the history of labor. It is as follows : Act of 1867.

SECTION 1. No child under the age of ten years shall be employed in any manufacturing or mechanical establishment within this commonwealth, and no child between the age of ten and fifteen years shall be so employed, unless he has attended some public or private school under teachers approved by the school committee of the place in which such school is kept, at least three months during the year next preceding such employment : provided said child shall have lived within the commonwealth during the preceding six months ; nor shall such employment continue unless such child shall attend school at least three months in each and every year ; and provided that tuition of three hours per day in a public or private day school approved by the school committee of the place in which such school is kept, during a term of six months, shall be deemed the equivalent of three months' attendance at a school kept in accordance with the customary hours of tuition ; and no time less than sixty days of actual schooling shall be accounted as three months, and no time less than one hundred and twenty half-days of actual schooling shall be deemed an equivalent of three months.

SECTION 2. No child under the age of fifteen years shall be employed in any manufacturing or mechanical establishment more than sixty hours in one week.

SECTION 3. Any owner, agent, superintendent, or overseer of any manufacturing or mechanical establishment, who shall knowingly employ, or permit to be employed, any child in violation of the preceding sections, and any parent or guardian who allows or consents to such employment, shall for such offense forfeit the sum of fifty dollars.

SECTION 4.   It shall be the duty of the constable of the
commonwealth to specially detail one of his deputies to see
that the provisions of this act and all other laws regulating the
employment of children or minors in manufacturing or mechanical establishments, are complied with, and to prosecute
offenses against the same ; and he shall report annually to the
governor all proceedings under this act ; and nothing in this
section shall be so construed as to prohibit any person from pros-
ecuting such offenses.

SECTION 5.   Chapter two hundred and seventy-three of the
acts of the year eighteen hundred and sixty-six is hereby repealed : provided, this act shall not affect any proceedings now
pending.

SECTION 6.   This act shall take effect sixty days from its
passage.

It will be seen that the act of 1866 was repealed by
this last law, but it established on a broader basis the
principles announced the year before.   In 1867 a special
state constable was appointed to enforce the provisions
of the schooling act just quoted.

Repeal of act of
1866, but its
principles were
established.

CHAPTER XXII.

LABOR LEGISLATION.

THE commission on the hours of labor which had been established in 1866 and 1867 made a report, which was signed by the five commissioners, and after presenting some statistics concerning the hours of labor, they concluded that the ten-hour system was generally adopted in mechanical employments and that eleven hours was the general rule in cotton factories. After presenting the arguments, pro and con, for a reduction of the hours of labor, touching in their considerations upon such points as province of law, law of usury, overwork, hasty meals, labor-saving machinery, elevation of labor, etc., they arrived at the conclusion, regarding an eight-hour law, that it should not be adopted, and for the reasons, as they considered, that it was unsound in principle to apply one measure of time to all kinds of labor; that if adopted as a general law it would be rendered void by special contracts; that a very large proportion of the industrial interests could not observe it; and, finally, that if restricted to the employees of the state of Massachusetts it would be manifestly partial and therefore unjust; and the commission took the ground that the change desired could be better brought about by workingmen outside the legislature than by legislators themselves. The commission did recommend, however, that a change be made in the statutes concerning the schooling and work of children in manufacturing districts, in

Report of Massachusetts commission of 1866 and 1867.

Its recommendations.

such way as to give them twice the amount of schooling then required, and this, it thought, could be secured by adopting in full what is known as the "half-time sys-

tem." The commission recommended that an inspector or inspectors be appointed to attend to the enforcement of the laws then in existence, and their duty should be to look after the children put to apprenticeship or otherwise bound to service by the state, to see that they were properly cared for according to the terms of indentures ; and it made this further recommendation, that provision be made for the annual collection of reliable statistics in regard to the condition, prospects, and wants of the industrial classes.

The second commission also made a majority and a minority report, and they found that the act of 1866, which has been quoted, and which provided that no child under ten years of age should be employed in any manufacturing establishment within the commonwealth, was generally disregarded. Eleven hours was found to be the rule in factories, and the commissioners remarked that such toil each day for six days in each week was more than women and children ought to be required to perform. The commission recommended that the exist-

ing laws be so amended as to insure the execution of provisions which forbid the employment of children between the ages of ten and fourteen, and that the employment of all persons under the age of eighteen years in factories for more than ten hours each day or sixty hours per week be prohibited. It also recommended that a bureau of statistics be established for the purpose of collecting and making available all facts relating to the industrial and social interests of the commonwealth.

On the general question of the reduction of the hours of labor, however, the commissioners did not believe in lawmaking. They thought public sentiment should induce the employer to shorten the hours in certain trades, especially in the winter season. They argued strongly in favor of making the hour the unit of time in relation to labor, and suggested that it might be well to enact that no contracts for labor not made upon the hour standard should be recognized in law. The commission concluded that it could not recommend the enactment of any law restricting the hours of labor for the adult population of the commonwealth.

In 1869, following the recommendations of the commissions, the legislature of Massachusetts established the Bureau of Statistics of Labor. Between 1866 and 1869 there was no particular attention given to labor reform, so far as legislation was concerned, in any of its phases. The establishment of the Bureau of Statistics of Labor in 1869 marked the beginning of a new movement in this country. That bureau was authorized to collect, assort, systematize, and present in annual reports to the legislature, statistical details relating to all departments of labor in the commonwealth, especially in its relation to the commercial, industrial, social, educational, and sanitary condition of the laboring classes, and to the permanent prosperity of the productive industry of the commonwealth. The experience of this office has led to the establishment of bureaus in thirty-one other states and of the United States Department of Labor. An influence has grown out of the work of these bureaus and department which has extended over the world, so that the experience of American states in collecting and publishing information relating to industrial affairs has been repeated in England, France, Germany, Belgium, Italy, Russia, Austria, and other states of continental Europe, and in New Zealand and Canada.

Establishment of first bureau of statistics of labor.

The United States and 31 states now have such officers.

Foreign bureaus of statistics of labor.

Facts which the American offices have been able to lay before the public have assisted largely in securing legislation on the one hand, and of preventing injurious legislation on the other.

Ten-hour law of 1874.

The attempts to secure legislation relative to the hours of labor were renewed in 1870 with great earnestness, and each year saw a repetition of attempts to secure the enactment of a ten-hour law ; but these attempts proved unsuccessful until 1874, when the act establishing the hours of labor at sixty per week for women and for children under eighteen years of age was passed. This law provides that no minor under the age of eighteen years and no woman over that age shall be employed by any person, firm, or corporation in any manufacturing establishment more than ten hours in any one day, except when it is necessary to make repairs to prevent the stoppage or interruption of the ordinary running of the machinery. The law also provides for penalties in case of violation.

Workingmen's trains.

In 1872 Massachusetts passed a law to secure cheap morning and evening trains on railways for the use of workingmen. No other state in the Union is known to have ever made this attempt, or, at least, to have succeeded in passing such a law. The roads running trains out of Boston to the suburbs followed the requirements of the law, and ever since on some of the roads, where they have been petitioned for the trains, these workingmen's trains have been run. In England they are known as "parliamentary trains."

Ten-hour law in Massachusetts.

The legislation of 1874 establishing the ten-hour system for women and for children under eighteen years of age did not entirely quiet the ten-hour agitation, and subsequently new legislation has been secured reducing the time below sixty hours per week. The legislation of

1876 reconstructed the laws relating to the employment of children and the regulations respecting them, yet preserved the principles involved in the earlier legislation.

In 1877, following the general provisions of the English factory acts, the legislature enacted a law relating to the inspection of factories and public buildings, under the provisions of which all dangerous machinery, such as belting, shafting, gearing, drums, etc., must be securely guarded ; and it also provided that no machinery, other than steam-engines, shall be cleaned while running. The ventilation and cleanliness of factories are also secured. Hoistways, hatchways, elevators, well-holes are, under the law, to be provided with and protected by good and sufficient trap-doors, etc., and all establishments three or more stories in height are to be provided with properly constructed fire-escapes. The law also provides that all the main doors, both inside and outside, of manufacturing establishments shall open outwardly whenever inspectors shall deem it necessary, and means of extinguishing fires must be provided in all such works. The law went beyond manufacturing establishments, and provided that all churches, schoolrooms, halls, theaters, and every building used for public assemblies should have such means of egress as the factory inspectors should approve, and that all doors to main entrances in such buildings should swing outwardly. Portable seats were prohibited in the halls or passageways of buildings during any entertainment or service. These provisions have remained in the laws of the commonwealth and have been incorporated in those of many other states. Factory inspectors are provided in many of the great manufacturing states, and they have an annual convention, during which they consider means for the safety of operatives, miners, and all employees engaged in manufacturing, mining, or mechanical pursuits.

Inspection of factories.

Safety of employees.

Great good has come from their deliberations. The commonwealth of Massachusetts has constantly amended the laws to which reference has been made, perfecting them, extending them, or restricting them when their provisions were found to be inoperative.

Factory laws of Massachusetts taken as for the whole United States.

This brief history of factory labor laws in the commonwealth of Massachusetts is the history of like legislation in various other states.*

Looking out more broadly now, it is found that certain changes have been made in the common law, growing out of the conditions of modern industry, and resulting in positive legislation which has changed the old common-law rules. The chief legislation in this

Employers' liability.

respect relates to employers' liability for personal injuries to their employees. Under the common law as it exists in England and America and in the greater part of the continent of Europe, where the Roman law is the prec-

Common-law rule.

edent, it is the rule that the principal is responsible for the acts of the agent, the same as if he performed the acts himself. There are, of course, many modifications of this rule under special circumstances, but the general rule is as stated. It is curious, however, to note that this rule does not apply, generally and in broad terms, where the person injured by the agent or employee of another is also an agent or employee of the same principal; that is, in simple terms, if A is the proprietor of a factory, a works, or a railroad, and B and C are employees of A, and B is injured through the carelessness or negligence of C, he cannot recover of the proprietor A, because B and C are what are known under the common law as co-employees, and the defense of co-employment would be set up in the courts of the common law,

---

* See reports of Massachusetts Bureau of Statistics of Labor, 1876, and subsequent years.

under which it would be claimed that A was not liable to
B for any damages resulting from injuries received Illustration of the common-law rule.
through the negligence of C. This doctrine, too, is
subject to modifications and restrictions, but the broad
principle is as stated. Of course if it could be proved
by B, who was injured through the carelessness or negligence of C, that the carelessness or negligence was
really that of the proprietor A, then he could recover,
but not otherwise.

It is usually assumed, under the common-law rule,
that the employee engages in the services of a company
or of an individual employer with a full knowledge of
all the risks, dangers, and responsibilities of the peculiar
employment, and therefore assumes those risks, responsibilities, and liabilities under any dangers which exist ;
but such risks which the employee takes are considered
only the ordinary risks. The rule does not apply where When rule does not apply.
the risk is not of such a nature as to be reasonably known
and assumed, nor does it apply under circumstances
where the risk is known to the employer but not to the
employee, nor where the employer is under a positive
duty and the injury results from neglect of that positive
duty, nor, as already remarked, when the injury is in-
curred through the negligence of the employer himself,
except, in the latter case, where the employee may have
contributed to the negligence.

This whole subject of the liability of employers for injuries to their employees is an exceedingly interesting
one, and offers very many opportunities for fine legal
distinctions and the application of what might be called
the philosophy of law. The reader must bear in mind
that while the rules of the common law are as have
been broadly stated, modifications and restrictions exist.
The one which is of interest at this point is that which

prevents the employee from recovering as against the employer when the employee is injured through the negligence or carelessness of a co-employee. This latter rule is a growth of recent years, and is what is ordinarily denominated "judge-made law"; that is, it is the result of the rulings of courts in various places, and not the result of statutory provision. It has grown up from the olden time and been projected into new conditions never contemplated when the rule was of value. The old rule has a good deal of reason in it under certain restricted circumstances, but when broadly applied it appears to many to be so inconsistent, and even ridiculous, that legislatures are beginning to restrict the common law by positive statutes.

"Judge-made law."

An illustration of how the old rule would work will, perhaps, best emphasize its absurdity. A man under former systems of industry, before the great factory system and the congregation of labor generally came into vogue—in fact, before the development of industries under our present methods—in working alongside of his fellow employee and all the employees working with the employer himself, might not reasonably claim damages for any injury received during the co-employment ; but to apply this rule when a brakeman on a railroad line, it may be hundreds of miles in length, by the negligence of a switchman whom the brakeman never saw, whose character he did not know when he entered the service, and to whose negligence the brakeman could not possibly have contributed, receives serious personal injury, appears, to the ordinary mind, the very height of absurdity. Under the old rule the brakeman cannot, under the circumstances just described, recover any damages from the railroad corporation, because the brakeman and the switchman are considered as co-employees of the same

How it works on a railroad.

principal. So in a factory, the attendant of a loom may be quietly and industriously attending to her business as In a factory. a weaver, and through the negligence or carelessness or drunkenness of one who attends the engine in the engine-house a thousand feet away, loses an arm ; under these circumstances the weaver cannot recover damages from the proprietor or owners of the factory under the common-law rule.

These illustrations show how thoroughly absurd that rule appears to many men and to many most excellent lawyers and judges. In order to remedy the difficulty recourse has been had to statutory provisions, by which the rule is abrogated or its application limited. The first attempt at such limitation was by the Parliament of Great Britain. After long agitation, investigations by parliamentary committees, and discussions in Parliament, a law Modification of common-law rule in England. in great measure abrogating the common-law rule was enacted in 1880 ; and that act called the attention of employers and employees everywhere to the inconsistencies of the common law. Many corporations resisted the enactment of laws which would tend, as they claimed, to the great increase of expenses of running their works or roads, and much fear was expressed on the passage of the bill through Parliament that the results would be disastrous to industry and prevent dividends on the stock of railroads. The experience of the English law, however, has not substantiated such fears, while one of the very best effects of the law has been to induce greater care in the selection of agents. It may be that this is the very greatest benefit that can be derived from such a statute, for the careful administration of the railroad service is one of the most vital features of railroad management, so far as the public is concerned ; and if the statutory limitation of the common law stimulates the selection of the very best skill in the employment of men, it certainly justifies its enactment. It is true that the financial disasters predicted have not occurred.

All the agitation in England relative to the subject has reappeared in the United States. Labor organizations demand it in their platforms and declarations of principles, learned writers have insisted upon the justice of it, and judges have indorsed it. The first law, however, following in any great degree the English legislation was quietly passed by the Alabama legislature February 12, 1885. The Massachusetts legislature, after several years of consideration and a very careful investigation of the law and facts by the Bureau of Statistics of Labor, passed an act to extend and regulate the liability of employers to make compensation for personal injuries suffered by employees in their service. This act was passed in 1887. These two states are the only states that have practically reënacted the English law of 1880. Many other states have, in some way and to some extent, weakened the force of the common-law rule. California, Colorado, Dakota, Florida, Georgia, Iowa, Kansas, Minnesota, Montana, Wisconsin, Wyoming, Illinois, Indiana, Kentucky, Texas, and it may be others, have in some way limited the old common-law rule.*

Modification in the United States.

Alabama.

Massachusetts.

Action in other states.

* The whole question of employers' liability is fully discussed in the report of the Massachusetts Bureau of Statistics of Labor for 1883 ; in the Eleventh Annual Report of the Bureau of Statistics of Labor and Industries of New Jersey, 1888 ; in the Fifth Annual Report of the United States Commissioner of Labor, 1889.

CHAPTER XXIII.

LABOR LEGISLATION (*Concluded*).

THERE has been a great change in the doctrine of conspiracy as applied to the efforts of workingmen to secure higher wages or to resist reduction. Prior to 1824 it was conspiracy and felony in England for laborers to unite for purposes which are now regarded in that country as desirable, not only for the safety of government but for the safety of capital and for the protection of the rights of workingmen.

While the doctrine of conspiracy, as derived from the English common law and applied in this country as modified by statute, has not, perhaps, undergone any radical changes, it is construed nevertheless much more liberally now than formerly. The trial of the journeymen boot and shoemakers of Philadelphia in 1806 furnishes a striking example. At that trial the recorder broadly asserted that "a combination of workmen to raise their wages may be considered in a twofold point of view ; one is to benefit themselves, the other is to injure those who do not join their society. The rule of law condemns *both*." *Changes in conspiracy laws.*

The doctrine has been construed and applied in rather a sporadic way as far back as 1821, when Judge Gibson of Pennsylvania expressed views more in accordance with the construction to-day than many judges who succeeded him. Judge Savage, in New York, in delivering an opinion, cited instances in cases supporting the *Sporadic construction in the past.*

statements that a confederacy or mutual agreement for the purpose of raising wages was an indictable offense at common law.

It is probably true that the doctrine of conspiracy was *Law of conspiracy not well understood.* so seldom invoked in the past that it was only imperfectly understood and that many belonging to the legal profession did not fully appreciate it. So, in view of the few precedents and adjudications, the decision in each individual case depended much, perhaps entirely, on the research and learning of the judge before whom the trial was made. As cases have multiplied in this country, however, the learning on the subject has become more widely known ; but the question of what combinations of workmen or employers may or may not do without subjecting themselves to indictment for conspiracy is still somewhat obscure, especially in those states in which the common law unmodified by statute still remains in force. Without modification by statute judges have modified its application, and so to-day a combination of workingmen for the purpose of united action in securing an increase of wages or for preventing a decrease is not considered conspiracy, nor the persons indictable as conspirators.

Perhaps as good an illustration of the present construc-*Present construction as illustrated in New York.* tion of the doctrine of conspiracy, as limited by statute, as can be given is contained in the decision of Judge Barrett of the Court of Oyer and Terminer of the city of New York*, delivered September 29, 1887, when certain members of the executive committee of one of the district assemblies of the Knights of Labor were on trial for alleged unlawful interference with employees of a manufacturer of that city. Judge Barrett states that the law, as expressed in the existing statute, permits orderly and peaceable coöperation, and, to render coöperation effective,

---

* Affirmed by Court of Appeals.

permits, logically, a resort to all lawful means of enforcement. He said that peaceable withdrawal from employment, commonly called a strike, however extensive, is
plainly such an incident. Violence, of course, is not,
nor is a threat of violence, whether direct or as implied
in a disorderly and turbulent strike ; and Judge Brady,
in delivering the opinion of the Supreme Court, to which
the case just cited had been appealed, stated that ''no
doubt exists of the right of workmen to seek by all possible means an increase of wages, and all meetings and
combinations having that object in view, which are not
distinguished by violence or threats, and are unlawful
therefore, cannot be reasonably condemned or justly interfered with.''

This fairly represents the attitude of the courts on the
doctrine of conspiracy as applied to combinations of work- Attitude ot
ingmen for lawful purposes. It is only recently, how- courts.
ever, that legislation in this country has been directed
toward strikes, boycotts, and conspiracies relating to the
raising of wages, etc. In many of the states where
the common law of England was in force men were
tried for, and often convicted of, conspiracy for attempts to coerce their employers by resorting to
strikes and their concomitants—the boycotting of non-
union men and those who employed them. In recent Of legislatures.
years a number of states and territories have endeavored
to make plain by statute how far a combination by employees to raise or maintain the rate of wages, or for kin-
dred purposes, is to be protected ; and, on the other
hand, what acts by such combinations or by individuals
will subject the perpetrators to punishment. Some states,
however, have made no such efforts, but of them it is
true that the common law on the subject of conspiracy
appears to be still in force and that in some others where

the common-law rule obtains the absence of statutory enactments on the subject may be accounted for by the comparative rarity of serious strikes or boycotts. This

Strikes, etc., do
not occur in
agricultural
communities.

is especially true in localities where agriculture is the chief pursuit of the people and where the mechanical, manufacturing, and mining interests are of little or no importance. In such communities strikes, boycotts, and conspiracies relating to wages are almost unknown.

Intimidation, violence, threats, and all such efforts

Peaceable or-
ganization not
conspiracy.

must accompany combinations now in most of the states in order to constitute a case of conspiracy under the law. Peaceable organization for peaceable and lawful purposes is no longer conspiracy. It is a piece of wisdom, therefore, that so many of the states have taken the pains to define by statute what shall constitute conspiracy.

In the early days of the development of mechanical in-

Truck system.

dustries, the truck system was introduced in different parts of the country east and west. It never had any existence in the South until since the war. By the truck system is meant the payment of wages in goods. Great manufacturing concerns, removed somewhat from trade centers, established stores where their employees could be supplied with the necessaries of life. The prime motive in the establishment of such stores was undoubtedly to accommodate the employees, because goods were brought directly to their own locality and they could get them easily and avoid great inconvenience ; but the habit soon grew of allowing employees to run an account at such stores, the consequence being that on settlement days many found that their wages had all been taken to pay the account, and that little or nothing was coming to

Evils of truck
system.

them. The temptation in this direction was twofold : First, the employees improvidently bought many things which they would not have purchased had they been obliged to pay in cash at the time of the purchase, and they thus exhausted their month's wages. Second, the "Pluck-me stores." temptation to the employer to charge exorbitant prices and thus secure a double profit—first, through the labor, and secondly, through the trade of his employees—grew to an alarming extent. The result was that these stores came to be known as "pluck-me stores," because the employee found himself plucked by trading at them.

To avoid the evils resulting from this truck system laws have been passed in many states making it unlawful for an employer to pay wages in goods. The legislation Laws against truck system. has not been entirely successful,* but it has been very beneficial. The system still exists in mining regions far from public stores. Could company stores be run in the interest of the purchasers, as they have been many times, much benefit would be secured. In one manufacturing town in Connecticut a great corporation established a general store for the supply of its people. It made very rigid rules fixing the price of all things to be sold, charging six per cent in advance of cost. The corporation had the advantage of being able to buy at first hands and for cash, and therefore at the lowest possible market prices. It invariably sold the goods at an advance of six per cent on such cost, out of which advance it paid all the expenses of the store. It went further, and provided that all profit beyond such expenses out of the six per cent advance on cost should be used in the establishment and maintenance of a library for the sole use of its operatives. Such a truck system, of course, would be beneficial, but the difficulties, obstacles, and temptations connected with the Instance of benefits. whole system render it obnoxious to workingmen everywhere, and law has stepped in to remove the offense.

Another very important branch of labor legislation

* In Illinois it has been declared unconstitutional.

Industrial con-
ciliation and
arbitration. which has been common to many states relates to industrial arbitration. To avoid labor difficulties, such as
strikes, lockouts, and boycotts, many devices have been
suggested, but no one of them has as yet proved effectual.
It is probably impossible to devise any measure which
will thoroughly prevent strikes ; and it may be that in the
progress of civilization such complete prevention would
not be desirable, but any measure which will prove effectual in reducing the number of controversies and in reducing their severity must commend itself to the minds of
all who believe in law and order and in the rights of men.

Industrial conciliation means the attempt on the part
of some properly constituted body, either through the
choice of the parties involved or of the lawmaking power,
to secure a settlement of grievances preferred by either
party, employer or employee, and thus prevent an out-
break or an open declaration of industrial war. Conciliation follows the Pauline plan of adjusting a difficulty
arising between two members of a church. It is there-
Founded on
highest prin-
ciples of ethics
and religion. fore founded on the very highest principles of religion and
ethics, and wherever attempted succeeds in large meas-
ure. Arbitration can be operative only after the issue
is defined between employer and employee ; that is,
after the difficulty is practically on. Conciliation seeks
to prevent open war : arbitration seeks to adjust difficulties after war is declared.

In France the *Conseils de Prud'hommes*, which have
been in existence for many years, endeavor to conciliate
employers and employees whenever difficulties arise, and
their work has been most beneficial. In England there
are voluntary boards of conciliation and arbitration created by mutual consent, and in those trades where they
have been created and efforts have been seriously made
to utilize them very satisfactory results have been secured.

In this country conciliation has not come into vogue to any great extent until recently, but legislatures have seen the necessity of creating state boards of arbitration, in order that such boards might be ready at any time either to offer their services or to contribute them on invitation. Fifteen states in the Union have enacted laws looking to the arbitration of labor troubles. So far, however, in only three or four states, notably New York, New Jersey, and Massachusetts, have boards of arbitration accomplished much.

Fifteen states have laws relating to arbitration.

The United States government, by an act approved by the president October 1, 1888, committed itself to the principle of industrial arbitration on interstate railroads ; that is, railroad lines extending from one state to another and whose traffic is known under the law as interstate commerce. Of course, the federal government has no right to legislate relative to the affairs of a state in such matters, but under the constitution it has a right to regulate commerce between the states, and therefore to make the attempt to prevent controversies arising on account of such commerce which in any way interfere with the peace and the prosperity of the inhabitants of different states.

Federal laws.

Arbitration is, of course, ethical, while its broad results may be economical in bearing. It is ethical because under it the relations of man to man and of man to society are involved. There are two kinds of arbitration, known as voluntary and compulsory arbitration. Voluntary arbitration takes place when employer and employee of their own motion consent to leave the details of their difficulties to some properly constituted board, which board may be the result of their own choice or one established by law. To secure the benefits of voluntary arbitration requires a very high moral stand-

Ethical basis of arbitration.

Voluntary arbitration.

ard, because there must be, in order to induce men to
resort to it, a moral recognition of the rights of others.
Many difficulties have been settled in this country and
abroad by resort to voluntary arbitration.

**Boards may
tender services.**
Another feature of this subject lies in the provision of
law in some states for the board of arbitration to tender
its services to the contending parties.   These services
may be accepted or rejected, but, in most of the cases,
when rejected the board still has the right to investigate
all the conditions leading to the difficulties and those
surrounding it after the break has occurred.   In this
way the public is informed of the circumstances and conditions surrounding the whole matter.   Much good comes
from this, because if the public can be made aware
promptly of the causes of a great strike and can ascertain from official sources just who is responsible for dis-
turbing the peace by inaugurating a great strike or lockout, sympathy is turned in the proper direction and public opinion, a very powerful judge, settles the matter.

**Compulsory
arbitration.**
On the other hand, compulsory arbitration, which appears to be a contradiction of terms, implies the forcing
of parties to submit their affairs to a court of arbitration.
To be effective such court must have all the rights, powers,
and privileges of a court of law or equity ; that is
to say, on the petition or complaint of one of the parties to a labor controversy the court must have the right
to issue its process summoning the other party into court
to show cause why the action sought by the petitioner or
complainant should not be taken.   Furthermore, the
court would have the right, under any system of compulsory arbitration, to consider all the matters pertaining
to the difficulty, to come to a conclusion thereon, and to
enter its judgment ; and after entering its judgment it
would have the right to enforce it, the same as any court

would have the right to enforce its judgment in a suit. The difficulties, complications, and embarrassments resulting from such a course of procedure would cause more injury to society than the progress of the controversy which one of the parties sought to have settled arbitrarily. There may be some modifications of the doctrine of compulsory arbitration applicable to great corporations which have a quasi-public function, like railroads, but so far no way by which the rule can be applied advantageously has been clearly seen.

Difficulties of compulsory arbitration.

The time is rapidly coming when the community will assert its rights to perpetual peace, and so bring to bear upon all parties engaged in industry a great moral influence which will secure all the benefits of voluntary arbitration and render the resort to any compulsory measures unnecessary. Such time will come only when the power of moral forces is recognized as essential in the development and evolution of economic forces.

There are many other directions in which legislation has aided in establishing the status of the wage-earner, but the illustrations given are sufficient to show intelligently the wide range and the deep significance of all such enactments and the tendency to the passage of restrictive laws under the modern system of industry, while the old restrictive laws of the colonial days have entirely or nearly passed out of existence.

Looking broadly now to the labor legislation as it has occurred in this country, it may be well to sum up its general features. Such legislation has fixed the hours of labor for women and certain minors in manufacturing establishments ; it has adjusted the contracts of labor ; it has protected employees by insisting that all dangerous machinery, hoistways, etc., shall be guarded ; it has prescribed that fire-escapes in factories and tenement

Summary of
labor legis-
lation.

houses shall be erected ; it has prohibited unsafe elevators ; it has created boards of factory inspectors, whose powers and duties have added much to the health and safety of operatives ; it has in many instances provided for weekly payments, not only by municipalities, but by corporations ; it has guarded the health of women employed in manufacturing, mechanical, and mercantile establishments by requiring seats for their use ; it has regulated the employment of prisoners ; protected the employment of children ; exempted the wages of wife and minor children from attachment ; established bureaus of statistics of labor ; provided for the ventilation of factories and workshops ; established industrial schools and evening schools ; provided special transportation by railroads for workingmen ; modified the common-law rules relative to the liability of employers for injuries to their employees ; fixed the compensation of railroad corporations for negligently causing the death of employees, and has provided for their protection against accident and death. Under it factory doors cannot be locked during working hours ; it has established boards of arbitration ; it has regulated, with more or less success, the pernicious custom of truck stores, and it has prohibited the employment of women and minors in manufacturing establishments between the hours of ten o'clock at night and six o'clock in the morning. All these provisions are not found in the statutes of all the states, but they are so general as to entitle them to be considered in the body of labor legislation.*

* Cf. Labor Laws of Massachusetts, Twenty-first Annual Report of the Massachusetts Bureau of Statistics of Labor.

CHAPTER XXIV.

LABOR CONTROVERSIES.

A STRIKE occurs when the employees of an establish- Strikes.
ment refuse to work unless the management complies
with some demand made upon it. A lockout occurs Lockouts.
when the management refuses to allow the employees to
work unless they will work under some condition dictated
by the management and which is opposed by the workmen. In effect, strikes and lockouts are practically the
same thing, the disturbances originating with one side
or the other in the case and taking their name accordingly. The strike is not a method belonging exclusively
to the modern system of industry, for it has occurred at
various times in the history of the world, wherever the
relation of employer and employee has existed. In
ancient times the strike was usually a practical insurrection or rebellion, during which many lives were lost and
sometimes governments overthrown.* Occasionally,
along through the course of history, labor riots and re-
volts are chronicled. As a general method, however, for
enforcing demands and for obtaining redress of real or
fancied grievances the strike has only recently assumed
much importance, and only isolated cases are reported in
our own country before the dawn of the present century.
The first recourse to the strike in this country occurred
in 1741, when a combined strike of journeymen bakers First strike in
occurred in New York City. An information was filed States.

the United

---

* For an account of such insurrections see " The Ancient Lowly," by C. Os-
borne Ward. Washington, D. C., 1891.

against the strikers for conspiracy not to bake until their wages were raised. On this they were tried and convicted, but so far as anything can be learned it does not appear that any sentence was ever passed. This strike may have occurred in 1740, but reference to it gives the year 1741 as that in which the information was preferred against the bakers.*

"Turnout" in Philadelphia in 1796.

There was an association of journeymen shoemakers in Philadelphia as early as 1792, and in May, 1796, a strike, or "turnout," was ordered by that organization for the purpose of securing an increase of wages, in which the strikers were successful. Another turnout was ordered by the shoemakers of Philadelphia in 1798. This strike was also for an increase of wages, and was successful. The next year (1799) the shoemakers turned out to resist a movement made by the master cordwainers of Philadelphia for a reduction of wages. The strike lasted about ten weeks and was only partially successful.

These four strikes are the only ones to which any reference can be found that occurred in this country prior to the present century. The condition of industry generally during the colonial days was not conducive to strikes. The factory system had not taken deep root, masters and men worked together, and so there was no opportunity for concerted action. Where two or three, or perhaps half a dozen, men were employed in one shop they were in such close relations to the employer and on such neighborly and domestic terms with him that differences, when occurring, were mutually adjusted after an exchange of views ; so there was no soil for the growth of the strike.

First notable strike in this century.

The first notable strike in this century occurred in November, 1803, in the city of New York, and is commonly

---

* See "Trial of the Journeymen Cordwainers of the City of New York." New York, 1810.

known as the "Sailors' strike." This strike has been generally considered the first one occurring in the United States, but recent investigations have developed those just mentioned. The sailors in New York at the time named (November, 1803) had been receiving ten dollars per month. They demanded an increase to fourteen dollars. In carrying out their purpose they formed in a body, marched through the city, and compelled other seamen who were employed at the old rates to leave their ships and join the strike. The strikers were pursued and dispersed by the constables, who arrested their leader and lodged him in jail, the strike thus terminating unsuccessfully.* .

"Sailors' strike" not the first.

In 1805 the Journeymen Shoemakers' Association of Philadelphia again turned out for an increase of wages. The demands ranged from twenty-five to seventy-five cents per pair increase. This strike lasted six or seven weeks, and was unsuccessful. The strikers were tried for conspiracy, the result of the trial being published in a pamphlet which appeared in 1806.†

Strike in 1805 at Philadelphia.

In 1809 a strike among the cordwainers occurred in the city of New York. The proprietors quietly took their work to other shops, and by this stratagem defeated the strikers ; but the action being discovered, a general turnout was ordered by the Journeymen Cordwainers' Association against all the master workmen of the city, nearly two hundred men being engaged in the strike. This general turnout was in November, 1809. At that time a stoppage of work in one shop by the journeymen

In 1809 at New York.

---

* Report of the Bureau of Statistics of New Jersey, 1885. See also J. B. McMaster : " History of the People of the United States," Vol. II. Mr. McMaster states that the strike occurred in October, 1802. It is believed, however, that the date given in the text is the correct one.

† Lloyd : " Trial of the Boot and Shoemakers of Philadelphia." The report of this famous trial can be found in the United States Supreme Court Library.

was called a "strike"; a general stoppage in all shops in a trade was known as a "general turnout." A member of a journeymen's association who did not keep his obligations to the organization was denominated a "scab."*

In 1815 at Pittsburg.

In 1815 some of the journeymen cordwainers of Pittsburg, Pa., were tried for conspiracy on account of their connection with a strike, and were convicted.

In 1817 at Medford, Mass.

In 1817 a peculiar labor difficulty occurred at Medford, Mass. Thacher Magoun, a shipbuilder of that town, determined to abolish the grog privilege customary at that time. Mr. Magoun gave notice to his people that no liquor should be used in his shipyard, and the words "*No rum!* NO RUM!" were written on the clapboards of the workshop and on the timbers in the yard. Some of Mr. Magoun's men refused to work, but they finally surrendered, and a ship was built without the use of liquor in any form.†

From 1821 to 1834.

The period from 1821 to 1834 witnessed several strikes, but rarely more than one or two in each year. These strikes occurred among the compositors, hatters, ship carpenters and calkers, journeymen tailors, laborers on the Chesapeake and Ohio Canal, the building trades, factory workers, shoemakers, and others. One of the most notable of these, for its influence upon succeeding labor movements, occurred in 1834, in the city of Lynn, Mass. During the latter part of the preceding year the female shoebinders of that town began to agitate the question of an increase of wages. The women engaged in this work usually took the material to their homes. The manufacturers were unwilling to increase the prices paid; so a meeting for consultation was held by more

---

* The People *vs.* Melvin and others, Wheeler's "Criminal Cases," Vol. II.

† McNeill: "The Labor Movement."

than one thousand binders. This was January 1, 1834. The binders resolved to take out no more work unless the increase was granted. The employers, however, steadily refused to accede to the demands, and finding no difficulty in having their work done in neighboring towns at their own prices, the strike, after three or four weeks, came to an unsuccessful termination.

In February of the same year a disturbance of short duration occurred at Lowell, Mass., among the female factory operatives. Their strike was to prevent a reduction of wages.

During the year 1835 there was a large number of strikes throughout the country, instigated by both men and women. The number of strikes by employees who desired some concessions regarding their wages or were otherwise dissatisfied with the conditions under which they were working had at this time become so numerous as to call forth remonstrant comments from the public press, the *New York Daily Advertiser* of June 6, 1835, declaring that "strikes are all the fashion," and, further, "It is an excellent time for the journeymen to come from the country to this city." From that period (1835) to the present time strikes have been common, often expensive, and sometimes destructive of much property.

Increase of strikes after 1835.

A detailed account of strikes is not necessary to illustrate the general tendency. As a rule, they have been for an increase or against a reduction of wages. An investigation conducted by the United States Department of Labor of all strikes occurring in the country from 1881 to 1886, inclusive (six years), shows that during that period 3,902 strikes occurred, affecting 22,304 establishments, the whole number of employees striking and involved in these disturbances being 1,323,203. In the year 1880, as shown by Mr. Joseph D. Weeks, in his excellent

Strikes from 1880 to 1887.

report to the United States census for that year, there were
610 strikes, the estimated number of establishments involved being 3,477.   In 1887, the year after the investigation by the United States Department of Labor referred to, according to information gathered from trade
papers, etc., there were 853 strikes, the number of
establishments involved being estimated at 4,862.

Taking these accounts for the years from 1880 to 1887,
we find that in the first year named 3,477 establishments
were affected by strikes, and that the number dropped
in 1881 to 2,928, and to a still lower point in 1882, when
the whole number of establishments affected was but
2,105.   In 1883 the number rose again, coming very
near that of 1881, or 2,759.   In 1884 there was a decrease, the number being 2,367, while in 1885 the number of establishments subjected to strikes was smaller
than in any of the years named except 1882, it being in
1885 2,284.   Eighteen hundred and eighty-six, however, was a prolific year, the whole number of establishments affected by strikes being 9,861.   The next year
there was a decrease to about 5,000.   The best information shows that the year 1886 was a turning-point for
several years.   The figures are not at hand, but the best
estimates and calculations made from various reports indicate that the number of establishments affected by
strikes constantly decreased until within two years, during which time they have been rapidly on the increase.
Official investigations now going on will determine the
number.   During the period from 1881 to 1886 the number of establishments involved, either by strikes or lockouts, was highest in the states of New York, Pennsylvania, Massachusetts, Ohio, and Illinois, these five states
contributing nearly 75 per cent of all the establishments
in the country affected by strikes and nearly 89.5 per

cent of all the establishments in the country affected by lockouts. These five states, at the period named, contained nearly 50 per cent of all the manufacturing establishments and employed 58 per cent of all the capital invested in the mechanical industries of the United States.

Some of the most noted strikes which have occurred in this country have had great influence upon economic affairs, in the organization of laborers, in calling attention to the relations of employers and employees, and in various other directions. During the period from 1881 to 1886, as has been stated, 1,323,203 employees were involved. Of this number 88.42 per cent were males and 11.58 per cent females. The number of successful strikes during that period was 46.52 per cent, while 39.95 per cent failed, and 13.47 per cent succeeded partially. A large number of the strikes and lockouts occurring during the years named were by organizations, the percentage being 82.24 of the whole. The causes for which strikes were undertaken were mostly for an increase or against a reduction of wages, four leading causes covering over 77 per cent of them all. These were for increase of wages, for reduction of hours, against reduction of wages, and for increase of wages and reduction of hours.

Influence of noted strikes.

Causes of majority of strikes.

The losses in strikes are enormous, as shown by the record of those to which reference has been made, when the strikers alone lost $51,814,723. The loss to employees through lockouts for the same time was $8,157,-717, making a total wage loss of nearly $60,000,000; the employers' losses for the same strikes and lockouts were over $34,000,000—a series of disturbances representing a loss of over $94,000,000 in a brief period of six years. No statement could more thoroughly exhibit the wastefulness of a method than do these figures. But

Losses by strikes.

General losses
not ascertain-
able.

no facts can ever be ascertained and no estimate formed concerning the losses to individuals indirectly related to establishments in which strikes or lockouts have occurred. Their indirect effect on the great commercial interests of the country can be referred to only in general terms.

CHAPTER XXV.

HISTORIC STRIKES.

SINCE 1877 some historic strikes have occurred—strikes from which influences have been felt in various directions and far beyond the parties engaged in the particular controversies.

The first of these great historic strikes occurred in 1877, although many very severe strikes had taken place prior to that year. The great railroad strikes of 1877 began on the Baltimore and Ohio Railroad at Martinsburgh, W. Va., the immediate cause of the first strike being a ten per cent reduction in the wages of all employees. This, however, was but one of many grievances. The wages, already low, were made yet lower by irregular employment. Men with families were permitted to work only three or four days per week, and two or three days each week they were forced to spend away from home, at their own expense, often being obliged to pay one dollar per day for board at the company's hotel, leaving them but little money for domestic use. The wages, payable monthly, were often retained two, three, or even four months. The tonnage of trains was increased, and the men were paid only for the number of miles run, irrespective of the time consumed in running. In most instances the strike affected only the freight trains. There was rioting, destruction of property, and loss of life at Martinsburgh, Baltimore, and various places in Pennsylvania. The state militia at Martinsburgh and

Railroad strikes of 1877.

On the Baltimore and Ohio.

Causes.

301

Pittsburg, sympathizing with the strikers, affiliated with them and refused to fire upon them.   The United States troops were promptly ordered from the eastern garrisons, and on their appearance the mobs fled.   In Cincinnati, Toledo, and St. Louis mobs of roughs and tramps collected and succeeded in closing most of the shops, factories, and rolling-mills in those cities.   In Chicago the communists made formidable demonstrations.   In those places, and in Syracuse, Buffalo, West Albany, and Hornellsville, N. Y., the mobs were dispersed by the state militia without violence or destruction of property.

The great strike at Pittsburg in 1877 on the Pennsylvania.

The Pennsylvania Railroad Company also had a memorable strike accompanied by riots and much violence and destruction of property.   Some time after the panic of 1873 this road reduced the wages of its employees ten per cent, and on account of the general decline in business made another reduction of ten per cent in June, 1877.   The employees of the different roads having their *termini* at Pittsburg commenced agitating the question of a strike on account of these reductions, which agitation resulted in the formation of a "Trainmen's Union."   Through the agency of this organization a

Events leading to it.

general strike was arranged to take place at noon on June 27, 1877, on the Pennsylvania Railroad, the Pittsburg, Fort Wayne and Chicago Railroad, the Allegheny Valley Railroad, the Pan Handle Railroad, and the branches of these roads.   The movements of the general strike were to be directed from Allegheny City.   On the 24th of June about forty members of the union were sent out to notify others on the different roads of the time when the strike was to take place, and on the night of June 25, at a meeting of the members of the union of the Pan Handle division, it was developed that a portion of them were dissatisfied with the proposed strike, and also that some member or members had divulged the plans of the union to the railroad authorities. In view of these facts, measures were at once taken to prevent the strike, word being sent to all points possible to be reached in the short time left.

The members of the union felt that they had met with defeat, and this left them very much dissatisfied. But the great strike of July 19, at Pittsburg, was not a *Special cause.* strike of the Trainmen's Union, nor did this union, as an organization, have anything to do with either that strike or the one of July 16, on the Baltimore and Ohio Railroad, at Martinsburgh. Early in July the Pennsylvania Railroad issued an order that all freight trains from Pittsburg east to Derry should be run as "double-headers," the order to take effect July 19. A "double-header" consists of thirty-four cars, and is hauled by two engines, a plan which had the effect of enabling the company to dispense with the services of one half of their freight conductors, brakemen, and flagmen on the Pittsburg division of the road. On the morning of July 19 several early trains left Pittsburg as "double-headers," but when the time arrived for the 8:40 a. m. train to leave, the men, consisting of two brakemen and one flagman, refused to go out on a "double-header," and the train *Objection to "double-headers."* did not leave the yard. The dispatcher made up two crews from the yardmen, as none of the regular trainmen would take their places, but the strikers threw coupling-pins, etc., at these men as they were endeavoring to make up the train, and so they were forced to desist. The strikers numbered only twenty or twenty-five men, but they took possession of the switches over which the trains would have to move, and refused to let any trains pass out. Their numbers increased gradually, men who came in on freight trains and others being induced to join the strikers.   By midnight of the 19th the crowd of strikers and sympathizers had increased to several hundreds.

The story of this great strike is a long one.   The sheriff of the county could not persuade the crowd to disperse, and the governor of the state of Pennsylvania was called upon for troops, the military authorities sending three regiments of infantry and a battery of artillery to Pittsburg.   The strikers increased in number, mobs gathered, and it is estimated that on the 20th there were four or five thousand men in the vicinity of the station.   Here were all the elements for a disastrous experience.   On the 21st rioting began, and while the troops were getting into position many of the guns of the militia were seized and bayonets twisted off.   The troops made no impression upon the crowd.   The mob grew more noisy, defiant, and boisterous, and stones and other missiles were thrown at the troops.   Pistol shots were fired by the crowd and the troops fired on the mob.   Several persons were killed and wounded, inquests being held on twenty-two persons in all, most of whom were killed by the soldiers at Twenty-eighth Street.   The firing, when it became regular, dispersed the crowd, which fled in all directions and left the troops in possession of the ground. But after a few hours, all attempts to move trains being abandoned and the troops needing rest and food, the mob came together again, and having obtained arms by breaking into two or three gun stores, began, soon after dark, to fire upon the roundhouse and machine-shops and in at the windows at any soldiers who might be inside, and later, fire was set to cars on the adjoining tracks, the mob running the burning cars down the track nearest the roundhouse, to set it on fire, if possible.

On the morning of the 22d of July the mob obtained

Rioting and violence.

Attempts to move trains abandoned.

possession of a field-piece and was ready to fire on the roundhouse, but the military officers notified the strikers that if they attempted to discharge the piece they would be fired upon in turn. They paid no attention to the warning, and when one of them was seen with the lanyard in his hand, ready to discharge the cannon, they were fired upon by the troops, and several of the mob fell, the rest dispersing. Later Gatling guns were brought into action, and the sight of them scattered the mob. These attacks and counter attacks, the gathering and dispersing of the mob, and the firing of trains were kept up until Monday, the 22d, as stated, when two regiments were marched through the principal streets of the city of Pittsburg for the purpose of overawing any disposition toward riotous conduct which might still exist. A citizens' committee was also organized during the previous Sunday, and this committee exerted considerable influence in quelling disturbances. Nevertheless, cars were set on fire and attempts were made to fire the station ; but members of the citizens' safety committee interfered and put a stop to the destruction. This was about the last attempt at violence at Pittsburg, although it was several days before order was fully restored.

From the very beginning of the strike the strikers had the active sympathy of a vast proportion of the people of Pittsburg. About 1,600 cars (mostly freight), including passenger and baggage cars, with such of their contents as were not carried away by thieves, 126 locomotives, and all the shops' materials and buildings, except one or two small ones, of the railroad company, from above Twenty-eighth Street to the union station, were burned on Saturday night and Sunday. The tracks from the union station, out to and beyond Twenty-

Use of Gatling guns.

Citizens' committee.

Damages resulting from strike.

eighth Street, were nearly all ruined by fire, the rails being warped and twisted and the ties burned.   It has been estimated by competent persons that the damage, including loss of property and loss of business consequent upon its interruption, which was inflicted by the mob at

Loss of railroad company.

Pittsburg amounted to $5,000,000.   The actual loss of the railroad company alone, not including the freight they were transporting, has been estimated at $2,000,-000.   It is impossible to state the number of men thrown out of employment, in the aggregate, by these strikes, nor the total value of the property destroyed through the resulting riots, but the chief of the Bureau of Industrial Statistics of Pennsylvania, in his report for 1880-81, makes the following statement concerning the cost of the Pittsburg riot :   Total amount of claims as presented to Allegheny County, the courts having decreed that that county was liable for all the losses sustained through the riots, $3,592,789.33 ; total amount actually paid by compromise and judgments at the date of the report named, $2,765,891.89.

The whole country was greatly excited during and after these strikes.   The question was constantly asked, How can such affairs be prevented or the causes leading to them removed ?   They were both unsuccessful.

Telegraphers' strike of 1883.

The next great strike was that of the telegraphers, which occurred in the year 1883.   There were involved in this strike the majority of the commercial telegraph operators of the entire country.   It extended to the linemen of the commercial companies, and then to a few railroad operators ; but the information relative to the facts is meager.   This strike took place to secure the abolition of Sunday work without extra pay, the reduction of day turns to eight hours, and the equalization of pay between the sexes for the same work.   The operators also demanded a universal increase of wages. The strike commenced July 19 and ended August 23, 1883, although it was declared off on the 17th of August. It was unsuccessful, the loss to employees being $250,000, while they expended $62,000 in assistance to destitute fellow-operators. The employers lost nearly $1,000,000. The whole number of persons involved in the strike was 6,270. One of the companies made a provisional agreement with the Brotherhood of Telegraphers, and in accordance therewith resumed business. As the other companies were resisting the strike, the company which made this agreement secured a handsome profit on account of the increased volume of business brought to it.

Not successful.

Another of what have been called "historic" strikes was that on the Southwestern or Gould system of railways, which occurred in the years 1885–86. The first of the strikes on this system took place in March, 1885. At this time and during the months preceding, the shopmen on the Missouri Pacific Railroad in Missouri, Kansas, and Texas became very much dissatisfied with the wages they were receiving, and about March 9 nearly four thousand of them struck for a restoration of the wages paid the preceding September, since which date reductions amounting in the aggregate to from ten to fifteen per cent had taken place. The strike was begun at Sedalia, Mo., March 7, 1885, and in two days became general all over the system, and during its continuance freight traffic was virtually suspended. The strike came to an end, however, on the 16th of March, 1885, at ten o'clock in the evening, and on the next day, the 17th, work was generally resumed. This result was brought about very largely through the efforts of the governors of Missouri and Kansas and other state officials upon this basis : "The company agreed to restore to its

Strike on Gould system, 1885-6.

Beginning and end of strike.

Basis of settlement.

striking employees . . . the same wages paid them in September, 1884, including one and one half price for extra time work, and to restore all of said employees to their several employments without prejudice to them on account of the strike.'' The company, on its part, also agreed, and voluntarily, that ''hereafter said rates will not be changed except after thirty days' notice thereof, given in the usual way.'' The strikers in this affair very generally had the sympathy and moral support of the public, for it was conceded on all sides, with few exceptions, that the employees had justice and right with them. This concession was because of the fact that the reductions of wages complained of were made at times when there was no corresponding decrease in the business or earnings of the company.

Second strike on Gould system, 1886.

The second strike on the Gould system took place in March, 1886, a year later than that just recited. The trouble began at Marshall, Texas, on the Texas and Pacific Railroad, and grew out of the discharge of the foreman for alleged incompetency. This foreman was prominent in the local assembly of the Knights of Labor, which order subsequently inaugurated the great railroad strike, the discharge of the foreman being the alleged

Causes therefor.

cause. The claim was made that the discharge of the foreman in this way was in violation of the agreement of March, 1885, made at the settlement of the strike through the influence of the governors of Missouri and Kansas, as just stated. Other violations were also claimed. During the entire month of March all freight traffic was virtually suspended on the roads involved, and about ten thousand men were out of work, nearly all being strikers. On March 28 the strike was declared off, and the hope was entertained that negotiations would be perfected between the officers of the roads and the representatives of the employees ; but the railroad officials declined to treat with the men, except individually, and on the 5th of April the order declaring the strike at an end was re- voked.   The backbone of the strike was broken by that time, however, and traffic was resumed, but under police protection for a time.   Many of the men had returned to work, while new men in sufficient numbers to carry on the traffic assumed the places of those who were still out. While the strike of March, 1885, was, as stated, gener- ally considered to be a just one, that of March, 1886, was regarded as ill judged, no adequate cause existing therefor.   The disastrous result and the lack of public sympathy displayed for the strikers bring the two strikes into sharp contrast.

Disastrous result of strike of 1886.

At Homestead, Pa., in July, 1892, there occurred a most serious affair between the Carnegie Steel Company and its employees, at what is known as the Homestead works, growing out of a disagreement in the previous month in regard to wages.   The parties were unable to come to an agreement that was mutually satisfactory, and the company closed its works on the 30th day of June and discharged its men.   Only a small portion of the men were affected by the proposed adjustment of wages.   The larger portion of them, who were mem- bers of the Amalgamated Association of Iron and Steel Workers, were not affected at all, nor was the large force of employees, some three thousand in number, who were not members of that association.   The company refused to recognize the Amalgamated Association of Iron and Steel Workers as an organization, or to hold any conference with its representatives.   Upon the fail- ure to arrive at an adjustment of the wage difficulty, the company proposed to operate its works by the employ- ment of non-union men.   The men, who could not se-

Homestead strike, 1892.

Failure to make an adjust- ment.

cure recognition, refused to accept the reduced rates of
wages and also came to the determination that they
would resist the company in every attempt to secure
non-union workers.

The history of the events at Homestead shows that
the lodges composing the Amalgamated Association proceeded to organize what was styled an "advisory committee," to take charge of affairs for the strikers. All
employees of the company were directed to break their
contracts and to refuse to work until the Amalgamated
Association was recognized and its terms agreed to.

The works were shut down two days prior to the time
provided by the contract under which the men were
working, and, as alleged, because the workmen had seen
fit to hang the president of the company in effigy. July
5 the officers of the company asked the sheriff of the
county to appoint deputies to protect the works while
they carried out their intention of making repairs. The
employees, on their part, organized to defend the works
against what they called encroachments or demands to
enter ; in fact, they took possession of the Homestead
steel works. When the sheriff's men approached, the
workmen, who were assembled in force, notified them to
leave the place, as they did not intend to create any disorder, and that they would not allow any damage to be
done to the property of the company. They further

offered to act as deputies, an offer which was declined.
The advisory committee, which had been able to preserve the peace thus far, dissolved on the rejection of
their offer to serve as deputies and conservators of the
peace, and all of their records were destroyed.

The immediate cause of the fighting which later on
took place at Homestead was the approach of a body of
Pinkerton detectives, who were gathered in two barges

on the Ohio River, some miles below the works. When the Pinkertons arrived the workmen broke through the mill fence, intrenching themselves behind steel billets, and made all preparations to resist the approach of the Pinkerton barges, and they resisted all attempts to land, the result being a fierce battle, brought on by a heavy volley of shots from the strikers. The Pinkertons were armed with Winchesters, but they were obliged to land and ascend the embankment single file, and so were soon driven back to the boats, suffering severely from the fire by the strikers. Many efforts were made to land, but the position of the men they were attacking, behind their breastworks of steel rails and billets, was very strong, and from this place of safe refuge the detectives were subjected to a galling fire. This opening battle took place on the 5th of July, about four o'clock in the morning, and was continued in a desultory way during the day. It was renewed the following day. A brass ten-pound cannon had been secured by the strikers and planted so as to command the barges moored at the banks of the river. Another force of one thousand men had taken up a position on the opposite side of the river, where they protected themselves, and a cannon which they had obtained, by a breastwork of railroad ties. A little before nine o'clock a bombardment commenced, the cannon being turned on the boats, and the firing was kept up for several hours. The boats were protected by heavy steel plates inside ; so efforts were made to fire them. Hose was procured and oil sprayed on the decks and sides, and at the same time many barrels of oil were emptied into the river above the mooring-place, the purpose being to ignite it and then allow it to float against the boats. Under these combined movements, the Pinkertons were obliged to

Use of cannon.

Attempts to burn boats used by detectives.

throw out a flag of truce, but it was not recognized by the strikers. The officers of the Amalgamated Association, however, interfered, and a surrender of the detectives was arranged. It was agreed that they should be safely guarded, under condition that they left their arms and ammunition, and having no alternative, they accepted the terms. Seven had been killed and twenty or thirty wounded.

On the 10th of July, after several days' correspondence with the state authorities, the governor sent the entire force of the militia of the state to Homestead. On the 12th the troops arrived, the town was placed under martial law, and order was restored. There had been much looting, clubbing, and stoning, and as the detectives, after surrender, passed through the streets they were treated with great abuse. Eleven workmen and spectators were killed in the fights.

Congress made an investigation of this strike, but no legislative action was ever taken. Some indictments were made and lawsuits ensued. The mills were gradually supplied with new people, but the strike was not declared off until November 20, 1892.*

The Homestead strike must be considered as the bitterest labor war occurring in this country prior to that which took place at Chicago later on, in 1894.

---

* A brief but very excellent account of this strike can be found in Appleton's "Annual Cyclopedia," 1892, and a more extended account appears in the report of the Pennsylvania Bureau of Industrial Statistics for 1892.

CHAPTER XXVI.

THE CHICAGO STRIKE, 1894.—BOYCOTTS.

PROBABLY the most expensive and far-reaching labor controversy which can properly be classed among the historic controversies of this generation was the Chicago strike of June and July, 1894. Beginning with a private strike at the works of Pullman's Palace Car Company at Pullman, a suburb of Chicago, it ended with a practical insurrection of the labor employed on the principal railroads radiating from Chicago and some of their affiliated lines, paralyzing internal commerce, putting the public to great inconvenience, delaying the mails, and in general demoralizing business. Its influences were felt all over the country, to greater or less extent, according to the lines of traffic and the courses of trade. The contest was not limited to the parties with whom it originated, for soon there were brought into it two other factors or forces.

The Chicago strike of 1894.

The original strike grew out of a demand of certain employees of the Pullman Company, in May, 1894, for a restoration of the wages paid during the previous year. The company claimed that the reduction in the volume of business, owing to business depression, did not warrant the payment of the old wages. On account of the increased production of rolling-stock to meet the traffic incident to the World's Fair in 1893, orders for building new cars were not easily obtainable, a large portion of the business of the Pullman Company being contract business in

Origin of the strike.

the way of building cars for railroad companies generally. This state of affairs resulted in a partial cessation of car-building everywhere in the country, the Pullman Company suffering with all others. The demand of the employees, therefore, was not acceded to, and on May 11, 1894, a strike was ordered. Several minor grievances were claimed to have existed and to have led to the action of the strikers, who had joined the American Railway Union, an association of railway employees which had achieved a partial success in a contest with the Great Northern Railroad a few weeks previous to the Pullman strike. The Railway Union espoused the cause of the Pullman employees on the ground that they were members thereof. This union numbered, as alleged, about 150,000 members. It undertook to force the Pullman Company to accede to the demands of its employees by boycotting Pullman cars ; that is to say, they declared that they would not handle Pullman cars on the railroads where such cars were used unless the Pullman Company would accede to the demands made upon it. The immediate antagonist of the Pullman Company in the extended controversy was, therefore, the American Railway Union.

Another force was soon involved in the strike, which was, very naturally, an ally of the Pullman Company. This was the General Managers' Association, a body of railroad men representing all the roads radiating from Chicago, and it was through the necessity of protecting the traffic of its lines, as claimed, that it made its contest with the American Railway Union. These roads represented a combined capital of more than $2,000,000,000, and they employed more than one fourth of all the railroad employees in the United States. These three great forces, therefore, were enlisted in a strife for supremacy,

Grievances claimed by men.

Boycott of Pullman cars.

Railway Managers' Association.

and they alone, without reference to the conditions and circumstances attending the strike or accompanying it, constitute it one of the historic strikes of this age.*

According to the testimony of the officials of the railroads involved, they lost in property destroyed, hire of United States deputy marshals, and other incidental expenses, at least $685,308. The loss of earnings of these roads on account of the strike is estimated at nearly $5,000,000. About 3,100 employees at Pullman lost in wages, as estimated, probably $350,000. About 100,000 employees upon the twenty-four railroads radiating from Chicago, all of which were more or less involved in the strike, lost in wages, as estimated, nearly $1,400,000. Beyond these amounts very great losses, widely distributed, were suffered incidentally throughout the country. The suspension of transportation at Chicago paralyzed a vast distributive center, and imposed many hardships and much loss upon the great number of people whose manufacturing and business operations, employment, travel, and necessary supplies depend upon and demand regular transportation service to, from, and through Chicago. The losses to the country at large are estimated by Bradstreet's to be in the vicinity of $80,000,000. Whatever they are, whether more or less, they teach the lesson of the necessity of preventing such disasters, and the strike illustrates how a small local disturbance, arising from the complaints of a few people, can result in involving so much of a large country. When the American Railway Union took up the cudgel for the Pullman strikers and declared their boycott as against Pullman cars, and the General Managers' Association took every means to protect their interests and prevent the stoppage

Losses growing out of Chicago strike.

Losses to the country.

---

* For an extended account of this strike see the report of the United States Strike Commission (Senate Ex. Doc. No. 7, 53d Congress, 3d Session).

of transportation, the sympathies and antagonisms of the whole country were aroused. The attempt was made to induce all trades in Chicago to join in a great sympathetic strike, but this attempt was not successful.

The inevitable accompaniments of a great strike were brought into play at Chicago. Riots, intimidations, assaults, murder, arson, and burglary, with lesser crimes, attended the strike. In this, as in some of the other historic strikes, troops were engaged. The city police, the county sheriffs, the state militia, United States deputy marshals, and regulars from the United States army were all brought into the controversy. The United States troops were sent to Chicago to protect federal property and to prevent obstruction in the carrying of the mails, to prevent interference with interstate commerce, and to enforce the decrees and mandates of the federal courts. They took no part in any attempt to suppress the strike, nor could they, as such matters belong to the city and state authorities. The police of the city were used to suppress riots and protect the property of citizens, and the state militia was called in for the same service. The total of these forces employed during the continuance of the strike was 14,186.

Many indictments have grown out of the difficulties occurring at Chicago, and the courts are at the time of writing considering the cases. But all the attending circumstances of the strike point to one conclusion—that a share of the responsibility for bringing it on belongs in some degree to each and every party involved. The strike generated a vast deal of bitter feeling—so bitter that neither party was ready to consider the rights of the other. The attacking parties claimed that their grievances warranted them in adopting any means in their power to force concessions. This is the attitude of all strikes. The other parties, on the other hand, claimed that they were justified in adopting any means in their power to resist the demands of the attacking party. The probability is that neither recognized the rights of the public to such an extent as to induce them to forbear bringing inconvenience and disturbance to it. It was the most suggestive strike that has ever occurred in this country, and if it only proves a lesson sufficiently severe to teach the public its rights in such matters and to teach it to adopt measures to preserve those rights, it will be worth all it has cost. This, perhaps, is the lesson of all the strikes that have been called "historic." This is not the place to discuss the merits of any of them or of the claims of either or any of the parties to them.

Lessons of the Chicago strike.

Other great strikes have occurred which, considered with those that have been described, constitute 1894 the era of vast labor controversies. The Lehigh Valley Railroad strike, which occurred in December, 1893 ; the American Railway Union strike on the Great Northern Railroad, which occurred in April, 1894 ; the great coal strike, which occurred in the same month, and the Chicago strike of June and July, all crowded into the space of seven months, are sufficient to make that brief period memorable, and they all call emphatic attention to the necessity of some sane method of preventing like occurrences, or at least of reducing their number and their severity. The lessons have been expensive, the losses great, the demoralization certain, the bitterness intensified, but out of all this comes the great moral lesson that there must be found a way to deal with such affairs without the presence of the sheriff and all that the sheriff stands for. This work deals with history, not with philosophy ; with the growth and development of industries and their accompanying conditions, not with

Other great strikes.

political economy, nor with remedies for bad conditions, and so the discussion of alleged solutions must be avoided.

Strikes and lockouts, as already stated, are similar in their character.   There is another weapon used in labor controversies, known as the "boycott."   This term was coined from the name of one Captain Boycott, an agent in Ireland of Lord Erne's Lough Mask estate, who in 1880 evicted a large number of tenants.   The tenants, with their neighbors, refused all further intercourse with Captain Boycott and his family, and declined to work for him or trade with him, or to allow any one else to do so.*   So now, when there is any organized attempt to coerce a person into compliance with any demand, through a combination pledged to abstain, and pledged further to compel others to abstain, from having social intercourse with him or to trade with him, or there is an organized persecution of any person or company, to be used as a means of coercion or intimidation or of retaliation for some act, or there is an organized refusal to act in any particular way, such action, in any of these cases, is called a "boycott"; that is to say, the person or party against whom any of these actions is directed is put into the position in which Captain Boycott found himself.

It is only the name in this connection which is of recent origin.   The process is very old, for whenever, for any purpose, a number of persons by agreement decide to let another severely alone in order to bring him to terms, that person has been boycotted; but the method has often been considered an evidence of the loftiest patriotism.   It all depends upon the cause and upon the popular estimate of the cause.   The tea episode in Boston Harbor and the efforts of the colonists, through their

* Johnson's "Universal Cyclopedia."

pledges, to prevent the importation of foreign goods and thereby force the consumption of home-made goods, are instances of the boycott. As Dr. Ely, in his work, "The Labor Movement in America," remarks : "The boycott has been employed against obnoxious individuals from time immemorial. In 1327 the citizens of Canterbury, England, boycotted the monks of Christ's Church, meeting in an open field, and passing these resolutions among others : 'That no one, under penalties to be imposed by the city, should inhabit the prior's houses ; that no one should buy, sell, or exchange drinks or victuals with the monastery, under similar penalties.'"

Instances of the boycott.

The abolitionists boycotted slave-made products ; the temperance people have used the same method to repress the liquor nuisance ; the pulpit has tried hard to boycott Sunday newspapers, and recently there has been established in the city of New York a society, consisting of women occupying excellent social positions, pledged not to purchase goods of houses which do not furnish proper conveniences for their saleswomen. Railroad companies have boycotted their men time and time again ; working people have boycotted railroads, dealers, and manufacturers ; railroads combine and boycott other railroads ; and so the method has grown to be a familiar one with all classes, and one that is used in various ways. When the boycott is carried to a certain extent or the combination seeking it amounts to a conspiracy to unlawfully prevent or restrain another, or to accomplish any unlawful purpose, it becomes a criminal offense, and is actionable. Many states have enacted laws relating to it ; but these laws practically admit, by their very language, the use of the boycott. For instance, the state of Illinois, in its statute relating to boycotting and blacklisting, provides that

When the boycott is criminal.

If any two or more persons conspire or agree together, or the officers or executive committee of any society or organization or corporation shall issue or utter any circular or edict as the action of or instruction to its members, or any other persons, societies, organizations, or corporations for the purpose of establishing a so-called boycott or blacklist, or shall post or distribute any written or printed notice in any place, with the fraudulent or malicious intent wrongfully and wickedly to injure the person, character, business, or employment or property of another, ... they shall be deemed guilty of a conspiracy; and every such offender, whether as individuals or as the officers of any society or organization, and every person convicted of conspiracy at common law, shall be imprisoned in the penitentiary not exceeding five years, or fined not exceeding $2,000, or both.

In all such laws it is to be remarked how cautiously the framers have used the words "fraudulent," "malicious," "wrongfully," "wickedly," etc., because should any number of persons agree not to purchase goods of a particular trader, or agree to avoid certain cars, or not to buy a certain paper, they could not be convicted unless it was shown that they did it maliciously, etc. The boycott is recognized as one of the accompanying conditions of the expansion of industry and the complications arising therefrom. When the strike goes, through prevention or through increased intelligence, the industrial boycott will become feeble in its operation, and will have no terror for the trader, in whatever capacity he may act.

PART IV.

THE INFLUENCE OF MACHINERY ON LABOR.

PART IV.—THE INFLUENCE OF MACHINERY ON LABOR.

CHAPTER XXVII.

THE INFLUENCE OF MACHINERY ON LABOR.—DISPLACEMENT.

As SHOWN in the chapter on the planting of the factory system, the age of machinery found its birth in the development of spinning and weaving, and as these two arts lie at the very foundation of the industrial arts of the ancients, so they are to a large extent the basic arts of the modern system of industry. Until the decade of years beginning with 1760 the machines in use for weaving, as well as for spinning, were nearly as simple as those in use among the ancients, and there were no machines of any consequence, certainly none used with power other than hand or foot-power, in operation. Of course the principles of all simple, primitive processes are those still in force, but it is only since invention has been applied to productive processes that it has had any specific influence upon the labor of man, either in an economic or an ethical sense. It is proposed here to treat of the influence of machinery in these two respects —in its economic and in its ethical influence on labor ; and, first, as to its economic influence :

Birth of age of machinery.

This influence has been felt in two ways, and these ways are diametrically opposed to each other. The one, in popular speech, is called the "displacement of labor"

Effects of machinery.

and the other may be called the "expansion of labor." By the displacement of labor is meant what would be expressed more specifically by the term "contraction of

OLD-FASHIONED STAGE COACH.

labor"; that is, where a machine has been invented by which one man can do the work, with the aid of the machine, of several men working without its aid; and by expansion of labor is meant where, through invention, more men are called into remunerative employment than would have been employed had not such invention been made. In considering these economic bearings or influences of machinery we must deal with labor abstractly ; but in speaking of the ethical influence later on labor must be considered not only abstractly, but as to its influence on man as a social and political factor. In the highest sense the ethical influence of machinery becomes the most prominent feature of any treatment of the relation of machinery to or its influence upon labor ; but naturally the economic disturbances which have taken place through the introduction of finely-specialized machinery claim the first attention.

Meaning of " expansion of labor."

Ethical influence the most prominent.

No one can claim that labor-saving machinery, so called, but which more properly should be called labor-making or labor-assisting machinery, does not displace labor so far as men individually are concerned, yet all men of sound minds admit the permanent good effects of the application of machinery to industrial development. The permanent good effects, however, do not prevent the temporary displacement, which, so far as the particular labor displaced is concerned, assists in crippling the consuming power of the community in which it takes place. It is, of course, exceedingly difficult to secure positive information illustrating a point so thoroughly apparent ; yet from the fugitive sources which are at command a sufficient amount of information can be drawn to show clearly and positively the influence of machinery in bringing about what is called displacement.*

Displacement of labor.

* The specific facts in this chapter have been drawn from the First Annual Report of the United States Commissioner of Labor and from " Recent Economic Changes," by David A. Wells, LL. D. See also the address of the author at the celebration of the beginning of the second century of the American Patent System, at Washington, April, 1891.

In manufacture
of agricultural
implements.
In the manufacture of agricultural implements new machinery has, in the opinion of some of the best manufacturers of such implements, displaced fully fifty per cent of the muscular labor formerly employed, as, for instance, hammers and dies have done away with the most particular labor on a plow. In one of the most extensive establishments engaged in the manufacture of agricultural implements in one of the Western States it is found that 600 men, with the use of machinery, are now doing the work that would require 2,145 men, without the aid of machinery, to perform ; that is to say, there has been in this particular establishment a loss of labor to 1,545 men, the proportion of loss being as 3.57 to 1.

In small arms. In the manufacture of small arms, where one man, by manual labor, was formerly able to "turn" and "fit" one stock for a musket in one day of ten hours, three men now, by a division of labor and the use of power

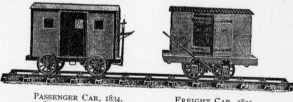

PASSENGER CAR, 1834.
Portage Railroad.

FREIGHT CAR, 1835.
Portage Railroad.

machinery, will turn out and fit from 125 to 150 stocks in ten hours. By this statement it is seen that one man individually turns out and fits the equivalent of forty-two to fifty stocks in ten hours, as against one stock in the same length of time under former conditions. In this particular calling, then, there is a displacement of forty-four to forty-nine men in one operation.

In brick-making. Looking at a cruder industry, that of brickmaking, improved devices have displaced ten per cent of labor,

while in making fire-brick forty per cent of the labor formerly employed is now dispensed with, and yet in many
brickmaking concerns no displacement whatever has
taken place.

The manufacture of boots and shoes offers some very
wonderful facts in this connection.   In one large and
long-established manufactory in one of the Eastern
States the proprietors testify that it would require five
hundred persons, working by hand processes and in the

In manufacture
of boots and
shoes.

FREIGHT AND PASSENGER CARS, 1848.
Jeffersonville, Madison and Indianapolis Railroad.

old way in the shops by the roadside, to make as many
women's boots and shoes as one hundred persons now
make with the aid of machinery and by congregated
labor, a contraction of eighty per cent in this particular
case.   In another division of the same industry the number of men required to produce a given quantity of boots
and shoes has been reduced one half, while, in still another locality, and on another quality of boots, being
entirely for women's wear, where formerly a first-class
workman could turn out six pairs in one week, he will
now turn out eighteen pairs.   A well-known firm in the
West engaged in the manufacture of boots and shoes
finds that it would take one hundred and twenty persons,
working by hand, to produce the amount of work done
in its factory by sixty employees, and that the hand-
work would not compare in workmanship and appearance by fifty per cent.   By the use of Goodyear's sew-

Instances of
displacement.

ing machine for turned shoes one man will sew two hundred and fifty pairs in one day. It would require eight men, working by hand, to sew the same number in the same time. By the use of a heel-shaver or trimmer one man will trim three hundred pairs of shoes a day, while formerly three men would have been required to do the same work ; and with the McKay machine one operator will handle three hundred pairs of shoes in one day, while without the machine he could handle but five pairs in the same time. So, in nailing on heels, one man, with the aid of machinery, can heel three hundred pairs of shoes per day, while five men would have to

Use of shoe machinery.

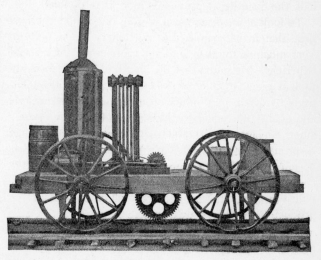

Model of the John Stevens Locomotive, the First in America. 1825.

work all day to accomplish this by hand. A large Philadelphia house which makes boys' and children's shoes entirely, has learned that the introduction of new machinery within the past thirty years has displaced employees in the proportion of six to one, and that the cost of the product has been reduced one half.

The broom industry, which would not seem to offer a large field for speculation in reference to displacement, has felt the influence of invention, for the broom-sewing machine facilitates the work to such an extent that each machine displaces three men. A large broom-manufacturing concern which a few years ago employed seventeen skilled men to manufacture five hundred dozen brooms per week, now, with nine men, aided by invention, turns out twelve hundred dozen brooms weekly ; so in this case, while the force is reduced nearly one half, the quantity of product is more than doubled.

In broom-making.

To look at a carriage or a wagon, one would not suppose that in its manufacture machinery could perform very much of an office, and yet a foreman of fifty years' experience has stated that the length of time it formerly took a given number of skilled workmen, working entirely by hand, to produce a carriage of a certain style and quality was equal to thirty-five days of one man's labor, while now substantially the same style of carriage is produced by twelve days' labor. Machinery has been employed in making the parts necessary to the construction of a carriage or a wagon, and thus has simplified the work and reduced the time essential for the production of the completed product.

Carriages and wagons.

In the manufacture of carpets there has been a displacement, taking all the processes together, of from ten to twenty times the number of persons now necessary. In the spinning of carpet material alone it would take, by the old methods, from seventy-five to one hundred times the number of operatives now employed to turn out the same amount of work, while in weaving there would be required at least ten times the present number.

Carpets.

A carpet-measuring machine has been invented which brushes and measures the product at the same time, and by its use one operator will accomplish what formerly required fifteen men.

Clothing.

Very many people would say that in the manufacture of clothing there has been no improvement, except so

MODEL OF THE STOCKTON AND DARLINGTON LOCOMOTIVE No. 1, BROUGHT FROM ENGLAND TO THE UNITED STATES IN 1826.

far as the use of the sewing machine has facilitated the manufacture ; yet in the ready-made clothing trade, where cutting was formerly done by hand, much of it is Use of dies. now done by the use of dies, many thicknesses of the same size and style being cut at one operation. So in cutting out hats and caps with improved cutters, one man is enabled to cut out a great many thicknesses at the same time, and he does six times the amount of work with such devices as could formerly be done by one man in the old way.

While the age of machinery began with improvements for the manufacture of textiles, so the manufacture of textiles, and especially cotton goods, offers perhaps as striking an illustration as any of the apparent displacement of labor. With a hand-loom a weaver used to weave from sixty to eighty picks* per minute in weaving a cloth of good quality, with twenty threads of twist to each one quarter square inch. With a power-loom he now weaves one hundred and eighty picks per minute of the same kind of cloth. Even in power machinery, a weaver formerly tended but one loom. Now one weaver minds all the way from two to ten looms, according to the grade of goods. In a large establishment in New Hampshire, improved machinery, even within ten years, has reduced muscular labor fifty per cent in the production of the same quality of goods. This, of course, is true in other localities given to the manufacture of cotton goods.

Textiles.

Product of power-loom.

In another line labor has been displaced to such an extent that only one third the number of operatives formerly required is now in employment. In the days of the single-spindle hand-wheel, one spinner, working fifty-six hours continuously, could spin five hanks† of number thirty-two twist. At the present time, with one pair of self-acting mule-spinning machines, having 2,124

Of spinning machines.

---

* PICK.—In weaving, the blow which drives the shuttle. It is delivered upon the end of the shuttle by the picker-head at the extremity of the picker-staff. The rate of a loom is said to be so many picks per minute.

† HANK.—A skein or coil of yarn or thread ; more particularly, a definite length of yarn, thread, silk, or the like bound up in one or more skeins. A hank of cotton yarn is 840 yards ; a hank of linen yarn is 3,000 yards.

spindles, one spinner, with the assistance of two small boys, can produce 55,098 hanks of number thirty-two twist in the same time.   It is quite generally agreed that there has been a displacement, taking all processes of cotton manufacture into consideration, in the proportion of three to one.   The average number of spindles per operative in the cotton-mills of this country in 1831 was

Displacement in cotton manufacture.

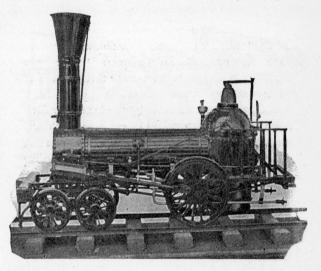

THE "GEORGE WASHINGTON" LOCOMOTIVE, 1835.   THE FIRST LOCOMO-
TIVE TO CLIMB A HEAVY GRADE IN THE UNITED STATES.

25.2 ; it is now over 64.82, an increase of nearly 157 per cent ; and along with this increase of the number of spindles per operative there has been an increase of product per operative of over 145 per cent, so far as spinning alone is concerned.   In weaving in the olden time, in this country, a fair adult hand-loom weaver wove from forty-two to forty-eight yards of common shirting per week.   Now a weaver, tending six power-looms in a

Product of hand-loom.

cotton factory, will produce 1,500 yards and over in a single week; and now a recent invention will enable a weaver to double this product.

Marvelous as these facts appear, when we examine the influence of invention as applied in the newspaper publishing business we perceive more clearly the magic of inventive genius. One of the latest sextuple stereotype perfecting presses manufactured by R. Hoe & Co., of

Printing.

THE HOE SEXTUPLE STEREOTYPE PERFECTING PRESS AND FOLDER.
Prints 72,000 4, 6, or 8-page papers per hour; 48,000 10 or 12-page papers per hour; 36,000 16-page papers per hour; 24,000 14, 20, or 24-page papers per hour; all the dimensions of the average daily newspaper, and delivered folded and counted.

New York, has an aggregate running capacity of 72,000 eight-page papers per hour; that is to say, one of these perfected presses, run by one pressman and four skilled laborers, will print, cut at the top, fold, paste, and count (with supplement inserted if desired) 72,000 eight-page papers in one hour. To do the press-work alone for this number of papers would take, on the old plan, a man and a boy, working ten hours per day, one hundred days. A paper now published in the morning, printed, folded, cut, and pasted before breakfast, would, before the edition could be completed under the old system, become a quarterly.

The modern press.

And so illustrations might be accumulated in very many directions—in the manufacture of furniture, in the glass industry, in leather-making, in sawing lumber, in the manufacture of machines and machinery, in the production of metals and metallic goods of all kinds, or of wooden-ware, in the manufacture of musical instruments, in mining, in the oil industry, in the manufacture of paper, in pottery, in the production of railroad supplies, in the manufacture of rubber boots, of saws, of silk goods, of soap, of tobacco, of trunks, in building vessels, in making wine, and in the production of woolen goods.

It is impossible to arrive at an accurate statement as to the number of persons it would require under the old system to produce the goods made by the present industrial system with the aid of invention and power machinery. Any computation would be a rough estimate. In some branches of work such a rough estimate would indicate that each employee at the present represents, on an average, fifty employees under the old system. In

many other branches the estimate would involve the employment of one now where three were employed. Looking at this question without any desire to be mathematically accurate, it is fair to say, perhaps, that it would require from fifty to one hundred million persons in this country, working under the old system, to produce the goods made and do the work performed by the workers of to-day with the aid of machinery. This computation may, of course, be very wide of the truth, but any computation is equally startling, and when it is considered that in spinning alone 1,100 threads are easily spun now at one time where one was spun under the old system, no estimate can be successfully disputed.

All these facts and illustrations simply show that there has been, economically speaking, a great displacement of labor by the use of inventions ; power machinery has Machinery
assists muscle. come in as a magical assistant to the power of muscle and mind, and it is this side of the question that usually causes alarm. Enlightenment has taught the wage-receiver some of the advantages of the introduction of inventions as his assistants, but he is not yet fully instructed as to their influence in all directions. He does see the displacement ; he does see the difficulty of turning his hand to other employment or of finding

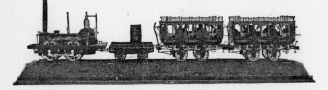

THE FIRST STEAM TRAIN RUN ON THE PENNSYLVANIA STATE RAILROAD, 1834.

employment in the same direction. These are tangible influences which present themselves squarely in the face of the man involved, and to him no philosophical, economic, or ethical answer is sufficient. It is therefore impossible to treat of the influence of inventions, so far Inadequacy of
individual basis. as the displacement of labor is concerned, as one of the leading influences, on the individual basis. We must take labor abstractly. So, having shown the powerful influence of the use of ingenious devices in the displacement or contraction of labor, as such, it is proper to show how such devices have influenced the expansion of labor or created employments and opportunities for employment which did not exist before their inception and application. A separate chapter is given to this part of the subject.

CHAPTER XXVIII.

THE INFLUENCE OF MACHINERY ON LABOR.—EXPANSION.

As INCREDIBLE as the facts given in the preceding

chapter appear to one who has not studied them, the
ability to crystallize in individual cases and show the
fairly exact displacement of labor exists. An examination of the opposite influence of inventions, that of the
expansion or creation of employments not before existing, reveals a more encouraging state or condition of
things, but one in which the statistician can make but very
little headway. The influences under the expansion of
labor have various ramifications. The people at large,
and especially those who work for wages, have experienced these influences in several directions, and contemporaneous with the introduction and use of inventions,
the chief economic influence being in the direction of
expansion, the other influences being more thoroughly
ethical, and these should be considered under that broad
title. The statistical method helps in some respects in
studying the expansive power of inventions, and especially in the direction of great staples used as raw material
in manufacturing processes and in the increase of the
number of people employed relative to the number of
the population. If there has been a great increase in
the consumption per capita of great staples for manufacturing purposes, there must have been a corresponding expansion of labor necessary for the production of
goods in like directions.

Taking up some of the leading staples, the facts show that the per capita consumption of cotton in this country in 1830 was 5.9 pounds ; in 1880, 13.91 pounds ; while in 1890 the per capita consumption had increased to nearly 19 pounds. These figures are for cotton consumed in our own country, and clearly and positively indicate that the labor necessary for such consumption has been kept up to the standard, if not beyond the standard, of the olden time—that is, as to the number of people employed.

Per capita consumption of cotton.

In iron the increase has been as great proportionately. In 1870 the per capita consumption of iron in the United States was 105.64 pounds, in 1880 it had risen to 204.99, and in 1890 to 283.38. While processes in manufacturing iron have been improved, and labor displaced to a certain extent by such processes, this great increase in the consumption of iron is a most encouraging fact, and proves that there has been an offset to the displacement.

Of iron.

The consumption of steel shows like results. In 1880 it was 46 pounds per capita, and in 1890, 144 pounds. The application of iron and steel in all directions, in the building trades as well as in the mechanic arts, in great engineering undertakings, and in a multitude of directions, only indicates that labor must be actively employed, or such extensions could not take place. But a more conclusive offset to the displacement of labor, considered abstractly, is shown by the statistics of persons engaged in all occupations. From 1860 to 1890, a period of thirty years, and the most prolific period in this country of inventions, and therefore of the most intensified influence in all directions of their introduction, the population increased 99.16 per cent, while during the same period the number of persons employed in all occupations—manufacturing, agriculture, domestic serv-

Of steel.

ice, everything—increased 176.07 per cent. In the twenty years, 1870 to 1890, the population increased 62.41 per cent, while the number of persons in all occupations increased 81.80 per cent. An analysis of these statements shows that the increase of the number of

Increase of population compared with increase in persons employed.

those engaged in manufacturing, mechanical, and mining industries, those in which the influence of inventions is most keenly felt, for the period from 1860 to 1890 was 172.27 per cent, as against 99.16 per cent increase in the total population. If statistics could be as forcibly applied to show the new occupations brought into existence by invention, it is believed that the result would be still more emphatic.

Influence of telegraphy in causing expansion.

If we could examine scientifically the number of created occupations, the claim that inventions have displaced labor on the whole would be conclusively and emphatically refuted. Taking some of the great industries that now exist, and which did not exist prior to the inventions which made them, we must acknowledge the power of the answer. In telegraphy thousands and thousands of people are employed where no one has ever been displaced. The construction of the lines, the manufacture of the instruments, the operation of the lines—all these divisions and subdivisions of a great industry have brought thousands of intelligent men and women into remunerative employment where no one had ever been employed before. The telephone has only added to this accumulation and expansion, and the whole field of electricity, in providing for the employment of many skilled workers, has not trenched upon the

Of electroplating.

privileges of the past. Electroplating, a modern device, has not only added wonderfully to the employed list by its direct influence, but indirectly by the introduction of a class of goods which can be secured by all persons.

Silverware is no longer the luxury of the rich. Through the invention of electroplating, excellent ware, with most artistic design, can be found in almost every habitation in America. The application of electroplating to nickel furnished a subsidiary industry to that of electroplating generally, and nickelplating had not been known half a dozen years before more than thirty thousand people were employed in the industry, where no one had ever been employed prior to the invention.

The railroads offer another grand illustration of the expansion of labor. It now requires more than three

Of railroads.

THE "PIONEER," FIRST LOCOMOTIVE IN CHICAGO.

quarters of a million of people to operate our railroads, and this means a population of nearly four millions, or one sixteenth of the whole population of the country. The displacement of the stage coach and the stage-driver was nothing compared to the expansion of labor

Number required to operate them.

All railroad
work leads to
expansion.
which the railroad systems of the country have created.
The construction of the roadbed and its equipment constantly involve the employment of great numbers—
armies even—of mechanics, while the operation of the
roads themselves, as has been stated, secures employment to more than three quarters of a million of people.

A MODERN LOCOMOTIVE.

The Empire State Express Engine No. 999 of the New York Central and Hudson River Railroad. This engine ran for a considerable distance at the
rate of 112½ miles an hour, hauling its regular train.

All this work of the railroads has not, in all probability,
displaced a single coachman ; on the other hand, it has
created the demand for drivers and workers with horses
and wagons through the great expansion of the express
business, of cab-driving, of connecting lines, and in other
directions, which could not have taken place under the
old stage-coach *régime.*

Influence
of the sewing
machine.
When the sewing machine was invented it was thought
that the sewing girl's day was over.   So it was in a certain respect.   She can now earn more money with less
physical exhaustion than under the old system.   Abomina-
bly poor as are the results of her efforts now, they are

far better than they would have been without this invention. But as a means of expansion of labor the sewing machine is a striking illustration. It has displaced no one ; it has increased demand, and it has been the means of establishing great workshops to supply the thousands of machines that are sold throughout the world.

The inventions of Goodyear, whereby rubber gum could be so treated as to be made into articles of wearing apparel, have resulted in the establishment of great industries as new creations. We need not in this place consider the great benefits through the use of waterproof clothing. The mere fact that great industries have arisen where none existed before is sufficient for our purpose. Much time might be taken up in simply accumulating illustrations showing the expansive force of inventions in the direction of creating new opportunities for remunerative employment. The facts given show conclusively that displacement has been more than offset by expansion. Yet, if the question be asked, Has the wage-earner received his just and equitable share of the economic benefits derived from the introduction of machinery? the answer must be, No. By this is meant his relative share, compared with that going to capital. In the struggle for supremacy in the great countries devoted to mechanical production it probably has been impossible for him to share equitably in such benefits. Notwithstanding this, his share has been enormous, and the gain to him such as to change his whole relation to society and the state, such changes affecting his moral position.

It is certainly true—and the statement is simply cumulative evidence of the truth of the view that expansion of labor through inventions has been equal or superior to any displacement that has taken place—that in those

Of rubber goods.

Displacement offset by expansion.

countries given to the development and use of machinery there is found the greatest proportion of employed persons, and that in those countries where machinery has been developed to little or no purpose poverty reigns, ignorance is the prevailing condition, and civilization consequently far in the rear.

Expansion of values.

The expansion of values as the result of the influence of machinery has been quite as marvelous as in any other direction, for educated labor, supplemented by machinery, has developed small quantities of inexpensive material into products of great value. This truth is illustrated by taking cotton and iron ore as the starting-point. A pound of cotton, costing at the time this calculation was made but 13 cents, has been developed into muslin which sold in the market for 80 cents, and into chintz which sold for $4. Seventy-five cents' worth of common iron ore has been developed into $5 worth of bar-iron, or into $10 worth of horse-shoes, or into $180 worth of table knives, or into $6,800 worth of fine needles, or into $29,480 worth of shirt buttons, or $200,000 worth of watch-springs, or $400,000 worth of hair-springs, and the same quantity of common iron ore can be made into $2,500,000 worth of pallet arbors.*

The illustrations given, both of the expansion of labor and the expansion of values, are sufficiently suggestive of

Machinery the friend of man.

a line of study which, carried in any direction, will show that machinery is the friend and not the enemy of man, especially when man is considered as a part of society and not as an individual.

---

* This calculation was made by George Woods, LL. D., of Pittsburg, Pa., and given by him in an address on " Technical Education," in 1874.

CHAPTER XXIX.

THE ETHICAL INFLUENCE OF MACHINERY ON LABOR.

ACCORDING to Mr. Herbert Spencer, ethics comprehends the laws of right living; and that, beyond the conduct commonly approved or reprobated as right or wrong, it includes all conduct which furthers or hinders, in direct or in indirect ways, the welfare of self or others; that justice, which formulates the range of conduct and limitations to conduct hence arising, is at once the most important division of ethics; that it has to define the equitable relations among individuals who limit one another's spheres of action by coexisting, and who achieve their ends by coöperation; and that, beyond justice between man and man, justice between each man and the aggregate of men has to be dealt with by it.

Spencer's definition of ethics.

This constitutes a very broad definition of ethics, and the propositions laid down by Mr. Spencer, taken by themselves, are such as no moral philosopher can for a moment reject, nor should they be rejected by economists, for a moment's reflection upon their bearing shows conclusively that material prosperity is best subserved by their incorporation as chapters in the laws of trade, commerce, and production. So the relation of the wage-receiver to his fellow-men and to society becomes ethical, purely so; but it is certainly ethico-economical, and his wages, the standard of his living; his working time, the cost of his living; his education, his interest in religious and literary matters, in art, and in all that adorns life,

Relation of wage-worker to society is ethical.

are features surrounding him which must be contemplated from the ethical point of view.   This thought is all the more emphatic when it is considered that invention has brought with it a new school of ethics.   It is the type and representative of the civilization of this period, because

MASONIC TEMPLE, CHICAGO.

it embodies, so far as physics and economics are concerned, the concentrated, clearly wrought-out thought of
the age.   Books may represent thought ; machinery or
invention is the embodiment of thought.   From an intellectual point of view, then, it becomes perfectly legitimate to speak of the ethical influence of inventions, and
no consideration of the relation of inventions to labor
or of the evolution of industry would be complete without showing in a more deeply philosophical sense their
ethical influence upon the individual laborer.

Machinery is the embodiment of thought.

We are living at the beginning of the age of mind, as
illustrated by the results of inventive genius.   It is the
age of intellect, of brain—for brain is king, and machinery is the king's prime minister.   Wealth of mind and
wealth of purse may struggle for the mastery, but the
former usually wins, and gives the crown to the Huxleys,
Darwins, Tyndalls, Proctors, Woolseys, and Drapers,
rather than to the men who accumulate great fortunes.
It is natural and logical that under such a sovereignty inventions should not only typify the progress of the race,
but that they should also have a clearly marked influence upon the morals of peoples, a mixed influence, to
be sure, as men are what we call good or evil, but on the
whole with the good vastly predominant.

Age of machinery the age of mind.

Under the old hand system of labor, or, to use a better term, the domestic system, which was displaced when
machinery came in and the factory system became fixed,
the most demoralizing conditions prevailed.   Those who
believe that the old system was better than the new find
something poetic in the idea of the weaver of old England, before spinning machinery was invented, working
at his loom in his cottage, with his family about him, and
from this reflection fall into the idyllic sentiment that the
domestic system surpassed the present.   This sentiment

has done much to create false impressions as to the results or influence of machinery. Goldsmith's Auburn and Crabbe's Village do not reflect the truest picture of their country's home life under the domestic system of labor, for the domestic laborer's home, instead of being the poetic one, was very far from the character poetry has given it. Huddled together in his hut, not a cottage, the weaver's family lived and worked, without comfort, convenience, good air, good food, and without much intelligence. Drunkenness and theft made each home the scene of crime and want and disorder. Superstition ruled, and envy swayed the workers. If the members of a family, endowed with more virtue and intelligence than the common herd, tried to so conduct themselves as to secure at least self-respect, they were either abused or ostracized by their neighbors. The ignorance under the old system added to the squalor of the homes under it, and what all these elements failed to produce in making the hut an actual den was faithfully performed, in too many instances, by the swine of the family. The reports of the Poor Laws commissioners of England are truer exponents of conditions than poetry, and show more faithfully the demoralizing agency of pauperism and of all the other evils which were so prolific under the hand system of work.

The influence of machinery at the particular time spoken of in the history of mankind is usually overlooked, and so, too, is the fact that if there is any one thing in individuals that the present age insists upon it is work—employment of some kind, for employment means the very best ethical condition of man. The lowest and the most harmful and the most expensive ignorance which can prevail in any community is ignorance of work, the want of some technical knowledge which

Marginal notes:

Condition under hand-labor system.

Employment means the best ethical condition of man.

enables a man to earn a living outside of a penal institution, and as ethics and practical religion most assuredly have much to do with everything that affects the conduct of life, the knowledge which enables a man to do his work well indicates his ethical relations. Poverty and pure religion cannot exist among the same people, for such a religion cannot prevail unless the people are engaged in that class of employment which tends to broaden all their faculties, to awaken not only their sense of duty to their kind, but also to develop their love of beauty, of art, and of all that adorns and ennobles life ; and such employment cannot be maintained without the vitalizing use of inventions which exhibit the enduring, the working, and the perfect embodiment of human ingenuity.

Religion demands high order of employment.

We are hardly aware of the silent working influence of machinery upon the morals of the world, but it is recognized in this particular thought that has been outlined, that poverty and religion are not now, as once, twin virtues. There are many other things to be learned from the influence of machinery which satisfy this thesis. Communism, which means the destruction of labor, can not coexist with machinery. Its use requires too much competition, both social and industrial, to admit of communism. The states, therefore, devoted to industries which require the use of machines to a large extent are safe from the inroads of communism and communistic socialism, for without machinery the world would necessarily retrograde to superstition and to ignorance, and the ingenuity of man would assume its old place among the unused faculties of the mind.

Communism cannot coexist with machinery.

The ethical effects of the division of labor which has resulted from the application of machinery are very marked. Trades are hardly essential now. The ap-

Benefits to apprentices.

prentice boy, if bright, can learn his trade in less than the time required in the old way, under which he cannot become a journeyman until he has been pronounced such by the time spent in his apprenticeship. After he becomes skilful his wages are usually exploited to the extent of his skill, and he is obliged to contribute more in the way of actual earnings than he receives. But this is not the worst result of the apprenticeship system. Finding that he is robbed by it, he finally undertakes to earn no more than he is paid, and so acquires habits of unthrift which follow him through life. These things have caused the apprentice boy to disappear practically from the industrial world. Through manual training

Effect of manual training.

and the results of the trade school, a boy can utilize his whole time, and as soon as he becomes accomplished or well equipped in his particular trade he can command the wages legitimately his due. He has had the experience of good training, and he has the advantage over the old apprentice, both in the saving of time and in the more immediate reward which his skill commands. But the ethical influences of machinery are shown in other

Gain in time.

directions, for with the diversity of employment which has resulted from its adoption there have come shorter hours of labor and consequently increased opportunities for mental and moral improvement. With this gain of time wages have been greatly increased and the cost of

In wages.

the principal articles of consumption constantly reduced.

In demand, cost, and increased product.

As to production, one illustration must serve for all, and this is drawn from the cotton industry. A fair adult hand-loom weaver can weave from 42 to 48 yards of common shirting per week; a weaver in a modern factory, tending six power-looms, can turn out about 1,500 yards per week. On the hand-wheel (one spindle) a spinner can turn off eight ounces of number ten cloth yarn in ten hours, or three pounds in one week ; the operator of the mule spinning machine can turn out over 3,000 pounds in the same time. All this means a corresponding decrease in price.

The hours of labor have been reduced from twelve or thirteen per day in the same industry to nine and one half in England and ten generally in this country. An examination of statistical tables will convince any one that for most divisions of labor in textile factories wages have been nearly doubled during the past sixty or seventy years, and such examination will show like results for very many other industries. *In reduction of hours.*

This inevitable ethical result of the application of machinery has been to enable man to secure a livelihood in less time than of old, and this is grand of itself, if no other advantage had been secured ; for it must be considered that as the time required to earn a living grows shorter civilization advances, and that any system which demands of a man all his time or the greater portion of it for the earning of mere subsistence must be demoralizing in all respects. The moral condition of man has been improved through the improvement of his health. In warm and comfortable clothing, in water-proof material, in heating and lighting, in a thousand ways, invention has carried with it more comfortable conditions, increased health, and an increased longevity, the average of life at present being ten per cent higher than in the olden time. Low grades of labor are constantly giving place to educated labor. The man who used to do the most detestable forms of work is being displaced everywhere by men of professional and technical training, who superintend some device brought into use by invention. So the constant promotion of luxuries to the grade of neces- *Increase in average life.*

saries of life marks the forward steps of civilization.

What once were luxuries to one class are now the necessaries of life to a class that might be considered below
the first.   This is illustrated by the fact that there was a
time when a linen sheet was worth thirty-two days of
common labor, and when a gridiron cost from four to
twelve days of labor.

Prior to the generation which precedes the present the
fastest time that could be made was through the speed
of man, or of horses, or of sailing vessels, except, perhaps, in the occasional transmission of intelligence by sig-
nals.   The very first change in the way of speed in transportation or in the interchange of intelligence came to the
world within the memory of men now living.   Engineering
enterprises are solving the problem of how to relieve
congested cities and of how to give to the wage-worker,
who must save time as between his lodging and his work,
the benefits of healthful surroundings in the country.

Rapid transit, through the application of electricity to
street cars, has in many cases added from one half to
three quarters of an hour of the day to the workingman's
available time.   This is the influence of invention, and a
moral influence, for it betters his condition, helps him
to a higher plane, facilitates social intercourse, and in
every way gives him better opportunities for enjoying all
that belongs to his environment.

Every machine that is invented marks some progress
in a useful art.   It accomplishes some useful end not before attained, or it does some old work better and
cheaper.   It makes more valuable the day's work of an
operative, and it adds to everything that makes life
agreeable, provided there is thrift and prudence behind
the worker.   If there is any ethical influence in the
study of or familiarity with works of art, certainly ma-

chinery has had a very deep ethical influence, for by the aid of mechanical powers the work of artisans is rapidly making the taste of the people artistic, for trained and inventive skill, as exhibited in machinery, puts art into wood and metal, showing "the highest discipline of the mental faculties, the direction and subordination of all its manifestations for some clearly-defined purpose." But it has gone beyond and has brought to the commonest person some of the results of the highest artistic skill in the world. Copies of great pictures, the works of the great masters, are familiar to the common people. Once only one man could own a great picture ; to him and to his friends all the joy that comes of beholding the artistic production was limited. To-day, while he owns the original, the people own the picture, and the artist and his influence serve all, and he is enabled not only to unlock the stores of art which the world holds, but by the cheapening of publication he can unlock the stores of knowledge.

Makes art common to all.

There is one feature which belongs to the ethical influence of machinery to which attention ought to be called. The argument is often made that by its use there is brought into industrial work an ignorant class of workers, but this argument is baseless. There is no more ignorance in the world on account of inventions, but by their perfection an ignorant class can often do perfectly what an intelligent class used to bungle over, and at the same time the intelligence of the ignorant is raised. The ignorant laborer of to-day is, in all that makes up condition, more than the peer of the skilled workman of a few generations ago, and the fact that as the country increases in wealth the numbers employed in miscellaneous industries, as has been shown in the preceding chapter, and what Mr. David A. Wells calls incorporeal functions

Machinery does not create ignorance.

—that is, artists, teachers, and others who minister to taste and comfort in a way that can hardly be called material—increase disproportionately to those engaged in the production of the great staples, answers the idea that inventions foster ignorance in production. Inventions have, indeed, superinduced the congregation of ignorant laborers, and thereby given the appearance of creating ignorant labor. The great fact remains that as ignorant laborers are brought together their condition attracts attention and the public proceeds at once to bring to them educational facilities. Invention was the cause of the better condition, for it was not until the factory system was thoroughly fixed as the industrial system of England that Parliament brought under educational influences the children of the factory. To machinery must be attributed the great extension of the facilities for educating the masses. The centers devoted to industrial pursuits are the centers of thought, of mental friction, of intelligence, and of progress.

It congregates ignorant laborers and then elevates them.

INDEX.

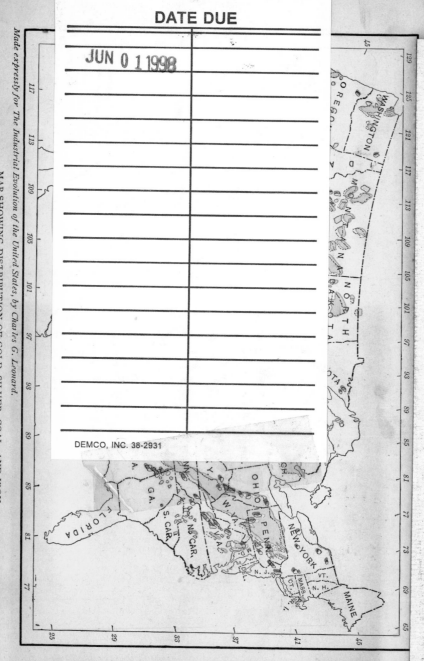

Made expressly for The Industrial Evolution of the United States, by Charles G. Leonard.

MAP SHOWING DISTRIBUTION OF GOLD, SILVER, COAL, AND IRON.